For my friend and colleague Karen Ellis

A History of Charitable Gift Planning

How Gift Annuities Shaped American Philanthropy

(1830–1959)

Ronald A. Brown

Ron Brown

ISBN: 1530197325

ISBN 13: 9781530197323

Library of Congress Control Number: 2016903313

CreateSpace Independent Publishing Platform, North Charleston, SC

Table of Contents

Preface

On Writing a History of Charitable Gift Planning

Gift planning has a history that can be useful in many ways. You may be interested in this book if you are a fundraiser for a nonprofit organization or a donor, attorney, investment advisor, actuary, financial planner, regulator, or student of American history.

In 2013, I launched a website entitled GiftPlanningHistory.org, in which I published essays that became the basis for this book. There are no other general histories of charitable gift planning, as far as I can tell. How did this book come about?

Like many people do, I threw myself into volunteer service following a personal tragedy, the death of my wife Lois in 1999. I suggested to Tanya Howe Johnson, then president of the National Committee on Planned Giving (NCPG; now the National Association of Charitable Gift Planners) that someone should write the history of the committee. A few weeks later, not to my surprise, Tanya said that writer should be me. I agreed immediately.

My volunteer research began in the year 2000. This seemed a worthwhile service on behalf of friends and colleagues raising money for American nonprofit organizations. How hard could it be to document the twenty-year history of a national association for which I had served as a board member and an enthusiastic participant?

My experience led me to believe that I could tell the stories well. I practiced gift planning at three universities (Princeton, Columbia, and Fordham), United Way of America, and the National Wildlife Federation. For eight years, I was a board member, research-committee chair, and a member of the rates committee for the American Council on Gift Annuities (ACGA). I served as the president of the Gift Planning Council of New Jersey and as a board member of the Planned Giving Group of Greater New York. I was a member of the CANARAS planned giving group from 2000 to 2017.

I've worked as a professional historian and as a writer. I served with the Naval Historical Center in Washington, DC; I received two Navy Achievement Medals for historical narratives and wrote similar histories for use by the Naval War College. As a student at Princeton and the University of Chicago, I studied the history of ideas and edited the newsletter of the Oriental Institute. I had long dreamed of writing full time.

When I began, it seemed that everyone working in the field knew (or thought they knew) that charitable gift planning began with the Tax Reform Act of 1969.[1] My first surprise came in reading the *Congressional Record* for that year. Members of the House intended to reform self-dealing abuses of charitable trusts that had been well-known for decades. Nonprofit organizations testified in the Senate about gift annuity programs going back more than one hundred years.

The history of NCPG would have to wait until I learned more about the roots of gift planning. I had a big day job and was raising a family, so I did research early in the morning and on weekends. Year after year flew by.

Gradually, I realized that the history of gift annuities and charitable trusts is not like a string of electric lights, each depending upon the continuing glow of all the ones before. There are discontinuities; traditions are forgotten, discarded, adapted. Rather than envisioning an unbroken process of progressive refinements in the techniques of gift planning, I found that it is more useful to think of people in each era using the tools available to realize their objectives.

There is much to enjoy and to learn in the adventures of gift planners long before the Tax Reform Act of 1969. The process resulting in a gift annuity contract in 1831 is complex and interesting. I aspired to show the meaning of these events for people engaged in similar processes today.

My first essay for GiftPlanningHistory.org had to be about the early years of the National Committee on Planned Giving. A simple chronology would not capture the drama. I needed to show why things happened as they did. I emphasized certain conflicts over control of professional training and certification; how a number of for-profit professionals began promoting charitable remainder trusts as tax shelters and investment vehicles; how a few professionals asked nonprofit organizations to pay finders' fees for the delivery of gifts; and related events that resulted in the code of ethics entitled *Model Standards of Practice for the Charitable Gift Planner*.[2]

With that promise met, I chose to write the history of American gift annuities. Everyone expects biographers to tell the story of the beginning of a life. Where and when was a person born; what experiences shaped their values? It is just so with historians. The starting point seemed clear enough when I began. Everyone knew (or thought they knew) that the American Bible Society had issued the first gift annuity in 1843.[3] Again, a commonly accepted fact of history proved not to be so.

The birth of gift annuities turned out to be a story of patriotism, religious controversy, political logrolling, and persistence. In 1831, Yale issued an annuity to the artist John Trumbull in exchange for his best paintings of the American Revolution. A gift annuity financed the country's first college art gallery.

My next big surprise came in 2007. I had read that the ACGA was founded in 1927. Just before I became chair of its Research Committee, I found microfilm copies of the first few reports from the Conferences on Gift Annuities in the archives of the New York Public Library. I was stunned to discover that ACGA began as a national reform movement in response to a wave of extremely risky nonprofit gift annuity programs in the 1920s.

What behavior by gift annuity donors and nonprofits in the 1920s needed to be reformed? The answers to that question led to the recognition of an actuarial revolution in American fundraising.

Notes

1   This limited view of the history of gift planning persists. On the website for the National Association of Charitable Gift Planners, a page entitled "Our Story" begins, "Born with our profession. In 1969, Congress passed the Tax Reform Act, changing the way Americans could make charitable contributions. This was the major impetus for the creation of the field of planned giving. During the 1970s, the planned giving profession was in its infancy, but by the end of the decade many organizations were beginning to see the field's potential." Downloaded from https://charitablegift-planners.org/history on May 17, 2017.

2   My essay entitled "The First Ethical Standards for Gift Planners: A Fledgling National Association Earns its Wings" can be found at Brown 2017.

3   See, for example, Schoenhals 1992.

Acknowledgments

I am grateful to the Sterling Memorial Library at Yale University for making available Benjamin Silliman's manuscript *Reminiscences*, letters by Silliman and John Trumbull, and other materials from Yale's archives. Except as otherwise noted, images of Trumbull's paintings used in the text were downloaded from the website of the Yale University Art Gallery, which has placed the images in the public domain.

The account of the American Bible Society's annuity campaign is based on primary sources in the society's archives. I am particularly indebted to Kristin Hellman, manager of library services for the ABS, for making available the minutes of the Ways and Means Committee, the series of historical essays written by ABS in the 1960s, and other documents.

The New York State Insurance Department provided an important letter from 1923 on the question of granting legal sanction for gift annuities issued by nonprofit organizations.

A large portion of the book draws on the reports published soon after each of ten Conferences on Gift Annuities held from 1927 to 1959. I incorporate reports from similar conferences held by the Committee on Financial and Fiduciary Matters of the Federal Council of Churches, the Methodist Church, and the National Council of Churches, as well as minutes of the Committee on Gift Annuities from 1937 to 1964.

Since there is no previous book on the history of charitable gift planning, this one depends heavily on synthesizing the work of researchers in many related fields. Credits are noted in the footnotes. Debits are entirely my responsibility. Please send any questions or corrections to me at rbrown.pghistory@gmail.com.

Many people provided encouragement for my research, most notably Andre Donikian, Peter Doyle, Catherine Gletherow, Professor Stanley N. Katz, Regina Ketting, Peter Kimball, Robert F. Sharpe Jr., Conrad Teitell, and Jonathan Tidd. Peter Jay Siris gave me extremely helpful suggestions for organizing and presenting the material. Several editors at CreateSpace provided expert assistance throughout. I am grateful to Lee Hoffman, his late brother Marc, and Randy Fox for publishing my original essays through their Planned Giving Design Center. I've learned much of what I know about gift annuities from Frank Minton and have benefitted from the professional expertise and benevolent guidance of William D. Zabel, Esq.

I thank the staff of the Princeton University Library, where much of the research was conducted. The Writers Room in New York City provided a quiet sanctuary in recent years. My beloved wife Margaret, who died in November of 2016, endured innumerable discussions about gift planning and provided invaluable feedback.

The graphic design for this book is by Gretchen Fuller of InktoBook.com, and the index was created by Heather Dubnick.

My website designer is Amy Hepler. Special thanks to the 2,471 subscribers to GiftPlanningHistory.org who were registered as of July 2017. The essays first published there have been revised and expanded, and much new material was added for this book.

We ought to be aware of untold stories. What matters most about gift annuities is that they fund services for people in need of help. Lives are saved or made more tolerable by shelters and soup kitchens, churches and synagogues, hospitals and nurseries, private schools and colleges. People who are helped rarely know that a gift annuity made some of these services possible.

There are untold stories about annuitants themselves. Thousands of families receive annuity payments that are financial lifelines during economic recessions, job losses, or deaths of breadwinners. And stories could be written illuminating how nonprofit managers grapple with the challenges of maintaining healthy annuity programs.

This book is not the end of the story of gift annuities—it is a beginning.

Introduction

Charitable gift annuities are familiar to many donors and nonprofit organizations: in exchange for a gift, a nonprofit provides fixed payments for one or two people's lives. About four thousand American nonprofits issue gift annuities.[1] The value of gift annuity reserve funds under management is more than $3 billion.[2]

A fundamental challenge for nonprofits issuing annuity contracts is to offer payment rates high enough to attract gifts, but not so high that little or nothing is left at the end of an annuitant's life to support a philanthropic purpose. George Huggins expressed this well:

> We want to provide income that will be attractive to donors and yet at the same time provide funds to further the work of our organization. The larger the annuity allowance, the greater is its value and the smaller is the gift portion. What is the happy medium? That is the gist of the problem confronting us today.[3]

Important benefits motivate America's nonprofit organizations to develop and continuously update a voluntary national process for determining annuity payment rates. Nonprofit fiduciaries need businesslike methods judged to be credible by donors, attorneys, financial planners, actuaries, nonprofit boards and staff, courts, state regulators, and federal and state legislators. Cost savings is a motivator: each nonprofit does not have to hire its own actuary to set rates. Also important is general acceptance that competing for donors by offering deals on higher rates could lead to financial disaster and loss of credibility in the whole enterprise of charitable gift annuities.

Donors and nonprofits entering into binding legal contracts make leaps of faith that the American system of gift annuities is safe for the annuitants and cost effective for nonprofit organizations. Gift planners may not be aware of the extent to which each element of marketing, administering, investing, and regulating gift annuities functions as part of a complex, national system that developed over many years.

The American system of gift annuities was not always as sound as it is now. Its fundamentals were constructed to manage the risks of life insurance and commercial annuity contracts and adapted to meet the needs of nonprofit fundraising.

This book consists of four sections:

1. A BRIEF HISTORY OF EARLY LIFE-INCOME GIFTS

For at least 1,400 years, people have made gifts for philanthropic purposes and received payments back for life. The opening section sheds light on how some elements of American gift annuities are part of a long tradition, and others are new.

Life annuities were common enough in ancient Rome to have their own mortality tables and legal regulations. The idea of raising money for nonprofit organizations by adding a philanthropic purpose to annuity contracts was introduced in the Middle Ages. By the 1920s, charitable gift annuities had become by far the most popular form of life-income gifts in the United States, and they remain so today. *Important Events in the History of Charitable Gift Annuities* (appendix I) is a chronology of selected highlights.

2. THE GIFT ANNUITY THAT FINANCED AMERICA'S FIRST COLLEGE ART GALLERY

To the best of current knowledge, modern gift annuities began in 1831 with a gift of his best paintings of the American Revolution by the artist John Trumbull in exchange for a $1,000 annual payment from Yale for his life. Our country's best visual records of the men, women, and events of the struggle for independence were preserved through a planned gift.

Fortunately for us, Benjamin Silliman recorded the story of Trumbull's gift. In his *Reminiscences*, written more than twenty-five years after the events described, Silliman tells how he orchestrated the gift-planning process. His task was neither easy nor simple. Yale had no money to pay Trumbull's annuity and had no art gallery in which to exhibit his paintings.

Trumbull's attorney Peter Jay invented suitable legal documents for Trumbull's annuity (appendixes II and III). Trumbull published the documents in his *Autobiography*,[4] making them available to professional advisors and nonprofit organizations for generations to come.

3. AMERICAN GIFT ANNUITIES, MARKETING, AND THE LAW (1831–1926)

The ingenuity of donors and their advisors shines brightly in the gift proposals for life-income trusts and annuities considered by the American Bible Society in the 1830s and 1840s. In this formative period of American philanthropy, the *Bradish Report*, written for the ABS Board in 1848 (appendix IV) is the earliest known example of a nonprofit organization grappling with the policy question of whether to encourage life-income gifts.

In the 1800s, American companies embraced actuarial science to measure longevity and manage the financial risks of commercial annuity contracts and life insurance policies. Their business model became extremely successful. At the dawn of the twentieth century, assets under management by US life insurance companies far exceeded assets managed by banks.

Nonprofit gift annuity programs flourished in the 1920s. These are illustrated by examples of *annuity bond* advertisements published by nonprofit organizations. The international annuity bond campaign by the American Bible Society, which produced 4,615 gift annuity contracts between 1920 and 1930, is explored in-depth for the first time.

Charitable gift annuities narrowly escaped legal prohibition by the State of New York. Thanks to an intervention by Dr. Gilbert Darlington of the Bible Society and George Huggins, the right of nonprofit organizations to issue gift annuity contracts was validated by the New York Insurance Law in 1925.

4. GEORGE HUGGINS AND THE CONFERENCES ON GIFT ANNUITIES (1927–59)

An emergency meeting of leading nonprofit organizations in 1927 addressed a crisis: too many nonprofits were issuing annuity contracts with too little understanding of the risks. Huggins presented an "ideal plan of conducting the annuity business" based on actuarial principles (appendix V).[5]

The years from 1927 to Huggins's death in 1959 were a crucible in which America's gift annuity model was refined by an economic depression and a great surge in human longevity.

What a time this was! The expansionary decade of the 1920s was shattered by the stock market crash and Great Depression.

Not so well known to many people today, but bedeviling to annuity fund managers, was the steady decline in interest rates from 1920 to 1946,[6] which threatened to bankrupt nonprofits issuing annuities based on return assumptions that turned out to be overly optimistic.

The outbreak of the Second World War in 1939 made economic forecasting extremely challenging, as the federal government exercised greater control over inflation and interest rates than economists expected. The aftermath of war brought a surge of new capital and aggressive investment strategies for gift annuity reserves.

Ample documentation of what leaders of national nonprofit organizations were thinking and doing in Huggins's era is found in reports that were published after each of ten Conferences on Gift Annuities held between 1927 and 1959. Two fundamental concerns dominated the agendas: "First, how long may we reasonably expect to have to make the annuity payments; second, what rate of investment income can we earn on the [reserve] funds?"[7]

At the conferences, economists and bankers would survey the current economy, provide investment advice for the country's annuity fund managers, and forecast future earnings.[8]

Before Huggins, no standardized models existed that would enable a nonprofit organization to compare its practices with those of its peers to determine whether gift annuities were effective ways to raise money. Legislators, judges, and regulators struggled to understand the differences and similarities between nonprofit annuity bonds and commercial investments. There was little public-policy guidance for valuing the charitable interests of life-income gifts or protecting the financial interests of nonprofits and their annuitants.

Thanks to Huggins, Americans have confidence in applying statistical ideas and methods to charitable fundraising, such as collecting and analyzing massive amounts of data on gift-annuitant mortality to determine the average length of an annuitant's life—thus, how much money a nonprofit may reasonably expect to pay.

The extent to which statistical reasoning was embraced by nonprofit organizations is shown in a conference presentation in 1955:

> The fact is, the donor is a statistic based upon millions of cases. Therein lies the strength of our gift annuity program and protection to the donor.[9]

Once enough people make the same kinds of life-income gifts, reliable statistical averages can be derived from experience. With the knowledge of gift averages, or norms, people can apply the wisdom of experience to the structure of gifts, assign present values to proposed or existing gifts, maintain adequate reserve funds, adjust payment rates for new gifts, promote life-income gifts to the right audiences, and monitor the financial health of annuity programs. Appropriate laws and regulations can be adopted. Best practices can be developed and modified as needed to achieve successful outcomes.

After Huggins's presentation in 1927, specialists responsible for understanding, marketing, and managing nonprofit gift annuities needed advanced training. In 1928, Gilbert Darlington observed that gift planning had become "technical and precise work," requiring well-trained professionals:

> It cannot be attempted by the ordinary annuitant without help and assistance from someone who is familiar with what must be done to get the proper result.[10]

Today's nonprofit organizations swim in Huggins's sea of actuarial science like fish in water. Actuarial methods are enshrined in federal policy, providing the only acceptable rules for calculating the tax benefits of a gift to charity that provides payments for the uncertain terms of beneficiaries' lives. The business model he introduced guides everyone who enters a gift annuity contract, manages a life-income gift program, or protects the rights of annuitants and charitable-trust beneficiaries.

It is time to see how this all got started.

NOTES

1   "Our best estimate is that upwards of 4,000 charities currently issue gift annuities. The number could be higher." "Methodology," in ACGA 2005, 2.

2   In the national survey conducted by ACGA in 2013, 299 nonprofit organizations reported a total of $2,435,179,161 in annuity funds under management, but that is far less than the actual amount. See "Market Value of Total Annuity Reserves," in ACGA 2014, 48. Reserve fund values are snapshots of a process in motion. New gifts are coming in, and money is sent out from reserve funds for use by the organization as annuitants pass away.

3   George Huggins, "Gift Annuity Rates and Mortality Experience," in Various 1955, 28.

4   Trumbull, 1841.

5   Huggins, "Actuarial Basis of Rates," in Various 1927b.

6   The yields of long-term, high-grade American bonds turned down in 1920, "declined most of the time for twenty-six years, and reached their all-time lows in 1946" (Homer 2005, 334). In a message to the author in June 2015, Mr. Sylla noted that the economic crisis of 2007–2009 resulted in even lower yields than in 1946. On July 6, 2016, the *Wall Street Journal* reported that "the yield on the benchmark 10-year U.S. Treasury note fell to its lowest level ever Tuesday, a new milestone in a three-decade downward run that even veteran traders never thought would go so far or last so long" (Min Zeng, "Is This Key Rate Going to Fall to 1%?" *WSJ*, C1).

7   George Huggins, "Gift Annuity Rates and Mortality Experience," in Various 1955, 28.

8   For example, as World War II broke out in Europe, a conference presentation by Dr. Marcus Nadler of the NYU Graduate School of Business

was titled "Rates of Yield on Invested Funds Under Existing Conditions, and the Probabilities as to the Future." Other common conference topics included marketing, law, taxation, and accounting.

9   John Rosengrant, "Correct Terminology," in Various 1955, 24.

10   Darlington, "Legislation and Taxation," in Various 1929b, 8.

Section 1

A Brief History of Early Life-Income Gifts

The concept of annuities that can be purchased by an individual to ensure income for an entire life is of ancient origin: an early form of commercial annuity was a useful financial tool in Assyria and Babylon.[1]

Annuities were regulated by Roman law. The legal scholar known as Ulpian (whose full name was Domitius Ulpianus and who lived from about 170 to 223 CE) published a surprisingly accurate mortality table for valuing annuities given through a person's will. The value of fixed, lifetime payments could be determined only at the death of the person whose estate purchased the annuity, based on the ages of the annuitants at that time. Under Roman law, family members had the right to inherit not less than 25 percent of an estate. There was a practical need for accurate annuity valuations to protect their interests.[2]

Ulpian's mortality table was used for some 1,400 years. George Huggins commented on Ulpian's table in his report for the ninth Conference on Gift Annuities (hereafter COA) in 1955:

> The earliest known reference to any estimates of the value of
> life annuities arose from the provisions of the Falcidian Law

1

of the Roman Empire; but the tables of values used were the result of conjecture rather than statistical investigation, and the element of interest was not taken into consideration.[3]

Commercial annuitants purchase life annuities for equivalent prices, which are purely economic exchanges with no gift elements. Life-income gifts for philanthropic purposes are also quite ancient. One of the most important and influential examples of gifts that involve payments back to a donor for life with a surplus amount (*residuum*) for charitable purposes dates to the sixth century CE. Life-income gifts were encouraged in the rules of the monastic communities founded by Saint Benedict of Nursia (480–543). Benedictine monks encouraged wealthy parents to help prepare their sons and daughters for entering religious communities by giving property to the church rather than to their children.

While the monks preferred gifts with no strings attached, they acknowledged that some parents were unable or unwilling to make valuable gifts unless they received an assurance of cash payments from the religious community. Benedict's Rule 59 encouraged parents to make gifts in exchange for lifelong income: "[If parents] wish to gain merit by offering some alms to the monastery, they may make a formal donation of the property they want to give to the monastery. If they wish, they may reserve the income for themselves."

Benedict's Latin sentence ends in a very important word: "Vel certe si hoc facere noluerint et aliquid offerre volunt in eleemosynam monasterio donationem, reservato sibi, si ita voluerint, **usufructu.**"[4] (emphasis added).

A *usufruct* was recognized in Roman law: title to property is transferred to another person, who accepts an obligation to pay income from that property (its "fruits") back to the grantor, generally for life.[5] Benedict's rule encouraging life-income gifts to his community through a usufruct is an important example of how the medieval church adapted a Roman concept for charitable purposes.

Unlike an annuity contract, the rate of payments from a usufruct was not based on the grantor's age but was simply a pass-through of income from property, such as lease income from land. A monastic community that accepted a usufruct did not have a general obligation to make payments to the grantor. Since the principal of the property was never invaded, there was little financial risk for the community.

Another gift arrangement involved much greater financial risk for the issuing organization. Beginning around the year 1100, and for the next four hundred years, Catholic institutions, such as monasteries and hospitals, issued life-annuity contracts called *corrodies*.[6] While specific practices over that long era varied from time to time and from place to place, corrodies involved gifts of cash or real property (houses, farms, raw land) to a church-run organization in exchange for defined lifetime benefits that were general legal obligations of the organizations. Details of gifts and their specific benefits were recorded in contracts and sealed by the issuing institutions.

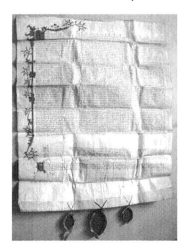

An illuminated and sealed corrody contract issued by Durham Cathedral in 1386.[7]

Depending on the needs of the donors and the ability and willingness of the organization to provide specific benefits, corrodians could receive food, shelter, firewood, clothing, candles, and/or drink, and, sometimes, cash payments for life.

Most frequently, especially in the earlier phase of their history, corrodies were given to secure places for donors and their families to live in retirement. Medieval historian Miri Rubin described why people arranged corrodies:

> Corrodians planned to spend their last days within a religious community, participating in its religious life, sharing its merit and enjoying the provision of all their physical needs. The entrant or his patron often granted a sizeable donation in perpetuity in return for sustenance until his death.[8]

These lifetime arrangements involved risks for the donor as well as for the institution. A donor might grow dissatisfied with the quality of a monastery's bread, ale, or leadership. Benefits could stop or be reduced because of a church's mismanagement or corruption.[9]

The hospital or monastery granting a corrody, for its part, committed to a lifelong relationship with a person or married couple whose personal behavior could be of concern. Most corrodies were arranged with people who were well known and acceptable to the religious community, but this was not always the case:

> A lady residing at Langley [P]riory had "a great abundance of dogs, insomuch that whenever she comes to church here follow her twelve dogs, who make a great uproar in church, hindering them in their psalmody, and the nuns thereby are made terrified." At Gracedieu [P]riory lived a Frenchwoman who "should be removed because of the unseemliness of her life, for she receives all alike to her embraces."[10]

4

Sometimes, a donor made a gift in exchange for guaranteed annuity payments from a trustworthy charity, with the intention of using the payments for living expenses. For example, in the years 1398–99, the financial records of Selby Abbey document a gift of eighty pounds from a textile merchant named John Tuch in exchange for lifetime annuity payments to him and his wife, Margaret.[11]

Payment rates for medieval corrodies, and for noncharitable annuities such as pensions, were not mathematically determined—no mortality data was available for statistical analysis—but instead depended upon sophisticated analysis of limited experience.[12]

The English practice of raising money for charitable purposes by issuing corrody contracts ended in the mid-1500s, when Henry VIII seized the assets of Catholic churches, monasteries, hospitals, and other institutions.

Philanthropic arrangements like corrodies should not be confused with the ancient practice of giving nonprofit organizations the rights to receive streams of fixed annuity payments from long-term leases of land. Annuity payments to charitable organizations were listed among the kinds of assets given to charity in the preamble to the Elizabethan *Statute of Charitable Uses* (1601), the foundation of the American law of charity:

> Whereas Landes Tenementes Rentes **Annuities** Profittes Hereditamentes, Goodes Chattels 4Money and Stockes of Money, have bene heretofore given limitted appointed and assigned, as well by the Queenes most excellent Majestie and her moste noble Progenitors, as by sondrie other well disposed persons...[13] (emphasis added)

These land leases were such important sources of income for nonprofit organizations in colonial America that the right to accept the gift of an annuity was often written into the charter of the organization. For example, in 1746, the trustees of the College of New Jersey (now Princeton University) were empowered "to have, accept and receive any rents, profits, **annuities,** gifts, legacies, donations and bequests" (emphasis added). In 1701, Yale College was empowered to receive annuities, but this referred to land leases, not life-annuity contracts.[14] Harvard College received payments from several land-lease annuities given to it in the 1600s.[15]

Annuity payments made *to* a nonprofit in a land lease work in the opposite direction from charitable gift annuities, which require payments *from* the nonprofit to an annuitant. Unlike corrodies and gift annuities, annuity lease payments to a nonprofit involve no obligation for the nonprofit to make payments during the life of an annuitant.

A working definition of gift annuities was provided in the preface to the report of the first Conference on Gift Annuities in 1927:

> As here used the word *annuity* has a technical meaning. It refers to the entire agreement and the execution of it, in accordance with which a person gives money, or other substantial equivalent, to an organization, which binds itself by contract, or agreement, to hold and administer the gift, and to pay to the donor an annual sum, varying according to the age and therefore according to the expected life of the donor, and ceasing only at the donor's death.[16]

Trusts that provide payments to people for life, with the remainder used for charitable purposes, belong to a different branch of the law from annuity contracts, though the history of annuities and trusts is occasionally intertwined.[17] As related below, in 1830, Peter Jay structured a proposed gift from John Trumbull to a new museum in Hartford as a trust, but he changed the structure to an annuity contract for the gift to Yale in 1831.

Luther Bradish's report on gift annuities for the American Bible Society in 1848 is now known as *On the Matter of Accepting Trusts* (appendix IV) because it was unclear to Bradish and his contemporaries how the State of New York would treat annuities issued by nonprofit organizations. Bradish asserted that if gift annuities are considered contracts, they are clearly sanctioned by law: "The transaction would be either—

1st Simply a matter of Contract;

2nd A Trust.

If simply a matter of Contract then no doubt could for a moment be entertained that it would be entirely lawful."

Bradish and the ABS Board were worried that New York would apply the law of trusts, so he devoted most of his argument to the defense of annuities as trusts.[18] He cited the precedent of a case heard in 1828 concerning a charitable trust in the will of Nicholas Anderson, appointing Saint George's Church as trustee:

> Nicholas Anderson, the Testator gave to St. Georges Church in New York a Legacy of Four thousand Dollars <u>in trust</u> that the same should be put out at interest or vested in Public stocks, and that the income thereof should be paid to his Housekeeper for life; and after her death the Income thereof to be applied to the purchase of a Church Library, the support of a Sabbath School in the church and other church purposes.[19]

Lack of clarity over charitable gift annuities as trusts or contracts persisted until enactment of the Tax Reform Act of 1969.[20] In 1931, the federal government and most state governments regulated gift annuities as life insurance contracts, but a leading expert observed that some charities were writing gift annuity contracts that paid actual net income to the beneficiary, instead of a fixed and certain amount:

If the contract agreed to pay only the income and no more, then it is questionable whether it is an annuity or a living trust. There seems to be a twilight zone between living trusts and annuities, and it may be necessary to clear up this twilight zone, because of regulatory legislation.[21]

In 1952, Gilbert Darlington saw a continuing need to urge charities to "draw clearly a distinction between (1) an annuity contract (2) a trust fund subject to life interest," citing significantly different tax treatment by the Prerogative Court of New Jersey.[22] The challenge of sorting out the tax implications of charitable trusts persisted through the ninth COA in 1955:

> Unlike charitable annuity contracts, living-income agreements are not easily defined. Primarily, the reason for this difficulty is that such agreements take a variety of forms and include provisions which are somewhat like annuity contracts and other provisions which are comparable to trust agreements.[23]

There is an important difference between the financial risk of annuities and that of trusts. Trusts protect a trustee against harm caused by greater longevity than expected or by poor investment performance. If the trust principal is exhausted, the trust simply terminates. This gives trusts an advantage over annuity contracts, which are general obligations of the issuers that usually require the payment of money in excess of the investment earnings on the original amount contributed.

Moreover, for more than a thousand years before the Tax Reform Act of 1969 introduced the now-familiar structures of the unitrust and annuity trust,[24] charitable life-income trusts operated as what we would call net-income trusts, paying out the actual income earned by the trust portfolios and thus providing greater margins of safety. A 1927 publication on charitable trusts even states that the amount going into a charitable trust will be *exactly* the same as the amount remaining at the beneficiary's death:

> [A person who creates a trust] may provide that during his life, or for a definite period of years during his life, he himself shall receive the income in its entirety or in part as he may select, together with all extraordinary dividends… In his trust agreement he may designate a charitable corporation as the final destination of the trust funds…To the trustor, who is in effect an annuitant, it yields the entire income. To the ultimate beneficiary it yields the entire principal…When the income in its entirety is paid to him, then his gift in its final form is exactly 100 per cent of its original amount.[25]

Unlike trusts, the remainder value of gift annuities is intended to be eroded by the required payments and may even cause the issuing organizations to suffer financial losses. Designed to consume a substantial part (but not too much) of a donor's original principal while making the required payments back, gift annuities involve financial risks for nonprofits as well as for annuitants expecting payments they would not outlive.

George Huggins captured the balance between the financial risks and rewards of annuity contracts in his first COA report in 1927:

> It is definitely contemplated that at least the major portion of the principal and interest earnings will ultimately be released for the purposes of the organization. Putting it another way, while the income [paid to an annuitant] is expected to exceed the interest earnings, and therefore cut into the principal, it must not cut in very deeply.[26]

Financial firms have devoted much effort to developing effective risk-management systems for life-annuity contracts. During the seventeenth and eighteenth centuries, mathematical advances in probability and statistics, and the systematic collection and analysis of mortality experience, led to the professional discipline of actuarial science.[27]

The ability to calculate with great precision the risks inherent in issuing annuity contracts based on the uncertain terms of human lives enabled American life insurance and pension companies to develop actuarially sound business models in the nineteenth century.[28] In 1927, George Huggins adapted some of these actuarial principles for use in nonprofit fundraising.

Everyone involved with John Trumbull's annuity in 1831 would have been quite familiar with the common practice of buying a life-annuity contract from an insurance firm. Benjamin Silliman and Peter Jay may or may not have had a deep understanding of the long history of mortality tables, annuity land leases, usufructs, and corrodies, but their innovative use of an annuity bond contract for a charitable gift depended upon common law and business practices built over many centuries of experience.

Notes

1   "The annuity has a record of possibly not less than 3,500 years of service (Kopf 1927, 264).

2   See especially the masterful analysis by Frier (1982, 213–51). For a discussion of commercial annuity contracts from Rome to the present, see Historic Records Working Party 1969.

3   Huggins, "Gift Annuity Rates and Mortality Experience," in Various 1955, 30.

4   Kardong 1996, 485–486. The author is grateful to Robert F. Sharpe Jr. for informing him about Benedict's rule.

5   For example, Ulpian's mortality table, published in the third century CE, was used to value a life annuity in the form of "a usufruct for life of income generated from property" (Frier 1982, 215).

6   Much historical research has been conducted on medieval corrodies. See, for example, Harvey 1993 and Rubin 1987. A particularly interesting treatment is Lewin 2003, 37–56.

7 *Grant of corrody, with bond and defeasance,* 1386 (DCD Reg. II f. 215r) from *A selection of medieval documents* at http://community.dur.ac.uk/medieval.documents/documents.htm, retrieved 7/30/16.

8 Rubin 1987, 172.

9 While he does not write specifically about corrodies, James J. Fishman (2007) describes numerous instances of bad fiduciary behavior in the Middle Ages and later. See esp. 41–49.

10 Harper 1983.

11 Tillotson 1988, 51.

12 Adrian Bell and Charles Sutcliffe apply a modern annuity pricing model to analyze the economics of medieval corrodies for the charities issuing them in Bell A. a. (2007, rev. 2009). The authors include a substantial bibliography on corrodies.

13 "The Statute of Charitable Uses and the English Origins of American Philanthropy" (2016) downloaded July 4, 2016. The preamble of the statute provides examples of true charity to clarify the differences between philanthropy and self-dealing. David C. Hammack's collection of foundational documents for nonprofits in the United States begins with this Elizabethan statute (Hammack 2000, 5–8).

14 "It is also further ENACTED by the Authority aforesd that the sd undertakers & Partners & their successrs be & hereby are further impowered to have accept acquire purchase or otherwise lawfully enter upon Any Lands Tenements & Hereditamts to the use of the sd School…& receiv all such Gifts Legacies bequests **annuities** [emphasis added] Rents issues & profits arising therefrom" (*Act for Liberty to Erect a Collegiate School* 1701).

15 Cited by Foster (1962). See table 35: Harvard College Stock, 1636 to 1712, 160: on May 3, 1652, Harvard recorded two annuities under "Capitalized Rents and Annuities."

16 Alfred Williams Anthony (Various 1927, 1).

17 There is no book documenting the long history of charitable-remainder trusts. For an international history of charitable trusts, see Helmholz (1998). Standard legal texts include Scott (1987), American Law Institute (2003), and Hess (1980–2017). See also many works by the legal historian Frederic William Maitland (such as Maitland 1909, reissued 1936 and 2011).

18   For a masterful analysis of "the development in New York of rules governing the transfer of property from individual donors to charitable trustees, associations and corporations," see Katz 1985.

19   In the Matter of Howe, etc., Executor, and Anderson, Deceased, 1828.

20   Public Law no. 91-172, 83 Stat. 487.

21   Hall 1931, 41.

22   Darlington 1952, 111–112.

23   Ralph L. Concannon, "Charitable Annuities and the New Tax Law," in Various 1955, 50.

24   An annuity trust pays a fixed dollar amount. A unitrust pays a fixed percentage of the trust's value.

25   Living Trusts: What They Are, What They Serve, Their Advantages, 1927, 4–9.

26   Various 1927b.

27   James Franklin traces the development of mathematical knowledge useful in "understanding the principles of probability and using them to improve performance" in Franklin (2001). On the history of actuaries, see Moorhead (1989) and the website of the Society of Actuaries: http://www.soa.org/about/history/about-historical-background.aspx.

28   "More important theoretical contributions to financial economics were made in the late 17th and early 18th centuries in solving problems of pricing life annuities. Around the middle of the 18th century, this led to a practical breakthrough in the related problem of devising and pricing life insurance" (Poitras 2000, 3). Also see Murphy (2010).

Section 2

The Gift Annuity that Financed America's First College Art Gallery

Professions such as law and medicine have their heroes: Clara Barton, founder of the American Red Cross; Justice Oliver Wendell Holmes Jr.; medical researcher Louis Pasteur. The profession of gift planning has Benjamin Silliman, a Yale scientist who championed a risky gift annuity in 1831, secured funding for America's first college art gallery, and endowed it with paintings by John Trumbull, "chief visual recorder" of the founding events of the United States.[1]

Silliman found solutions to familiar challenges: overcoming competition for the gift; persuading a legislature to grant public money to a private nonprofit; negotiating the terms of a contract to satisfy a nonprofit's doubts about the risks of a legal obligation to pay a fixed annuity; and the donor's concerns about the nonprofit's financial ability to do so and his desire to control the use of his gift.

Silliman told the story of Trumbull's gift in an extraordinary reminiscence, never fully published, written in a notebook twenty-six years after the annuity agreements were signed.[2] Begun on July 3, 1857, the day before Independence Day, Silliman's narrative describes negotiations that were "effected primarily through my agency, cooperating with colleagues and other friends."[3]

Discussions of a gift for Yale began in the summer of 1830 with Benjamin Silliman's visit to John Trumbull's Lower Manhattan apartment. Trumbull's greatest oil paintings filled the walls: an "unexpected vision," as Silliman noted in *Reminiscences*. There was his *Declaration of Independence*, with the faces of forty-two signers; soul-stirring scenes of the battles at Bunker Hill, Quebec, Trenton, Princeton, and Saratoga; *The Surrender of Lord Cornwallis at Yorktown*; *General Washington Resigning His Commission* (in Annapolis); and miniature portraits of leading American patriots.

The Battle of Bunker's Hill, June 17, 1775, *by John Trumbull (1786).*

Trumbull—seventy-four years old, widowed, and alone—confessed that expenses had far exceeded his income. Silliman asked what he intended to do with the paintings and recorded Trumbull's response: "I will give them to Yale College to be exhibited forever for the benefit of poor students provided the College will pay me a competent annuity for the remainder of my life." (All quotations in this section that are otherwise unattributed are from *Reminiscences*)

Thrilled by the offer, Silliman returned to New Haven and found President Jeremiah Day, his friends in the senior faculty, and "officers of the fiscal department" (later identified as "the Prudential Committee") generally receptive to the idea of a gift of Trumbull's paintings, but they depended on him to work out the practical details and return with an acceptable gift proposal. His odyssey began in the absence of formal legal authorization: "being as yet without authority from the college senate, the corporation of the institution, we had no power to make a binding contract."

Silliman's *Reminiscences* represents an extended description of challenges faced and resolved by a charitable gift planner in 1830–31. His primary goal was to explain how it came about that America's most important visual depiction of the people and events of its War for Independence was preserved forever at the college Silliman loved.

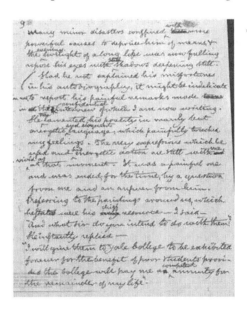

A page from Benjamin Silliman's Reminiscences.

The challenges would have given a lesser man serious doubts. Yale College was suffering a financial crisis yet agreed to pay Trumbull a life annuity of $1,000. This was a considerable sum in 1831, when the annual salary for college professors at Yale was $1,100.[4] At a time when no other college in America had an art gallery or any courses in art history, Yale contracted to build a gallery in the center of its campus, designed by Trumbull himself, to house more than fifty of his paintings—and agreed never to sell any of them.

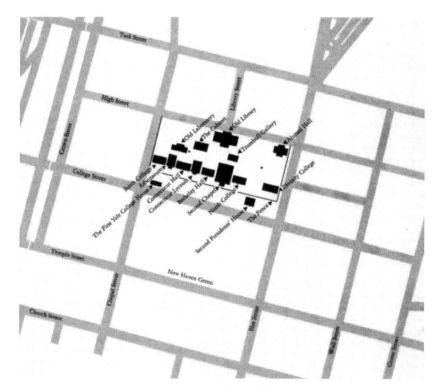

Located in the very center of Yale's Old Campus, the Trumbull Gallery opened to the public on October 25, 1832—and was already too small by 1842.[5]

Donor complications arose, naturally. Trumbull was persuaded by a wealthy Yale donor and family member to split his paintings between Hartford and New Haven. A year later, he changed his mind, deciding that a single gallery at Yale would be preferable after all. Creditors appeared: Trumbull had borrowed money against some of the paintings. Fearful of default on his annuity payments, Trumbull wrote to the president of Harvard and told him that if anything went awry with Yale, his alma mater in Cambridge would get the paintings instead.

There were legal questions. Few reliable precedents guided those deliberations. In the absence of an American public-policy framework for life-income gifts to a charity, what documents needed to be invented, with what terms and safeguards, for all parties to agree on the gift transfer?

Yale, Silliman, Trumbull, and Trumbull's lawyer, Peter Jay, considered several gift structures, including a charitable trust, and settled on two formal contracts: an annuity bond—an early example of adapting concepts from the world of commercial finance to a charitable life-income gift—and an indenture that spelled out Yale's obligations. (See appendixes II and III and the discussion below.)

A satisfactory explanation of America's most influential gift annuity begins with biographies of Silliman, the gift planner; Trumbull, the donor; and Jay, the professional advisor.

Benjamin Silliman, *by John Trumbull (1825).*

BENJAMIN SILLIMAN: GIFT PLANNER AND PATRIOT

Benjamin Silliman was Yale's first professor of science; he was an attorney, chemist, educator, writer, patriot, donor, life insurance executive, and entrepreneur who spent eighteen months as a volunteer fundraiser in pursuit of Trumbull's gift.

There is no evidence that Silliman had any artistic talent or a passion for education in the arts. What drove him to become the catalyst for this hard-won gift of historical paintings?

Silliman, born in 1779, was quite literally a child of the American Revolution. A brief review of his family's experiences illustrates why Trumbull's scenes from the War of Independence acted powerfully upon Silliman's imagination. In 1776, his father, Gold Selleck Silliman, was appointed brigadier general in command of the Connecticut militia. General Silliman fought battles in New York and in Danbury (Connecticut) alongside George Washington's army of regulars and became a prosecutor of disloyal colonists.

In May of 1779, General Silliman was abducted from his home in Fairfield, Connecticut, by local Tories (sympathizers with the king) and imprisoned by the British army. His pregnant wife, Mary Fish Noyes Silliman, was left to manage her household and four young boys during wartime as a single woman.[6] In July of 1779, she fled the family's home to escape from rampaging British troops, taking refuge in Beach's Tavern in the town of Stratford (now Trumbull), Connecticut. One month later, Benjamin was born in the tavern.

Mary Silliman pleaded unsuccessfully with Connecticut governor Jonathan Trumbull Sr. (father of painter John Trumbull) and General George Washington himself to act on the quick release of her husband from the clutches of the British. He spent a year in captivity. Released in May of 1780, he died in 1790, a month before Benjamin's eleventh birthday. Benjamin knew his heroic father only through childhood memories and stories told by others.

Though not wealthy, Mary was determined that her children should receive good college educations: all five boys graduated from Yale College, the alma mater of their father, Selleck (class of 1753), and grandfather Major Ebenezer Silliman (class of 1727).

Benjamin Silliman (Yale class of 1796), who taught at Yale from 1799 to 1855, considered bringing Trumbull's paintings to campus a fitting memorial for people like his father and the ancestors of other students, who fought to create a free and independent country. Silliman underscored the importance of the Trumbull Gallery in preserving images from the birth of the United States and, through the images, understanding the realities of this war:

> The pictures...are of inestimable value, and we are most fortunate in possessing them...Every passing year will add to their value and they will be still more highly prized by a remote posterity...The efforts, the sacrifices, the sufferings and the indomitable firmness of the men of that day in the great conflict, which, under God, secured our liberties and made us a great and prosperous nation, are in danger of being undervalued and forgotten now that almost three generations have been born since the blood of their fathers ceased to flow—the blood that was the holy sacrifice on the altar of liberty.

Silliman made himself a student of the war. Long before 1857, when he wrote the passage above, Silliman took responsibility for providing Americans with an aid to remember their Revolution. In 1819, he and his relative Daniel Wadsworth traveled from Hartford to Quebec. Silliman published an account of what they had seen and heard.[7] A 50-page set piece vividly describes the sites of important battles in and around Quebec, incorporating interviews with aging veterans from a generation that "is now almost passed away," who "speak in their own language" about "the places where they and their companions fought and bled, and where sleep the bones of the slain." Silliman hoped his personal narrative would renew the founders' values:

> To rekindle those [feelings] of genuine patriotism—should it revive in any one, a veneration for the virtues of those men who faced death, in every form, regardless of their own lives, and bent only on securing to posterity, the precious blessings, which we now enjoy...the time occupied in this sketch, will not have been spent in vain. History presents no struggle for liberty, which has in it more of the moral sublime than that of the American Revolution.[8]

Benjamin Silliman never served in uniform but compared himself to a military hero to dramatize his commitment: he was "resolving like Col. Miller at Lundy's Lane that I would try" to capture the prize.[9]

John Trumbull, The Death of General Montgomery in the Attack on Quebec, December 31, 1775 (1786).

Silliman mustered powerful intellectual and political capital for the task. He had studied law at Yale and was admitted to the

Connecticut bar in 1802. With encouragement from Yale president Timothy Dwight, Silliman changed course, joined the Yale faculty, was appointed a full professor at the age of twenty-three, and became one of America's greatest teachers of chemistry and natural history.[10]

He was an entrepreneurial businessman who worked as a consultant for several oil companies and served as a founder and president of the American Mutual Life Insurance Company of New Haven.[11]

Silliman was instrumental in founding the Yale Medical Institution, which received a grant of $20,000 from the state legislature in 1814.[12] This created an important precedent for a grant to Yale in 1831.

One of the best-known and most widely influential scientists of his time, Silliman earned the trust of Yale's leaders through his years of teaching and research, public speaking, and administrative service. In 1842, he agreed to become a leading spokesman for a Yale fundraising campaign.[13] President Theodore Dwight Woolsey called Silliman "our standing orator, the principal medium between those who dwelt in the academic shade and the great public."[14] Silliman College at Yale is named for him.

Silliman had a link to John Trumbull's family: he married Trumbull's niece Harriet and maintained a lifelong friendship with the artist. Silliman drew on all his political and personal capital to manage the gift-planning process.

John Trumbull, by Gilbert Stuart (1818).

COLONEL JOHN TRUMBULL: ARTIST AND DONOR

John Trumbull is generally recognized as the greatest historical painter of the American Revolution.[15] Trumbull knew many of the young republic's leaders and painted their portraits from life, thus inaugurating an American tradition of documentary realism. We know many of their faces today primarily—sometimes solely—through his paintings.[16]

Because of his gifts, Yale has by far the largest and best Trumbull collection—an extraordinary treasure. Eight oil paintings dramatize events from the Revolution. Trumbull executed these at the height of his powers, and they are known as the "National History" series. Congress commissioned Trumbull to paint large copies of four of these, which hang in the rotunda of the US Capitol. His *Declaration of Independence* graces the two-dollar bill.

John Trumbull, The Declaration of Independence in Congress, July 4, 1776 *(1786–1820). Note that Trumbull captured the faces of everyone in the room.*

Also part of the original gift to Yale were large portraits of General Washington (in his military uniform), Alexander Hamilton, and other leaders; thirty miniature portraits painted from life; and nine religious subjects copied from old masters— lesser paintings completed in his later years.[17] Trumbull gave many other paintings to Yale after 1831 and asked no compensation in return.

His family and personal connections permitted John Trumbull easy access to American, British, and French leaders; his Harvard education, personal experiences, and expert legal counsel made him a shrewd negotiator.

The Trumbull family of Hartford, Connecticut, was a leading political force. The family's influence facilitated Silliman's lobbying of the state legislature in the summer of 1831. John's father, Jonathan Trumbull Sr., was a hero of the Revolution. Governor of Connecticut from 1769 to 1784—one of only two colonial governors to remain in office after the signing of the Declaration of Independence—Trumbull served as a close friend and important supplier of troops and material to General Washington. Yale's Trumbull College is named for him.

John's brother, Jonathan Trumbull Jr., became the second Speaker in the US House of Representatives, and he was just finishing twelve years as governor of Connecticut in 1809, when Benjamin Silliman married his daughter.

John Trumbull was expected to follow his family into public service. Virtually blinded in his left eye by an accident when he was five, he still determined on a career as an artist. He became a student of the painter John Singleton Copley at Harvard and of Benjamin West in London.

Just nineteen years old when the Continental Congress adopted the Declaration of Independence, Trumbull joined the Continental army, sketched plans of the British fortifications at Boston, witnessed the Battle of Bunker Hill, served briefly as an aide to General Washington, and served a year as deputy adjutant-general to General Horatio Gates. He attained the rank of colonel, though he never commanded troops in battle.

Following the war, Trumbull served as secretary to Ambassador John Jay in London (together with Jay's son, Peter Augustus Jay) as the ambassador negotiated the terms of the Jay Treaty. John Jay had been appointed the first chief justice of the United States in 1789 and continued serving as the nation's highest judge while on his mission in Great Britain. His son Peter became Trumbull's lawyer for the gift annuity negotiations.

Trumbull's gift accomplished what he needed to do at the end of a long artistic career documenting the faces and major scenes of America's Founding Fathers. He is now recognized as the premier historical painter of the American Revolution,[18] and his four large paintings in the Rotunda of the US Capitol are among the country's best-known works of art. But in 1830, his works were becoming out of fashion. Prospects for selling the eight grand paintings in his National History series at an acceptable price were dim. The chances for keeping the paintings together after a sale were even less likely.

Trumbull saw Yale College as a place where his most important works would be conserved, respected, and exhibited together in perpetuity.[19] He expected that the sale of tickets to a new Trumbull Gallery would finance his annuity payments and provide scholarship aid for needy students.

With the negotiations completed and all documents signed, on September 27, 1832, Trumbull boarded a steamboat carrying his paintings from New York to New Haven and personally directed the hanging of his works in the newly completed Trumbull Gallery (which he had designed) on the Yale campus.

He returned to live alone in New York, but in 1837, he moved in with the Silliman family in New Haven and lived cordially with them until 1841. While in New Haven, at the request of several Yale undergraduates, Trumbull delivered the earliest art history lectures given at a college in the United States.[20] While Trumbull was in his eighties, he wrote the first book-length autobiography by a major American painter. He moved back to his apartment in New York upon the autobiography's publication in 1841.[21] His autobiography included a very short account of the gift to Yale, consisting primarily of the texts of the indenture and annuity bond contracts.

Trumbull's wife, Sarah, had died some years earlier. He had her body reinterred beneath the Trumbull Gallery. Upon Trumbull's own death in 1843, Yale honored his wish to also be buried below his gallery. When Yale opened its Street Gallery in 1866 and moved Trumbull's paintings there, the couple's remains were reinterred below the new building. The present Yale University Art Gallery was built in 1928, and it was renovated and expanded in 2012. Again, Yale honored Trumbull's request to be buried in a tomb below his paintings.

Trumbull Gallery Broadside from about 1850[22]

25

Portrait of Peter Augustus Jay.[23]

PETER AUGUSTUS JAY: LEGAL INNOVATOR

Peter Augustus Jay (1776–1843) was uniquely qualified to represent his friend and client John Trumbull in designing the legal and financial architecture of his gift. That Jay was the major author of the Yale documents is made clear in a letter from Trumbull to Silliman dated November 10, 1836: "Our contract was drawn with admirable simplicity and precision by my friend, Peter A. Jay."

Born in 1776, eldest son of John Jay, Peter served with Trumbull as a secretary for his father in 1794–95, while the elder Jay negotiated a far-ranging postwar treaty with Great Britain. Peter Jay realized the importance of preserving Trumbull's visual documentation of the American Revolution.[24]

Educated, like his father, at King's College (now Columbia University), Peter Jay became a practicing attorney, legal scholar, and a founder and vice president of the New York Law Institute.[25]

In the first decades of the nineteenth century, public protections for American investors and depositors were uneven or nonexistent. Jay successfully prosecuted the Life and Insurance Company in 1827 for fraudulent sale of what it called "bonds," which, in fact, were tools in a Ponzi scheme that resulted in the company's bankruptcy and contributed to a financial panic in 1826.[26]

Working-class people suffered from the lack of reliable banks for depositing money.[27] Jay's great-grandson tells that in 1814, Peter lent his sister's money to Trinity Episcopal Church in lower Manhattan (where he served as a vestryman) to preserve her capital, because that well-endowed nonprofit organization provided a safer harbor than any available bank:

> At that time there were no savings-banks or other institutions allowing interest on deposits, and the inconvenience of having funds uninvested can be seen from the following, written by Mr. Jay to his sister in 1814: "I have not yet disposed of your money. If there were any reasonable hopes of peace I should purchase bank stock. But in the present state of things I think that would be risking too much, and have agreed to lend it to Trinity Church…I preferred this arrangement as being upon the whole the most secure."[28]

Peter Jay was deeply involved with three institutions that issued annuity contracts:

1. He chaired a Legacy Committee for the **American Bible Society,** which considered accepting a gift annuity in 1831. In 1843, the Bible Society embraced Jay's annuity bond to create a template for gift annuity programs used by thousands of nonprofit organizations today.

2. The **New York Corporation for the Relief of Widows and Children of Clergymen of the Protestant Episcopal Church in the State of New York** was a nonprofit corporation chartered by King George III in 1769 to provide annuities for the surviving families of Episcopal clergy, who were "with great difficulty able to provide for their families, so that their widows and children are often

left in great distress."[29] Jay served as treasurer, the most important professional and power position.[30]

The Episcopal population grew to such an extent that in 1806, New York established its own relief organization apart from Pennsylvania and New Jersey. Conceived several decades before actuarial science was applied to retirement plans in the United States, the fundamental laws of the New York Corporation began with a section entitled "Laws Relative to Annuities," which illustrates how an experienced issuer of life annuities managed financial risk through general rules that did not account for life expectancies at various ages. Ministers were expected to pay annual premiums of eight, sixteen, or twenty-four dollars. Their surviving widows received life annuities equal to five times the annual premium, regardless of their ages.

Since the corporation could not calculate the values of individual contracts,[31] there were rules for reducing an annuity when a minister had paid premiums for fewer than fifteen years and when a widow remarried. There was also a rule for increasing payments when the annuity reserve account experienced a surplus: "After the annuities chargeable on the Corporation shall have been paid, one half of the surplus product of the fund shall be equally divided among all the widows and children of contributors…and the remainder shall be added to the capital stock."[32]

As treasurer, Jay ensured that the rules for premium payments and annuities were observed, managed the investment of the "capital stock," provided an annual accounting to the corporation, and acknowledged "the occasional donations of benevolent persons" whose gifts increased the pool available for annuity payments to widows and orphans.

3. His high-level involvement in a new life insurance company gave Jay useful professional awareness of the

power of actuarial science. In 1830, the same year in which John Trumbull offered his paintings to Yale, Jay became a founding stockholder and trustee of the **New York Life Insurance and Trust Company**, together with other leading New Yorkers.[33]

Under the direction of President William Bard, a professional actuary, NYL&T was one of the first companies to create a business model and marketing strategies based on the best available actuarial principles and demographic data. William Bard, founder of the NYL&T in 1830, was the first actuary to be president of an American financial-services firm. Bard used mortality data aggressively to price and promote its life insurance policies, capturing a substantial share of the rapidly growing market.[34]

The Death of General Mercer at the Battle of Princeton, January 3, 1777. *George Washington's pivotal victory. One of the National History series of paintings given to Yale College by John Trumbull in 1831.*

YALE'S CASE FOR A GRANT
FROM CONNECTICUT

Immediately following the end of classes in May of 1831, Professor Silliman went to Hartford and spent a month lobbying the Connecticut legislature for a grant to Yale.

Yale needed outside funding because the college had no appropriate space in which to exhibit Trumbull's paintings and had no capital for a new building. In fact, Yale's fundraising appeals during the early 1800s make clear that the college was in desperate financial straits, lacking money for core services: hiring qualified instructors, stocking the campus with books and equipment, and providing financial aid for poor students.

In 1818, Yale published a fundraising pamphlet ("its first general request for funds in the college's history"[35]) by James L. Kingsley that described in detail the college's financial needs.[36] The lack of money made it increasingly difficult to maintain the college's excellence:

- Only one professorship was endowed, and that only partially.
- The library was aging and small.
- There was not enough financial aid: "A large portion of the students, especially from Connecticut, have a bare sufficiency to pay the expenses of their education, and not a few of them are indigent."
- Competition for students was growing because of the new colleges that were established in the region, including Middlebury (in Vermont), Williams (in Massachusetts), and Hamilton and Union (both in New York).

Most troubling to Kingsley, and challenging for Silliman's appeal to the legislature in 1831, was that Yale College had received no public funding from Connecticut since 1796. Kingsley observed that other states had been far more generous. The Massachusetts constitution, for example, provided for "the most liberal grants" to Harvard College, while New York had granted $750,000 in recent years to Columbia, Hamilton, and Union Colleges. South Carolina had made capital grants of $200,000 for buildings at its college over the previous twenty years, plus $12,000 annually "from the publick treasury" for support of its faculty.

While it had been generous to Yale for the first seventy-five years of its existence, Connecticut no longer recognized a duty to support the only college in the state: "The College, from its foundation [in 1701], to the commencement of the revolutionary war [1776], received from the legislature an annual grant. At this time, on account of the publick necessities, the grant was discontinued."

Connecticut had made its last grants to Yale in 1792 and 1796 as the college, its potential students, and their parents recovered from the economic difficulties of the War for Independence. The pamphlet points out that in 1792, "the whole annual income of the College from permanent funds, which could be appropriated to the support of instruction, was less than one thousand dollars." From 1792 to 1818, Yale had "accumulated so little property, that its whole annual income from perpetual funds, is now less than four thousand dollars."

Despite the need for funding, and the examples of other, more "enlightened" states, no grant from the Connecticut legislature came to Yale in 1818. In 1822, Yale appealed again to the legislature, without success.

With the help of gifts and bequests from individual donors, Yale did make some progress in building its endowment, although that progress was halted in 1825 by a financial crisis caused by the failure of the Eagle Bank. Bolstered by confidence in the men behind this bank, Yale had received special legislation from Connecticut that allowed the college to "invest more than the statutory limit of $5,000 in one bank. Then it proceeded to pour money into the stock of the bank, even borrowing money to do so...the bubble burst in September 1825, and with it went some $21,000 of the funds of the college."[37]

Yale historian Brooks Mather Kelley detailed the extent of the college's crisis: "Total endowment income, exclusive of library funds, had fallen to only $1,800. Debts amounted to over $19,000."[38] But the legislature turned down Yale's request for funding in 1825 and again in 1830.

In 1831, the very year in which Silliman was trying to put together financing for Trumbull's new gallery and life annuity, Yale launched a sorely needed endowment campaign to raise $100,000 from its alumni. Silliman faced a complex challenge in making the case for a grant.

Remembering his lobbying efforts, Silliman wrote that "we were afraid on all hands, that it would be impossible to extract any money from the treasury of the State." The only hope was for the college to benefit from a bonus from the charter of a new bank: "possibly the Legislature might give us a dividend of an expected bonus to be paid for the charter of a Bank at Bridgeport."

Despite Yale College's long history of rejection by the state legislature, Silliman appealed to Hartford in 1831 because he knew from experience that windfall income could become available to a worthwhile cause when the state approved the charter of a bank.

There were other charitable suitors at the time of the Bridgeport bank charter in 1831. How did Silliman position Yale College to receive its first public funding since 1796?

A SURPRISING RELIGIOUS TWIST IN PUBLIC GRANTSMANSHIP

Benjamin Silliman left much unsaid in his *Reminiscences*. His description of providing a suitable gallery, for example, is workmanlike: "There was no apartment in Yale College adapted to the exhibition of the Paintings...a building must therefore be constructed and the means must be obtained."

Whom could Silliman persuade to fund an art gallery on Yale's campus at a time when the study of art was not part of any college curriculum in America? Endowing a college with basic materials for teaching and research in the natural sciences was challenging enough, but that was a more likely undertaking than housing a collection of historical paintings.

There was also the challenge of financing cash payments to Trumbull. A full year after Trumbull's offer to give his paintings in exchange for "a competent annuity for life," Silliman was still seeking people to underwrite Yale's annual payment obligations, which he described as an "insuperable difficulty" and a "formidable" challenge for the cash-poor college. As we will see, he was not entirely successful in doing so, nor was he able to secure a single capital gift from Yale donors. It would fall to the State of Connecticut to rescue the entire plan from failure.

For thirty-five years, Yale's constant and fruitless pleading had not overcome resistance to using public revenues for the operation of a private college. Silliman succeeded where previous generations had failed.

What went on in Hartford in May of 1831? Silliman wrote fewer than four hundred words about the month he spent influencing members of the state legislature. This is disappointing, given the importance of the grant.

Silliman attributed his success to, as he put it, "Fortunate Coincidence." That is true in a certain sense: it was purely an accident of timing that money appeared in 1831 in the form of windfall income to the state from issuing a corporate charter to a new bank in Hartford.

It was no accident that, among all the possible recipients, Connecticut approved a grant to Yale from the unforeseen bonus. Silliman had lobbied energetically for the grant: "We were much engaged in canvassing and in every way preparing our respective cases—and happily with success."

It is impossible to understand and appreciate the success of Silliman's mission in Hartford without having some historical perspective. Silliman delivered a winning argument for a grant to Yale as a politically acceptable counterweight to a grant to Washington College in Hartford. Funding for Trumbull's gallery was made possible by fundamental shifts in religious and political currents, which drove Yale, the Episcopal Church, Washington College, and elected officials toward a unique compromise.

It was inevitable that Benjamin Silliman would be cast in a leading role to seize the opportunity for Yale. Twenty years earlier, Professor Silliman had helped organize the Yale Medical Institution. The new professional school was chartered by the state in 1813.

Within a year, in a totally unrelated development, a group of leading citizens, primarily representing the Episcopal Church, petitioned the legislature to issue a corporate charter to the Phoenix Bank of Hartford.

In negotiations with the founders of Phoenix Bank, the Connecticut legislature required the bank to follow a well-established practice of paying a percentage (5 percent, in this case) of the bank's initial capitalization to the state. The bank "bonus" would be distributed by the legislature as grants to community organizations. This was quite acceptable to the bank founders, whose written petition to the General Assembly specifically requested a grant of $10,000 to the Bishop's Fund of the Episcopal Church, and a grant of $20,000 to the Yale Medical Institution/Connecticut Medical Society.[39]

The terms of the bank petition worked out as planned for Yale—not so for the Episcopalians. To summarize a long and complicated religious history: since Yale's founding in 1701, the college had had an unbroken string of Congregational Church ministers as presidents. That church's power over public policy was waning by 1815, but Congregationalism (a branch of the Presbyterian Church) effectively remained the state religion of Connecticut.[40] For many years, friends of Yale in the legislature had refused to grant a charter to an Episcopal college in the state, partly because the Episcopal Church was the American arm of the Anglican Church of England, and partly because Yale's supporters wanted no competition from another college.[41]

Despite the presence of a growing number of Episcopalian representatives elected to the General Assembly, intolerance toward their church resulted in overturning the terms of the Phoenix Bank petition. Opponents successfully blocked the proposed grant of money destined for an Episcopal college—even though the source of the money was the Episcopalians' own bank. In 1815, the legislature approved a grant for Yale's medical school but denied a grant to the Episcopal Church.

The bank's founders were outraged by this betrayal.[42] Members of the Episcopal Church and other citizens sympathetic to their cause fought an energetic public battle in the newspapers over the "Bishop's Bonus." A bitter exchange of letters lasted for two years and produced several lengthy compilations devoted to the controversy.[43] Largely because of these public arguments, and the effect they had on mobilizing people who challenged the religious establishment, in 1823, the Connecticut legislature reversed course and approved a charter for Washington College, named for the iconic general and first president in order to be noncontroversial.[44] The college's name was changed to Trinity College in 1845.

General George Washington at Trenton, *by John Trumbull (1792).*

The Bishop's Bonus controversy was fresh in the minds of all concerned with the Bridgeport Bank charter and grant requests in 1831. Few wanted to repeat the traumatic experience of 1815. When the Bridgeport Bank came along, Episcopalians and their sympathizers recognized the opportunity for a somewhat more enlightened legislature to redress their grievances.

Benjamin Silliman was thrust back onstage for the second act of a familiar religious drama. He humbly admitted, "Probably my application [to the Connecticut legislature] would have been unsuccessful had not the Episcopal Church been at the same time [in] the arena."

John S. Whitehead, a historian of the rapidly shifting balance of forces among private education, sectarian religion, and public policy in Connecticut, made a stronger assertion. He asserted that Yale's grant was a side effect of actions taken by the Episcopal Church and Washington College: "Supporters of the Episcopal college maneuvered an educational bank bonus through the [Connecticut] assembly in 1831 [that] netted Yale $7,000."[45] The leading man for the Episcopal side was Charles Sigourney, the founding secretary of the Washington College board of trustees. Sigourney, it turns out, was very well-known to Benjamin Silliman and the Connecticut legislature.

Charles Sigourney, co-lobbyist with Benjamin Silliman[46]

Writing about his time lobbying in Hartford, Silliman credited three allies. Two were young Yale alumni who served in the state legislature at the time. State Senator Truman Smith, esquire, class of 1815, was serving his first term in 1831, while State Representative Judge Romeo Lowrey, class of 1818, was a very junior member. Silliman wrote that both men had "cooperated heartily with me" and that "we ought ever to remember [them] with gratitude." The third ally, and by far the most important, was Charles Sigourney.

Silliman recorded almost nothing in his *Reminiscences* about Sigourney's credentials, other than that he represented the Episcopal Church:

> Charles Sigourney Esq. of Hartford and myself became thus coadjutors—he for the Episcopal Church and I for Yale College.

> Mr. Sigourney was a shrewd sensible man and was very active in promoting his object. He had great influence with those who were in sympathy with him and his cause...

> Mr. Sigourney and myself pulled indeed on different ropes attached to the same machine, but pulled in the same direction, so effectually, that with the aid of our friends both within and without the Legislative Halls, we succeeded in moving the carriage of State.

Silliman does not say that Charles Sigourney, the chief lobbyist for the Episcopal Church in 1831, was author in 1814 of the legislative petition to create the very Phoenix Bank that was the source of the Bishop's Bonus controversy.[47] Sigourney became president of Phoenix Bank and served in that capacity from 1821 to 1837.

Thus, Silliman, a devout Congregationalist and member of the American Bible Society[48] (ABS), and Sigourney, an official of

Christ Episcopal Church and a leading volunteer for Washington College, became partners, pleading before the legislature in 1831 for a share of the bank bonus.

The champion for the Episcopal cause was one of Hartford's leading merchants and founder of an eponymous hardware store.[49] There could be no doubt of Sigourney's Episcopal bona fides: he served as a senior warden of Christ Church,[50] and by 1831, he had served for ten years as president of what was known as Hartford's "Episcopal Bank." Sigourney was a founder and the first secretary of Washington College. He contributed $1,000 in 1823 to its support.[51]

Providing no details of the "sausage making" involved in a month of lobbying state legislators, Silliman aptly characterized his partnership with Sigourney without reference to religious controversies or personal histories. We now understand what he meant in writing that he and Sigourney had "pulled indeed on different ropes attached to the same machine, but pulled in the same direction." A grant to Yale made a grant to the Episcopalians more palatable politically for some Congregational legislators,[52] while supporters of the Episcopal Church and for the idea of "disestablishment" gladly accepted a deal that included Yale.

Political considerations illuminated the unrestricted grant made to Yale. There were two reasons why Silliman could not campaign openly on behalf of what he wanted most. First, he chose not to awaken criticism in the legislature by disclosing that Yale would use the public's money for such a suspicious purpose as constructing an art gallery. Better to roll with the tide of political compromise than endanger the grant through too much specificity.

The second reason for pursuing an unrestricted grant had to do with timing. While the college had authorized Silliman in May of 1831 to petition the legislature for a grant, at that time, he had no legal authorization from the Yale Corporation to come to terms with Trumbull on an annuity contract. The roster of subscribers to safeguard Trumbull's annuity payments was probably not completed until August of 1831. The Yale Corporation approved the general terms of its commitment to Trumbull in September and signed specific legal documents in December. While Silliman was meeting with elected members of the legislature in May, he was unable to present a case for a grant dedicated to constructing an art gallery in New Haven.

Fortunately, a specific case was not needed. Connecticut provided an unrestricted grant of $7,000 to Yale College and a grant of $3,000 to the Bishop's Fund. Quoting his letter to Trumbull dated June 4, 1831, Silliman wrote in his *Reminiscences* that "I have succeeded in obtaining a grant for $7,000," but he could not put Trumbull's fears to rest. Silliman still had work to do in convincing Yale to allocate part of the grant for construction: "Out of this I shall make it my business to obtain from our corporation enough to erect the Building which I have no doubt can be ready by mid summer of next year 1832."

In September of 1831, the Yale Corporation did allocate part of the state grant to building the Trumbull Gallery, eventually spending $5,000. Discussing these decisions, Silliman recorded one of his very rare passages to express frustration with the college bureaucracy:

> The primary estimate [for construction costs] was for $2500—but it rose to $3,000 and by a movement of the Corporation themselves to $3,500. Our worthy and vigilant friend Mr. [Stephen] Twining [the Yale treasurer and a subscriber for Trumbull's annuity payments], always laudably anxious for the most economical application of the funds of the college, was much annoyed that the charges ran up to $5,000, but I felt differently.

> My only regret on that subject is that the entire sum of $7,000 which I earned by my own efforts aided by my

friends in the Legislature, had not been expended upon the Building.

Silliman was justifiably proud of his accomplishments as a grant seeker. Yale's grant in 1831 was the first the college had received from the legislature since 1796, and the last that Yale and private colleges such as Harvard, Dartmouth, and Columbia would receive from their respective state governments until Reconstruction following the Civil War, more than three decades later.[53]

Because Yale's pockets were empty, Silliman, after his success in securing the first major piece of his plan, turned to his next challenge.

FINANCING TRUMBULL'S ANNUITY

Arranging a life annuity for Trumbull was a more difficult task than Silliman admitted in *Reminiscences*. He began writing about his financing solution under the heading "Provision for the Annuity," as follows:

This first difficulty [i.e., Daniel Wadsworth's proposal for a second Trumbull gallery in Hartford] being removed, it became important to make provision by subscription [pledge], for the annuity, as this might form an insuperable difficulty with the Corporation of the College; for although they were liberal to the utmost of their ability, we knew that the income of the Institution was so fully pledged that a thousand dollars per ann. [annum, or year], which was the amount expected by Col Trumbull might appear a formidable addition to their already expanded civil list.

Silliman portrayed self-motivated financial volunteers: "Several of the friends of the proposed Gallery however came forward promptly, & Mr. Wadsworth was magnanimously the first to pledge his name and his means." In fact, Silliman labored for nearly a year between his discussion in Trumbull's New York apartment in the summer of 1830 and his first major victory, the Connecticut grant in May of 1831.

During this time, Silliman solicited other Yale donors, including Arthur Tappan. Like Trumbull, Tappan was passionate about funding scholarships. Trumbull wrote to Silliman, wishing him a positive response from Tappan, who, in 1828, had pledged $4,100, payable over four years, for the education of poor Yale scholars.[54] Tappan declined to underwrite Yale's annuity payments.

Silliman presented events out of their proper chronological order. Wadsworth's vexing proposal for creating a second Trumbull gallery in Hartford was not the first "difficulty" to be removed. It was virtually the last. A letter from Trumbull to Silliman describes how Trumbull firmly decided against the idea in late November of 1831. Negotiations over the ill-conceived Hartford gallery consumed enormous amounts of many people's time and energy but were nevertheless quite important in crystallizing many of the legal and financial questions involved in the complicated and innovative gift arrangements later developed with Yale.

We have seen that Silliman removed the first difficulty by lobbying successfully for a grant from the Connecticut legislature. On September 13, 1831, the Yale Corporation allocated part of the grant toward constructing the Trumbull Gallery, but not before Silliman rounded up five men, who each agreed to underwrite a specific share of the $1,000 annuity as needed for the first six years of Trumbull's payments.

Daniel Wadsworth was the only subscriber with substantial personal assets. The others included three top Yale College officers and a leading faculty member: President Jeremiah Day pledged $100, Secretary Elizur Goodrich[55] $250, and Treasurer Stephen

Twining $150.[56] Professor Silliman himself pledged $250, as did Wadsworth.

Theodore Sizer, Trumbull's editor and a director of the Yale University Art Gallery, remarked that these were "certainly liberal contributions from administrative officers and college professors."[57] They were not gifts, however, but loans to be provided as needed and to be repaid by Yale from admission fees collected by the Trumbull Gallery.

Yale's indenture refers to this financing arrangement as follows:

And if the profits of such exhibition shall not, during the life of the said John Trumbull, be sufficient to discharge the said annuity, then the said parties of the second part may borrow as much money as may be necessary for that purpose, and the profits of the said exhibition, after the decease of the said John Trumbull, shall be applied to discharge the principal and interest of the debt which shall thus have been incurred.

Silliman dutifully recorded further details of the annuity financing by quoting from his letter to John Trumbull:

In a letter of mine to Col Trumbull dated Aug 15, 1831 I remark "It is expected that the corporation will take the annuity upon themselves after six years, but if necessary, the gentlemen named above will go on beyond six years; **the income of the gallery is to be pledged to the redemption of this debt.**" (emphasis added)

It is quite likely that personal pledges from the president, secretary, treasurer, and leading faculty members of the college were intended to demonstrate to other Yale faculty and staff that none of the college's money would be diverted from teaching and research. Silliman alluded to their official capacity in quoting from his letter to Trumbull of August 15: "Our responsibility is limited to ourselves and to our continuance in office." He also made it clear that under the terms of the indenture, Yale had full legal responsibility for repaying any loans needed to finance the annuity payments: "the corporation are our indorsers [*sic*]."

All parties to the Yale agreements hoped and expected that admission fees to the Trumbull Gallery would defray the cost of payments to Trumbull and, in time, become a source of scholarship grants for Yale students. There could be no guarantee of sufficient revenue from admission fees in the years to come. Could the cash-poor college demonstrate to Trumbull, his legal advisor, and underpaid members of the faculty and staff its ability to manage the financial risk of a contractual annuity obligation of $1,000 per year, paid in quarterly installments over the uncertain duration of an annuitant's life? Everyone looked to Benjamin Silliman to mitigate the risk of financing Trumbull's annuity—and Silliman delivered.

But, in the years after gift negotiations ended, was net income from the Trumbull Gallery sufficient to pay his annuity? Silliman provided several accounting reports that listed income and expenses from the Trumbull Gallery, which Sizer summarized well.[58]

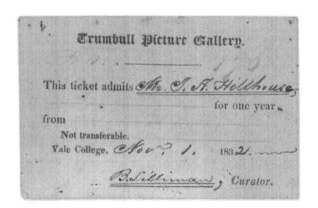

Admission ticket #176 was issued on November 1, 1832, one week after the Trumbull Gallery opened on October 25.

In its best year, which was the year of its opening in 1832, the net income was $930. Trumbull followed reports on the cash flow closely. In a letter acknowledging receipt of his fourth annuity payment, Trumbull wrote, "I am very much pleased…that the year's receipts of the Gallery so nearly balanced the Annuity. I hope that hereafter it may exceed it."[59]

Sizer noted that the second year's receipts were $847.50 and, in the third year, "much less," due to a cold winter. Time passed, and Trumbull's popularity among the undergraduates faded, as did appreciation of their grandparents' (or great-grandparents') war. The admission fee, set at twenty-five cents, was a barrier to attendance. No other campus facility charged a fee.

Silliman filed an accounting with the Yale treasurer in 1863, showing that income and expenses from the Trumbull Gallery, weighed against Trumbull's annuity payments of $11,250, had resulted in a net profit for the college:

> The gross receipts for 24 years, $12,467.78, have exceeded the amount paid for the annuity by $1,217.78. The average expenses have been about $189 per annum—for the last 3 years $67.70 annually…The building cost $5,000 and the College gained $2,000 in the operation in addition to the building which was in fact a "gift to the College"—the net average over expenses has been $334.37 per ann. applicable to the wants of poor students.[60]

A major reason why annual operating expenses were so low is that Silliman himself served as curator of the Trumbull Gallery, an in-kind donation of his services (see broadside above).

It is important to note that in his accounting, Silliman did not mention Treasurer Stephen Twining's death in 1832 affecting Trumbull's annuity payments through 1843. In fact, Silliman did not mention the subscribers at all but balanced admission fees against annual expenses in his accounting report. If he or other subscribers had helped finance the annuity payments, Silliman surely would have reported that fact. Perhaps Yale did not enforce the loan subscriptions, because in the years after the documents were signed, college officials felt the full weight of their legal obligation. Yale, not the subscribers, issued and signed the annuity bond and indenture.

Once the Trumbull Gallery became a real presence in the center of Yale's Old Campus, and the college saw that there was a steady cash flow from admission fees, its leaders may have trusted that future admissions would repay any then-current shortfall. Rather than calling for personal loans from the college president, secretary, and treasurer, the annual shortfall could be met by borrowing from other college accounts. After all, the elderly painter was seventy-six years of age when his annuity began. How much longer was he likely to live?

One final note on Trumbull's overhanging debt is that Silliman wrote that Trumbull had borrowed money against some of his paintings and that his gift to Yale had placed them "beyond the reach of earlier claims." Serving as Trumbull's executor, Silliman sold five large copies of the National History series to Daniel Wadsworth for his Atheneum. The originals remain in the Yale collection to this day, as Trumbull directed. Silliman records that as executor, he used the sale proceeds "to cancel all those claims by a full payment, from funds which became available in my hands."

A TRUMBULL GALLERY FOR HARTFORD?

The legal documents for the annuity were signed eighteen months after the conversation in Trumbull's New York apartment, typical for a complex gift-planning process. In recording his extended negotiations, Silliman was careful to check his sources (which were voluminous): "I have now lying before me about forty letters addressed by me to Col. Trumbull" from the period 1831–32, as well as "other letters addressed to persons more or less interested."

Silliman wrote that "no small part" of this correspondence related to the proposal for a second Trumbull gallery in the family's hometown of Hartford. This was suggested by the amateur artist and patron of the arts Daniel Wadsworth and some of his friends, including the banker Alfred Smith. (Wadsworth, who had also married a Trumbull niece, was one of the wealthiest men in Connecticut. Today he is best known as the founder of the Wadsworth Atheneum in Hartford.[61]) This group, "having a just appreciation" of Trumbull's paintings, "early manifested an interest" in making a case for Hartford and "entered warmly into the deliberations and discussions."

Although Silliman gamely recorded that "we had him and his friends with us as efficient allies and coworkers," a few pages later he admitted that "from the first suggestion of a plan for dividing the Paintings, I regretted that it should have been proposed." Fans of Trumbull's paintings would have to travel to both Hartford and New Haven (not an easy task in those days), since neither gallery could offer a complete collection. From the perspective of a gift planner who was managing relationships and legal and financial issues, Hartford's entry complicated Silliman's negotiations immensely.

In John Trumbull's curious autobiography, published when he was eighty-five, there is no hint of Silliman's protracted efforts to arrange Yale's annuity. Trumbull's very brief account begins and ends with a friend from Hartford: "The thought occurred to me, that in an age of speculation, it might be possible, that some society might be willing to possess these paintings, on condition of pay by a life annuity...I hinted this idea to a friend (Mr. Alfred Smith, of Hartford)—it took—was followed up, and resulted in a contract."[62]

Trumbull explains nothing about how his conversations with Alfred Smith of Hartford resulted in his paintings hanging in New Haven. Silliman corrected the record: negotiations began in Trumbull's New York apartment in the summer of 1830. Wadsworth and Smith intervened near the end of 1830 by offering a second gallery and an additional annuity.

Wadsworth's proposal was that Yale would receive the paintings originally offered to Silliman, and Hartford would receive new, large-format copies of the National History series to be painted by Trumbull. In exchange, Yale and the trustees of the Hartford gallery would each pay Trumbull a life annuity.

Trumbull found this suggestion attractive. A letter from him to Wadsworth dated January 7, 1831, refers to Wadsworth's plan: "I read your proposition with the attention it merited." It also alludes to legal counsel: "intending after fair deliberation to reply advisedly (as the Lawyers say)." Trumbull told Wadsworth that he was hard at work on new paintings intended for Hartford, and that he was giving "every hour [he could] to advance my preparation for your City."

Trumbull's support for a Hartford gallery put Silliman in a difficult position. Not only was Trumbull the captain of his paintings' fate, but Wadsworth and his friends were major donors to Yale:

> From a delicate respect to the wishes of Mr. Wadsworth and his friends which were favored by Col. Trumbull, I acquiesced, and put forth my best efforts to carry the scheme into effect, nor did I reveal to any one the doubts which I felt…I felt my own position to be a difficult one as Mr. Wadsworth and other gentlemen in Hartford had on former occasions made liberal contributions to Yale College, and any coolness on my part would have appeared equally uncourteous and ungrateful.

Negotiations between Hartford and Trumbull became increasingly specific. A letter from Trumbull to Silliman dated April 13, 1831, spoke of very concrete legal arrangements: "What I have said of the Ownership & Trustees for the part of the Collection intended for Hartford, is I trust sufficiently explicit."

Trumbull's use of the legal concept "trustees" in relation to ownership of the Hartford paintings is important to note here. The source of this concept was his lawyer, Peter Augustus Jay, who was an unsung hero in the negotiations. ("Jay" will henceforth refer to Peter Augustus Jay unless otherwise noted.) We will return to the Hartford plan after describing the state of negotiations with New Haven.

As summer loomed in 1831, two very large parts of Silliman's gift plan for New Haven were still missing. Because Yale had no money to build a gallery, Silliman would appeal to the Connecticut legislature in May for public funding, but the prospects for success there were far from certain. Yale also had no money to pay Trumbull's annuity.

Trumbull and Jay had taken the lead in developing the practical details of a gift exchange with Hartford. Wadsworth and the men of Hartford had deep pockets. Would the Hartford plan become the model for Yale—or its alternative? Trumbull had asked Yale to go all-in to construct a gallery and pay him a life annuity. Could he be certain that the college could carry out the plan?

Silliman must have known that if Yale faltered, Hartford would stand ready to buy the Trumbull collection. In May of 1831, he provided Trumbull with a positive report on Yale's progress. In response, Trumbull wrote to Silliman on May 28 that he had instructed his lawyer to arrange a bequest to Yale as a safeguard:

Your last letter detailing the doings of your Prudential Committee etc I have placed in the hands of my friend P. A. Jay for the purpose of drawing a Will, which in case I should be removed before the arrangement can be entirely completed, may insure to Yale College the possession of the small paintings etc according to the plan of the room which I gave; to be applied to the Education of poor Scholars.

This written commitment of an intended bequest to Yale in case of Trumbull's untimely death must have heartened Silliman. Trumbull expressed very different sentiments to Harvard later in the summer of 1831.

In his autobiography, which Trumbull published ten years later (1841), he somewhat perversely wrote that he originally considered Harvard to be the recipient of his paintings and guarantor of his life annuity but decided in favor of Yale because it was "poor." As he noted: "I first thought of Harvard College, my alma mater, but she was rich, and amply endowed. I then thought of Yale—although not my alma, yet she was within my native state, and poor."[63]

Trumbull did not publish his letter of September 16, 1831, to President Josiah Quincy of Harvard, in which he first voiced his odd rationale about Yale's lack of money. Greater than his concern about money was Trumbull's distrust of Yale's fidelity. Trumbull expressed to President Quincy a plan to include a provision in his Yale annuity agreement to benefit Harvard in case of a "perversion" of his intentions:

I have Conveyed my original paintings of Subjects of the Revolution, with others, to the President and Fellows of Yale College—burthened with payment of an annuity to me during my Life:—and afterward the income which may be derived from the Exhibition of them to be applied forever to the Education of poor Scholars—to guard against the possibility of a perversion to any other purpose in any future time I wish to insert a Clause in virtue of which (in case of such perversion) the whole may pass into the possession of my Alma Mater, Harvard, to whom I should have offered the donation in the first instance had she not been very rich and Yale very poor. It is necessary to know accurately the Legal Style and title or Appellation of Harvard for the purpose—may I beg you to give me as soon as may be this information.[64]

49

Jay must have encountered other clients who wished to provide permanent safeguards against the misuse of their gifts to charity after their deaths. Whether Jay included Harvard in an early draft of Yale's indenture is unknown. In the documents executed in December of 1831, which contain no mention of Harvard, Trumbull retains the right to take back the paintings if Yale defaults on its responsibilities during his life. The college, for its part, swore that any net income from selling tickets to exhibitions of Trumbull's paintings "shall be sacredly applied to the purposes before mentioned [i.e., the education of poor scholars], and to no other."

Trumbull should have trusted Yale to honor his intentions. It has done so with great care since 1831.

John Trumbull's gift to Yale in 1831 included thirty miniature portraits of men and women of the Revolutionary War era. Notable are President John Adams, Chief Justice John Jay, and George Hammond, British envoy to the new United States of America.

HARTFORD TRUST SUCCEEDED BY YALE ANNUITY BOND CONTRACT

As early as the spring of 1831, Jay's legal arrangements between Trumbull and the city of Hartford were well advanced, and Trumbull was sharing the details with Yale. For example, Trumbull wrote to Silliman on April 13, 1831, referencing an exchange of letters:

> On the other side is duplicate of what I wrote to you on the 4th...I have this moment rec'd yours of the 11th by which I see that you had not then rec'd it.

> What I have said of the Ownership & Trustees for the part of the Collection intended for Hartford, is I trust sufficiently explicit.

By the end of August of 1831, there was no final agreement between Yale and Trumbull, but Jay and Trumbull had drafted terms for a trust arrangement with Hartford. Yale's annuity bond and indenture contracts, which were signed in December, would incorporate verbatim virtually all the terms of the Hartford plan without the trust structure.

Trumbull, Jay, and the Yale Corporation must have exchanged correspondence and developed an early draft in August. Trumbull wrote to Silliman on September 3, saying, "It appears to me that there is a complexity in the actual form which would require still much writing to bring into a simple form, which at the same time a few minutes of conversation may set all right." He told Silliman that he would travel from New York to New Haven to take a meeting with him and Yale treasurer Stephen Twining: "I have determined to come to you on Tuesday or Wednesday of next week [i.e., September 6–7, 1831]—whichever will be most convenient to you and Mr. Twining."

It is very likely that the main topic of the meeting in New Haven in early September was a discussion of the terms that Trumbull and Jay were working out with Wadsworth and his Hartford colleagues. Silliman recorded that Trumbull provided him with a legal memorandum dated September 5, 1831, entitled "Plan for a Gallery of Col Trumbull's Paintings to be established in Hartford." This plan was "now before me in his own hand writing." Silliman considered this memorandum of such importance that he copied nearly the whole document by hand on pages 13–18 of his *Reminiscences*, condensing its first paragraph by omitting the names of trustees other than Wadsworth and some of Jay's legal terms.[65] His copy of Trumbull's memorandum begins, "I propose to convey to Daniel Wadsworth etc. etc. etc. of the city of Hartford, as Trustees, for the uses and on the conditions hereinafter recited—The Paintings of which a list is subjoined."

There were three parties to the Hartford gift: Trumbull, the Hartford trustees, and Yale. In exchange for twenty-one listed paintings, the trustees (under Trumbull's direction) would erect a building to house and exhibit the paintings and pay Trumbull a specific life annuity: "An annuity of $500 shall be secured, to be paid to me yearly, in four quarterly payments, during my life— The Paintings shall be publicly exhibited, and the proceeds of such exhibition shall be applied toward the payment of such annuity."

The annuity payment period would begin upon Trumbull's completion and delivery of the twenty-one paintings. If Hartford's annuity payments were not made on time, Trumbull wrote, "I reserve to myself the right of returning, taking possession of and removing such paintings; without being required or obligated to refund any sum which I may have previously received on account of said annuity."

Should ticket sales fall short, the Hartford trustees could borrow to make the annuity payments and use subsequent admission income to repay their borrowing "until the same [shall] be fully repaid with interest." Surplus income from the Hartford Gallery not required for Trumbull's $500 annuity during his lifetime, and in perpetuity thereafter, would be sent to Yale "for the Education of poor Scholars." The trustees named in the memorandum and their successors would hold the paintings in perpetuity, "never to be sold, divided, alienated or dispersed, but the income to be sacredly applied to the above [named] purpose."

The Jay/Trumbull legal memorandum of September 5, 1831, Silliman's effective lobbying for a grant of $7,000 from the State of Connecticut, and a successful subscription campaign to relieve Yale of the financial stress of a life-annuity obligation all spurred the Yale Corporation to action. On September 13, the Yale Corporation formally approved the gift plan in principle, subject to the development and approval of various legal documents. Silliman wrote, "At the meeting of the corporation in September 1831, the proposals for the Gallery were received with unanimous approbation, and money was voted for the erection of the Building...Contracts in due legal form were executed and interchanged."[66]

We should not, with Silliman, leap immediately to the annuity bond and indenture contracts, which were signed and sealed in December of 1831, three months after the Yale Corporation's approval in principle. There remained a sensitive negotiation between Yale, Trumbull, and Jay over specific terms. In a letter to Silliman on September 16, 1831, Trumbull reported that "Mr. Jay is preparing a draft of agreement, which will be sent to you for consideration as soon as possible."

DONOR WEIGHS THE ODDS AS FUNDRAISING JOINS THE "PROBABILISTIC REVOLUTION"

Without realizing the full implications in 1831, Silliman had led Yale to embark on a financial experiment with an uncertain result, whose success or failure in future years would involve the new actuarial science of mortality experience and mathematical probabilities. Writing in 1857, Silliman acknowledged the importance that life expectancy played in setting the terms of the pledge agreements. In establishing a term of years, Silliman had applied his best scientific judgment to arrive at a plausible and reasonably responsible hypothesis:

> The subscription was for the term of six years, which upon the ordinary valuation of human life might be presumed sufficient for a man who had already numbered seventy six years and might not pass eighty two—and it is probable that the gentlemen who gave their names would have become responsible for a longer term had it been deemed necessary.

Silliman wrote this sentence, packed with complex ideas, twenty-six years after Yale's president and secretary had signed the annuity bond and indenture. He wrote with the weight of experience and a much clearer understanding of what he, Trumbull, and Jay had gotten Yale into in 1831. With a slight touch of defensiveness, Silliman described the assumptions behind fixing the term of the subscription at six years, which "might be presumed sufficient" to manage longevity risk for a seventy-six-year-old who "might not pass" eighty-two.[67]

What Silliman did not say in his *Reminiscences* is that Trumbull lived for nearly twelve years after Yale signed its life-annuity bond. America's first gift annuitant was the first to outlive his life expectancy: instead of dying "on time"[68] in 1837, he lived twice as long as the expected six years, dying in 1843. Yale ended up sending Trumbull forty-five quarterly payments of $250, not the twenty-four payments that "might be presumed sufficient" for an annuitant who was seventy-six at the time of his gift. Put another way, Yale assumed it would pay Trumbull $6,000 but, in fact, paid him $11,250.

Silliman wrote that the subscribers "who [had given] their names" to underwrite Yale's financial commitment if the college had asked them to loan money during the first six years of the contract would probably have agreed to extend their responsibilities for "a longer term." Silliman did not claim that the subscribers would have signed on for Trumbull's life, which was an open-ended financial commitment. He did say that they probably would have done more after the first six years if Yale had asked.

Yale did *not* ask the subscribers for a loan in the first six years and did not call upon the subscribers to extend their pledges for any term beyond the original commitment.

None of the parties in 1831 could be sure that the net income from the new gallery would cover Yale's obligation to pay $1,000 per year to Trumbull for his life. What was certain is that, given the sorry state of its financial condition, the Yale Corporation could not take on this general obligation without its own safeguards. Securing loan commitments from the five subscribers for Trumbull's life expectancy allowed for the legal and financial fiction of an annuity reserve account. Silliman and Jay thus circumvented the "insuperable obstacle" of financing Trumbull's annuity.

There was a final twist to the Hartford chapter of the story. Silliman recorded that at some point, Wadsworth "suggested an occasional exchange of Paintings between the two galleries that they might be as near equality as possible." This new proposal must have come after the September 5 memorandum, since that contained no mention of exchanging paintings.

Trumbull wanted his historical paintings kept intact as a collection, to be neither sold nor loaned to other museums. Wadsworth, his nephew-in-law, persuaded him for a time to split the paintings between New Haven and Hartford, but he soon realized the difficulties this scheme would present: not being able to see the whole collection in one place, difficulties in travel, and the inevitable damage in moving paintings, among other factors. Trumbull eventually realized that one unified exhibition of his paintings had more artistic value and commercial potential than two galleries, each dependent on selling admission tickets.

On November 30, 1831, Trumbull sent a letter to Silliman regarding a draft agreement that Silliman had mailed to Trumbull that mentioned two schedules that were not enclosed. Trumbull wrote that he would "submit your draft to Mr. Jay, and may obtain his opinion before you can send us the schedules" that were missing from Silliman's letter. In the meantime, he said, "I have deferred sending you any answer."

In this letter of November 30, Trumbull reported that the original paintings promised to Yale were ready to be shipped, but he had decided against sending others to Hartford or painting copies of the National History series for Wadsworth's exhibition. That plan called for exchanging paintings from one place to the other from time to time, but the travel and rehanging issues "would unavoidably in a few repetitions occasion irreparable injury." His "first principle by which I have been activated in the whole negotiation" was "the desire to preserve the Labor of my Life, as far as possible."

He explained that his small paintings fit the proposed Yale gallery but "would be lost in the larger room prepared for Hartford."

Trumbull also eventually realized that the financial return for a great deal of artistic work would not justify the years required to gain an extra $500 annuity from Hartford, when he had a $1,000 annuity in the works from Yale for his existing paintings. Trumbull used the terminology of life expectancy and probabilities in expressing his view of the risks and rewards of painting large-scale copies for Wadsworth's exhibition in exchange for an annuity of $500:

But is it wise for me to enter into legal stipulations to complete a work, which cannot be finished in less than Four years of health, when I am entered on my 76th year, and four more will bring me to Eighty: __ by such stipulations I should feel myself bound to devote myself entirely to this work, and to decline all others ____ and what is the contemplated recompence for this unremitting labor?

Nothing unless I live to complete it: ____ and if I do complete it $500 for every year which may be granted me after Eighty: ____ in other words—Eight paintings at $2,500 each are worth $20,000 ____ I then sink a Capital of 20,000 dollars in the purchase of an annuity of $500, on a life past 80 ____ which may possibly, but not probably [be] received, for five years: ____ that is, I give Seven pictures to sell one, or $17,500 for $2,500.

Trumbull summarized the proposed relationship with Hartford as a business transaction: "This is the prudential view of my side of the Bargain, which a merchant would take."

The gift conversation with Silliman began when Trumbull was seventy-four. The painter was in debt, with a small military pension his only dependable income. Like many subsequent donors, Trumbull could make such a large gift only if he could rely on receiving lifetime payments in return. Trumbull's letters record his doubts about the extent to which he could rely on Yale and how likely it was that he would live long enough to receive sufficient value. He provides timeless insights into a gift annuity donor's thoughts.

These are the earliest recorded deliberations on whether a gift annuity contract is priced fairly and secured adequately, introducing the calculation of probabilities into American fundraising: how long is an annuitant likely to live? What are the probable costs of a life-annuity contract? And is it reasonable to expect that the benefits for a nonprofit organization will justify a legally binding financial obligation?

With the Hartford decision behind Trumbull, negotiations with Yale were nearing a final resolution. In his *Reminiscences*, Silliman recorded that once Trumbull decided in favor of a single gallery at the end of November of 1831, the artist *"appeared as of now* [emphasis added] about to surrender a valuable property."

In his *Autobiography*, Trumbull acknowledged that his annuity from Yale provided most of his income and gave him a warm glow of satisfaction, knowing he had helped future generations of deserving students: "Thus I derive present subsistence principally from this source, and I have besides the happy reflection, that when I shall have gone to my rest, these works will remain a source of good to many a poor, perhaps meritorious and excellent man."

Trumbull portraits of leaders from two southern states: Governor John Rutledge, Governor Thomas Pinckney, General Charles Pinckney, and General William Moultrie of South Carolina; and General Otho Holland Williams of Maryland.

THE TERMS OF THE YALE ANNUITY BOND

The annuity bond was the first of the two documents to be signed. The indenture noted that the bond had already been executed by Yale. Both are dated December 19, 1831, though Trumbull signed the indenture several weeks later. In a letter to Silliman dated December 30, 1831, Trumbull wrote:

> I have received yours of the 26th with the Bond and Deed enclosed duly executed by the College authorities (so far as I am a Judge)—but owing to the severity of the weather, I have not yet shown them to Mr. Jay—if when I have sent them to him he should state any objection, I will state it to you. So far as I can see, the intentions and requirements of both parties are completely expressed.

After the fact, Trumbull and Silliman downplayed the actual gift documents, though Trumbull reprinted them in his *Autobiography*, as if to ensure public recognition of the promises made to him by Yale. Of course, publication of these documents in 1841 made them available to any donor, attorney, financial planner, and charitable organization in the country as a model, and perhaps to be understood as a legal precedent.

Since the financial obligations in the annuity bond were all on Yale's side, it seems clear that Trumbull and Jay insisted on getting this commitment executed before proceeding to the more complicated conditions in the indenture.

There are two parts to the annuity bond. The first paragraph is a long sentence (just over a hundred words) that announced to the world ("Know all men by these presents") that the president and fellows of Yale were "bound" to pay John Trumbull "twenty thousand dollars lawful money of the United States of America," as certified by applying the corporate seal of the college. While the bond was binding to the officers of the Yale Corporation and "our successors," the subscription pledge bound its subscribers only while they remained in office.

The second paragraph is an even longer sentence (160 words) that set forth one condition: if Yale made timely and accurate payments of $250 per quarter to John Trumbull as long as he lived, then it would not have to pay him the $20,000 as a lump sum. The payments were due quarterly on the first days of January, April, July, and October. The initial payment would be made on October 1, 1832; since the document was signed in December 1831, this was a deferred-payment gift annuity. If Trumbull's payments were made on time, Yale's obligations of paying him a lump sum, and any annuity payments after his death, were void; otherwise, they would "remain in full force and virtue." The annuity bond was signed by President Day and sealed by Secretary Goodrich.

It is important to pause for a moment to reflect on this brief document and what it did *not* contain.

First, there was no mention in the annuity bond of a gift to Yale, nor a bargain sale of Trumbull paintings, nor the education of poor scholars. He would deliver his paintings once the new gallery was built—and there was also no mention of a gallery. Nothing in the annuity bond indicated that Trumbull would provide consideration to Yale of any kind. It was a single-premium annuity with no premium specified.

The bond was clearly issued by the president and fellows of Yale College as a general obligation. The five subscribers who underwrote the first six years of the annuity were not mentioned. The focus of the entire document was that Yale was bound to pay Trumbull $20,000 but would not be required to make that lump-sum payment on condition of paying him $1,000 for life in quarterly payments on a specific schedule.

There was no explanation in the annuity bond of where the figure of $20,000 came from. In fact, this was a legal and financial fiction[69]; Trumbull did not transfer $20,000 to Yale College to purchase a life annuity of $1,000. Nor did he loan Yale $20,000 in expectation of an interest income and the eventual return of his capital investment. His paintings could never be liquidated. Their monetary value for purposes of the annuity bond was purely the projected net revenue from future admission fees.

The closest analogy the parties could find for Trumbull's charitable gift annuity was an annuity bond, a contract depending upon a specific monetary exchange. The formalities of a bond required Yale to state that it owed Trumbull $20,000, even though it would have been exceptionally difficult, if not impossible, for Yale to pay $20,000 to anyone in 1831. The entire Yale endowment was worth roughly that amount, and parts of the endowment were encumbered by agreements with donors. Yale could not afford to set aside an adequate amount of money in an annuity reserve account to demonstrate the issuer's capacity to make future payments.

Failure to make the annuity payments would have devastating financial consequences for Yale, since the specified penalty was a "death threat": a $20,000 lump-sum payment to Trumbull and/or a return of his paintings. To protect against default, the college had to have those five subscribers who had pledged in their side agreement to underwrite Yale's annuity payments by providing whatever loans were necessary to make up a shortfall in admission revenue. Even with their written assurances, signing the annuity bond was a courageous act of faith by the Yale Corporation.

The amount of $20,000 was probably not calculated as the then-present value of Trumbull's life annuity. Yale could reasonably expect Trumbull to live for another six years, so it could expect to pay him a total of $6,000 during that time. A reserve of $20,000 would be too generous, as was demonstrated when Trumbull lived for more than eleven years and received payments totaling $11,250.

Perhaps $20,000 was a mutually agreed-on value for the paintings to be delivered by Trumbull. It is similar to the terms in Trumbull's letter to Silliman of November 30, 1831, on the terms of the Hartford proposal. In calculating the benefits from his proposed annuity from Hartford, Trumbull wrote that "eight paintings at $2,500 each are worth $20,000." The heart of his transfer to Yale was the set of eight paintings in the National History series.

The equivalency between the Hartford paintings and those headed to New Haven didn't quite work, since Trumbull knew that the quality and value of his original paintings of the American Revolution were much greater than the copies proposed for Hartford. Trumbull had also agreed to give Yale many more paintings in addition to the main prize. If any professionals had existed in 1831 who could have provided an independent appraisal of Trumbull's fifty-five paintings, the value at that time would likely have been much higher than $20,000.

It is possible that Trumbull had resolved that an acceptable bargain sale price for the lot was $20,000, which at a rate of 5 percent would have produced a $1,000 life annuity. Any additional value would be purely a gift to Yale. Trumbull confirmed his charitable intentions by contributing quite a few additional paintings (including twenty-eight more miniature portraits) to Yale after his annuity agreements, not asking for additional compensation.

Five years after negotiating terms with Yale, Trumbull expressed bitter regret at the amount of his annuity when he learned that the college had collaborated with the city of New Haven to raise $4,000 for the purchase of a paired work of statuary by the local artist Hezekiah Augur.[70] Trumbull was not a fan of sculpture. In 1830, he had told the artist Joseph Frazee that "sculpture would not be wanted in this country for yet a hundred years."[71]

His letter to Silliman dated November 10, 1836, is worth quoting at length, since it sheds some light on how Trumbull viewed the $20,000 amount at that point in time. He referred to the $4,000 paid to Augur, then calculated the capital amount he would have received if Yale had paid him $4,000 for each of his eight National History paintings (i.e., $32,000). With a capital sum of $32,000, Trumbull asserted that his annuity would have been $1,600 instead of the $1,000 he had negotiated in 1831. The high emotions experienced by the painter are indicated by his underlining and long blank lines:

> I rejoice to hear such a spirit of munificence exists respecting Mr. Augur. The difference between his Case and mine stands thus;—it is proposed <u>to pay him splendidly</u>: _____ If I had been paid as much for each of the Eight subjects of the Revolution (as important to Mankind surely as the [illegible] conduct of Jephthah) the gross amount would have been $32,000, which at 5 per Ct. would have given a perpetual income of $1,600 a year _____ instead of this, I have given them (to say nothing of the others) for a Life Estate of $1,000 per ann.: ____ when near 80 Years of age. ____

> The consolation of such a Sacrifice is the reflexion that after my death, I shall bestow the blessing of Education on many poor young men.

Despite his shock at the sale price for a modern sculpture, Trumbull did not suggest reopening his negotiations with Yale:

> I do not like Codicils:____the Constitution of the United States has been Codiciled and amended, until few know what it now is. Our contract was drawn with admirable simplicity and precision by my friend, Peter A. Jay, & cannot be misunderstood—I am not willing that it should be altered.

Trumbull's transfer of his paintings in exchange for a life annuity was not entirely a sale—nor was it a bond, since the "investor" never wished to see the return of his capital. The indenture characterized Trumbull's transfer of paintings equivocally, but began with Trumbull's charitable intent: "In consideration of his [Trumbull's] good will toward Yale College, and his desire to promote its prosperity, [he] hath granted, bargained, sold and conveyed...all the pictures or paintings mentioned in the schedule to this indenture."

Before leaving the subject of the annuity bond, there is a final note on Trumbull's annuity payments. These took the form of a series of forty-five letters from the Yale treasurer that contained bank drafts authorizing Trumbull to receive $250 from the City Bank of New York. The letters presumably were mailed within fifteen days of their payment dates, but not all of the letters were mailed on the first day of each quarter, as promised. A letter dated January 6, 1835, from Yale treasurer Wyllys Warner apologized to Trumbull for sending his payment a few days late: "Please excuse the oversight. I will endeavor to be punctual hereafter."

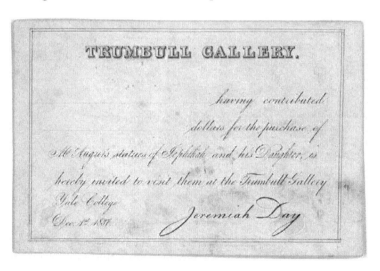

Donors to the acquisition of Hezekiah Augur's statuary pair Jephthah and his Daughter *received a pass like this one that included admission privileges to the Trumbull Gallery.*[72]

Trumbull painted portraits of notable women of the Revolutionary War era, including First Lady Martha Washington, her granddaughter Eleanor Custis, and two daughters of Pennsylvania Chief Justice Benjamin Chew, an important legal advisor to George Washington and other Founding Fathers.

THE TERMS OF THE YALE INDENTURE

Following a long tradition of indenture contracts, two identical originals were prepared and signed separately.[73] The last paragraph of the Yale indenture noted this formality:

> In witness whereof, the parties to these presents have interchangeably executed the same, that is to say, the said John Trumbull hath to one part of these presents set his hand and seal, and the said President and Fellows of Yale College, in New Haven, have to another part of these presents caused

their corporate seal to be affixed, on the day and year first above written.

An original indenture in the Yale archives is dated December 19, 1831, internally. There is no date next to the signatures. The document is signed by Trumbull in two places, with a word changed by Jay and signed by him, noting "Sealed and delivered by John Trumbull." The identical version printed in Trumbull's *Autobiography* is the one signed and sealed by Yale's President Day and Secretary Goodrich.

There were two parties to the indenture: Trumbull and Yale College. This was unlike the annuity bond, which was solely about Yale's obligations and signed only by the college president and secretary. The indenture contract also differed from the Hartford trust proposal that involved Trumbull, the Hartford trustees, and Yale College: the words "trust" and "trustee" were not used in the indenture. Apart from the concept of a trust, the indenture and annuity bond contained all the terms and conditions described in Trumbull's legal memorandum of August 15, 1831 plus several others.

The indenture began with a very long sentence of 319 words. First, it set out the basic terms. The contract was based on two elements of "consideration." One was the previously executed "bond or obligation," which specified the annuity amount to be paid to Trumbull by Yale, the payment dates, and the penalty in case of Yale's default. The other was Trumbull's charitable intent: his "good will toward Yale College, and his desire to promote its prosperity." Motivated by these considerations, Trumbull "hath granted, bargained, sold and conveyed" to Yale "all the pictures or paintings mentioned in the schedule to this indenture, annexed."

The indenture immediately made clear that the transfer of Trumbull's property was contingent upon two general conditions. First was that Yale must not be late in making its annuity payments in the full amount: "Provided always and nevertheless, and these presents are upon condition, that if the said annuity, or any part thereof, shall be behind or unpaid by the space of fifteen days next after any of the days of payment whereon the same ought to be paid, pursuant to the condition of the said bond..."

The other general condition was that Yale must strictly observe a series of additional promises that were spelled out in the second part of the indenture: "if default shall be made in any of the covenants or agreements herein contained..."

The annuity bond specified a penalty for Yale's failure to make the annuity payments on time and in the full amount: a $20,000 lump-sum payment to Trumbull. The indenture stated that if Yale should default on any of the specified promises, Trumbull had the legal right to demand the return of all of his paintings: "it shall and may be lawful for the said John Trumbull...to retake and repossess the said paintings...as in his first and former estate, any thing herein contained to the contrary notwithstanding."

The indenture then articulated three sets of Yale's obligations:

- **The gallery**: Yale agreed to build a fireproof gallery on its campus; to complete construction by October 1, 1832; to allow Trumbull to approve the gallery's "form and dimensions"; and to give Trumbull the power to "place and arrange" his paintings in the new gallery. The indenture did not name the Trumbull Gallery and did not require the permanent operation of a separate gallery building dedicated solely to Trumbull's paintings. The annuity bond called for payments to begin on October 1, 1832, when the gallery had to be completed.

- **Use of exhibition income**: Yale agreed to use any net income from gallery-exhibition fees to pay Trumbull's life annuity. All surplus fees during and after his life "shall be perpetually appropriated toward defraying the expense of educating poor scholars in Yale College, under such regulations as the said President and Fellows, and their successors, shall from time to time see fit to make." The indenture did not refer to a permanent endowed account (such as a "John Trumbull Scholarship Fund") but deferred to the college's judgment in applying net income toward "educating poor scholars." The indenture did provide one financial safeguard for Yale: the power to "borrow as much money as may be necessary" to make annuity payments to Trumbull. The college would be allowed to use future exhibition income "to discharge the principal and interest of the debt which shall thus have been incurred." The indenture was a general obligation of the Yale Corporation and did not mention the subscribers.

- **Permanent custody of Trumbull's paintings**: Yale agreed that the paintings given by Trumbull in exchange for his annuity "shall never be sold, alienated, divided or dispersed, but shall always be kept together, and exhibited as aforesaid… and that the profits of such exhibition shall be sacredly applied to the purposes before mentioned, and to no other."

The schedule that accompanied the indenture was "a list of the paintings thereby conveyed to the President and Fellows of Yale College, in New Haven." The main prize was the eight National History paintings: "original paintings of subjects from the American Revolution," enumerated by title. The collection also included nine lesser paintings of scenes from the Bible; four important portraits of Washington, Hamilton, and the afore-mentioned Rufus King and Christopher Gore; and "six frames, each containing five miniature portraits of persons distinguished during the Revolution."

Six frames (thirty miniature portraits) were thus committed to Yale. Another six had been allocated to Hartford under that unsuccessful plan. Trumbull also decided to give these twenty-eight miniature portraits to Yale. He installed all fifty-eight portraits in the new gallery in 1832.

Trumbull retained the right to approve the design for the gallery and to arrange how each painting would be hung in the exhibition. After the documents were signed, Trumbull insisted on designing the art gallery himself in neoclassical Greek style, which he did with the assistance of professional architect Ithiel Town.

Trumbull Gallery, Yale College, in 1832.

REFLECTIONS ON THE GIFT ANNUITY ISSUED BY YALE

With no fanfare announcing a new arrow in the quiver of non-profits in search of financial support, Jay drew upon his experiences with religious pensions, life insurance, and investments to create a gift annuity contract whose terms were shaped to achieve the objectives of a donor and a charity.

This is an important point that has often been misunderstood: gifts to a nonprofit organization in exchange for life payments were not created through legislation or administrative regulations. The idea of enacting a statute that would create a charitable annuity bond that borrowed from commercial law would not have occurred to public officials in New York or Connecticut. Annuity contracts issued by a nonprofit organization were first recognized under New York law in 1925.

In 1831 there was no public-policy framework or legal protection for a charitable gift annuitant or the charity that issued an annuity. No memorandum exists citing legal precedents for Yale's annuity in 1831, as Luther Bradish would write for the Bible Society in 1848. Nor is there a record of the degree of confidence felt by Jay or the Yale Corporation that the terms of an annuity bond appropriate for investors had effectively expressed the relationships between a donor and a charitable organization obligated to provide the donor with a life annuity.

Yale was chartered as a private college, not as a life insurance company. Like the charters of other nonprofit corporations, Yale was empowered to receive annuities, but this referred to land leases, not life-annuity contracts.[74] (See the discussion of early annuities in section 1.)

The absence of specific legal authority would trouble the ABS board a few years later. There were no "safe harbors" for a nonprofit to accept and administer a life-annuity contract.

In fact, certain public-policy considerations could have weighed against Trumbull's arrangements with Yale if the specifics of his gift had been challenged. Jay silently assumed the validity of an unsecured, general-obligation annuity bond issued by a nonprofit charitable corporation to a donor/annuitant in exchange for illiquid, tangible assets—a gift of paintings Yale agreed never to sell. A regular cash flow from admission fees to a new gallery of historical paintings was far less certain than would be acceptable for any revenue bond. Few, if any, board members of a financial services company would consent to such an arrangement, then or now.

Some elements of Trumbull's contract with Yale College were like a modern charitable gift annuity, and some were very different. Trumbull's annuity is like a modern gift annuity in that the specific responsibilities of the issuing charity were detailed in a legally binding contract. As with modern annuities, the payments promised to Trumbull were a general obligation of the issuing charity rather than being limited to the actual income that was generated by admission fees.

Like gift annuities today, the value of the assets that were funding the annuity (i.e., Trumbull's paintings) was greater than the value of his life payments. The fact that there is a gift element differentiates a charitable annuity from a commercial-life annuity, in which money purchases an investment of equivalent value.

Both the donor and the charity issuing the annuity expected that, over time, there would be surplus income from admission fees that would be applied toward helping the "poor scholars" of Yale College. The indenture referred to a bargain sale that demonstrated Trumbull's charitable intent: "In consideration of his good will toward Yale College, and his desire to promote its prosperity, [Trumbull] hath granted, bargained, sold and conveyed…all the pictures or paintings mentioned in the schedule to this indenture."

On the other hand, significant elements of Trumbull's annuity are quite unlike a modern gift annuity. For example, his contract with Yale was unique: the college intended to have just one annuitant, rather than mitigating longevity risk by spreading that risk across a pool of annuitants.

Yale set aside no annuity reserve account. The college used the fictitious $20,000 in its annuity bond contract. The assets used to fund Trumbull's annuity were unmarketable since Yale agreed never to sell the paintings.

Despite Jay's choice of terminology, Trumbull's gift arrangement with Yale was not an *annuity bond*. Unlike a bond investor,

Trumbull was making a gift, not a loan that would involve payments of interest in exchange for the use of investment capital.

The *annuity bond* metaphor[75] at the heart of these documents had a profound influence on subsequent life-income gifts in the United States. Peter Jay's metaphor dominated the country's thinking about gift annuities for nearly one hundred years, illustrated in section 3 by many examples of *annuity bond* advertisements published by nonprofit organizations early in the 1900s. Jay's terminology worked in 1831 and was used successfully by the ABS for many years,[76] but the analogy was inadequate and was eventually discarded.[77]

Over time, income from the gallery exceeded expenses, but fundraising was never Silliman's main objective. Bringing to Yale Trumbull's beloved paintings illustrating American independence was always the prize: "Lessons indeed they are in the art of painting but lessons still more important in the history of our country. Every passing year will add to their value and they will be still more highly prized by a remote posterity, should they be preserved to future generations."

Notes

1   Sizer 1967, inside front cover.

2   Benjamin Silliman, "The Trumbull Gallery: History of the Paintings, July 3, 1857," in Silliman 1857. Quotations not otherwise identified are from the *Reminiscences*.

3   Quoted by Sizer in *The Works of Colonel John Trumbull*, 168. Sizer observed that Trumbull "set down these words—then modestly crossed them out" in his notebook. Sizer was a scholar who served as director of Yale's Art Gallery (1940–47), published parts of Silliman's essay, and provided important contextual details.

4   Kelley 1974, 143.

5   "The day is not distant when another edifice, or an extension of the Trumbull Gallery, will be demanded." (Silliman 1842, 28). The map is from Holden 1967.

6   See Buel (1984). The TV movie *Mary Silliman's War* (1994) is based on this scholarly biography. Among the Silliman Family Papers in the Yale University Library is Benjamin's annotated copy of his mother's *Reminiscences, 1736–1813*.

7   Silliman 1820. Wadsworth, an amateur artist, provided engravings of several scenes.

8   John Trumbull used similar rhetoric explaining to President James Madison his selection of *General George Washington Resigning His Commission* for the rotunda of the US Capitol: "One of the highest moral lessons ever given to the world was that presented by the conduct of the Commander-in-Chief resigning his power and commission." Quoted by Jaffe (1976, 15).

9   The simile is from the War of 1812—the war of Silliman's generation against the British—and refers to a heroic charge of the Twenty-First US Infantry Regiment under Colonel James Miller at a battlefield west of Niagara Falls. Ordered to take a hill where deadly British guns were emplaced, Miller responded, "I'll try, Sir!" His successful uphill charge was a turning point in the bloodiest battle of that war. Silliman's comparison of himself with a legendary war hero, a contemporary of his, but written forty years after the Battle of Lundy's Lane, was a deep gesture of faith-keeping with his family's military virtues and a recognition of the degree of difficulty he faced in meeting the terms of Trumbull's gift annuity.

10   In 1818 Silliman founded the *American Journal of Science*, still active today. He started a natural-history collection—including fragments of a meteor he analyzed in 1807 and "Sillimanite" crystals he discovered—and was one of two professors who raised $14,000 in 1825 to buy the Gibbs Cabinet of minerals for Yale. These became the foundation for Yale's Peabody Museum.

11   Founded in 1847, the company was managed by Benjamin Noyes, a bad financial actor whom Insurance Commissioner Elizur Wright prevented from doing business in Massachusetts and who eventually landed in jail. Wright had been a student of Silliman's at Yale.

12   Founded in 1813 as a joint effort between Yale College and the Connecticut Medical Society, the institution is now known as the Yale School of

Medicine. "In 1810 the Connecticut General Assembly established the Medical Institution of Yale College, giving Yale and the Connecticut Medical Society shared jurisdiction over the training of physicians. The school opened its doors in 1813 with four professors and 37 students and conferred its first degrees the following year." See http://medicine.yale.edu/about/history.aspx.

13   Silliman 1842. As he spoke to a gathering of the Yale Alumni Association, Silliman used military metaphors to describe students who enrolled but did not graduate from Yale: "Some drop off from ill health; some from change of circumstances and destination; some to remove to other institutions; and not a few from the operation of the rules of discipline, which show no favor to the indolent, negligent, apathetic or vicious youth...From all these causes it happens, as in the armies of Napoleon, pushing forward in the forced marches of an arduous campaign, that many are enrolled who do not reach their destination...only the hardy and the brave live it through; the phalanx, thinned in numbers but tempered by hardship and toil, arrives on the field of conflict, with men of iron bodies and indomitable minds, and the shout of victory follows hard upon the cry of battle" (12).

14   Quoted by Kelly (1974, 171).

15   See Staiti 2016; Cooper 1983; Jaffe 1975; and Sizer 1967.

16   John Trumbull did not live to see a photograph. Benjamin Silliman's life (1779–1864), on the other hand, spanned all the way from the American War of Independence to the Civil War. Only four years after his *Reminiscences* (from 1857) celebrated the power of Trumbull's paintings to illustrate courage and patriotism, photographers like Mathew Brady would use their new technology to memorialize people and events in an even larger and equally important conflict.

17   See Appendix III for the schedule of paintings included in Trumbull's gift of 1831.

18   For example, in 2016 Trumbull's painting of John Adams was selected as the all-time best presidential portrait by Holland Carter, co–chief art critic for the *New York Times*. See Carter 2016.

19   In a letter dated September 5, 1821, Trumbull wrote to Rev. Jeremiah Day, president of Yale, that he was sending the college a newly painted

portrait of his father, Governor Jonathan Trumbull Sr., to replace one that he had painted many years earlier that was "utterly unworthy of the place it occupies" in the Yale Library. Trumbull said the new portrait was "a better resemblance, and more worthy to be preserved in a public & permanent Institution."

20   Sizer, *The Works of Colonel John Trumbull*, 174.

21   Trumbull 1841. Sizer (1967) calls this "the earliest extended account of an individual artist written and published in the United States" (173).

22   Yale University Art Gallery 2008, 81.

23   By John Wesley Jarvis—Own work Sclary, 7/15/09, Public Domain, https://commons.wikimedia.org/w/index.php?curid=7312806, retrieved 8/13/16.

24   Jay dedicated his life to public service. In addition to the nonprofit organizations mentioned in the text, Jay was deeply involved with King's College (trustee, 1823–43; chairman, 1840–42), New York Hospital (president, 1827–33), and the New York Historical Society (president, 1840–42).

25   Founded in 1828, the institute provided the first circulating law library in New York. Jay donated books from his own collection: "Many of the old classics of the law, rare and valuable reports and commentaries, were the gifts of the accomplished scholar, Peter A. Jay...One runs across Jay's name in the books and treasures of the Law Institute library frequently" (Winters 1892, 2–3).

26   Eric Hilt describes how in the 1820s, many New York firms such as the Life and Fire Insurance Company evaded bank regulations by using "an insurance corporation to engage in transactions normally reserved for banks" (Hilt 2009).

27   *Memorials of Peter Jay*, p. 77 (Knowles 1929). Jay drafted a charter and lobbied the New York legislature for an act of incorporation for the bank "to benefit the working classes, encourage thrift, and help such as might not be able to make safe investments for themselves." An innovation resisted by the banking establishment, the bank was an immediate and lasting success.

28   Jay 1905, 76–77.

29   The King's Charter is reprinted in Charter and Fundamental Laws of the Corporation for the Relief of Widows and Children of Clergymen of

the Protestant Episcopal Church for the State of New York (1807). The quote cited is from page 3. The first such organization in the American colonies was the Corporation for Relief of Poor and Distressed Widows and Children of Presbyterian Ministers established in 1759, often credited as the first American life insurance company. Robert Patterson of Philadelphia provided actuarial services and computed premiums for the Ministers Fund in 1792 (Moorhead 1989, 2).

30   The Episcopal bishop for the State of New York served as president of the corporation ex officio. A vice president, treasurer, and secretary were elected.

31   Elizur Wright was the first to calculate the present value of every individual life insurance contract issued by companies doing business in the state of Massachusetts.

32   Charter and Fundamental Laws 1807, 5.

33   The founding stockholders represented an "A-list" of New York financial and professional dignitaries: John Jacob Astor, Chancellor James Kent, Steven van Rensselaer et al. The Bard family was highly distinguished. See Hirsch 1941, 222–41. William Bard (class of 1797) became a trustee of King's College in 1840, while Peter Jay (class of 1794) served as chair.

34   Historian Sharon Ann Murphy credits Bard with the creation of the modern American life insurance industry: "With Bard at the helm, NYL&T would revolutionize the way life insurance companies operated in the United States, creating—virtually from scratch—the statistical basis for the long-term safety of the industry...NYL&T completely reinvented how life insurance was sold in America, establishing the model followed by all subsequent nineteenth-century competitors" (Murphy 2010, 14). Bard tried for many years to encourage insurance companies to pool their mortality data for the general good. See "In Search of an American Mortality Table" (Murphy 2010, 22–27).

35   Kelley 1974, 144.

36   Kingsley 1823. The pamphlet was reissued in 1823; this version added the need for a new dormitory and chapel.

37   Kelley 1974, 150.

38   Kelley 1974, 150.

39   The bank petition to the Connecticut General Assembly, dated February
      14, 1814, is reprinted in Burpee 1914, appendix I, 135–38.

40   According to a history of Trinity College (in Hartford), "Connecticut had
      been founded by tough-minded Puritans who were determined to build a
      new English Canaan from which Episcopacy was to be forever excluded"
      (Weaver 1967, 3).

41   The Goodrich family of Connecticut, whose male members were Yale
      alumni, was instrumental in both the Phoenix Bank bonus controversy
      and the financing of John Trumbull's annuity payments. The Reverend
      Elizur Goodrich Sr. (Yale class of 1752) served as pastor of the Durham,
      Connecticut, Congregational Church from his ordination in 1756 until
      his death in 1797, and had been one of many colonial Patriots "vigor-
      ously opposing a British threat to send an Anglican bishop to America"
      (see   http://oll.libertyfund.org/?option=com_staticxt&staticfile=show.
      php%3Ftitle=816&chapter=69311&layout=html&Itemid=27). His son
      Elizur Goodrich, member of the Yale class of 1779, was serving in the
      Council, or upper house of the legislature, at the time of the Phoenix
      Bank charter in 1815 and published several letters during the "Bishop's
      Bonus" controversy. Elizur became one of five subscribers recruited by
      Silliman in 1831 to underwrite Trumbull's annuity payments and signed
      the annuity documents as secretary of Yale. His brother, Chauncey
      Goodrich, Yale class of 1776, taught rhetoric and oratory at Yale from
      1779 to 1781, became a lawyer and served as a member of the US House
      of Representatives from 1795 to 1801 and as US senator from 1807 to
      1813. In 1813, the Connecticut Assembly appointed Chauncey Goodrich
      as lieutenant governor. He was serving in that office and as mayor of
      Hartford during the Phoenix Bank controversy in 1815. Chauncey was
      also a leading delegate to the Hartford Convention of 1814–15.

42   "The course pursued by the Legislature was felt by Episcopalians to be
      a violation of good faith and a blow aimed at their order" (Beardsley
      1868, 121).

43   Two of these compilations include Various1816a and Various 1816b.

44   In its centennial history, Phoenix Bank proudly claimed that the battle
      for its charter as the Episcopal Bank "secured for Connecticut its present

constitution and with it at last absolute separation of church and state" (Burpee 1914, 8).

45 Whitehead 1973, 111.

46 Burpee 1914, frontispiece.

47 The "elaborate bank petition to the Legislature [was] written by the Scotch-Huguenot American Charles Sigourney" (Burpee 1914, 16). Theodore Sizer, editor of John Trumbull's autobiography and a scholarly art historian, wrote extensively about Silliman's leadership in making the Trumbull Gallery a reality but did not publish a discussion of Sigourney's essential roles within the Phoenix Bank, Episcopal Church, and Washington College.

48 Founded in 1816, the ABS states its mission thus: "Through a world-wide network of Bible Societies and partners, our mission is to make the Bible available to every person in a language and format each can understand and afford, so all people may experience its life-changing message."

49 In 1819 Sigourney married Lydia (Huntley) Sigourney, a popular and important American poet commonly known as the "Sweet Singer of Hartford." Trumbull's nephew-in-law, Daniel Wadsworth of Hartford, was Lydia's principal patron, another fact not mentioned by Silliman or Sizer.

50 Weaver 1967, 17.

51 The founders of Washington College scrupulously avoided the appearance of creating an Episcopal seminary. In 1823, Sigourney wrote to Thomas Jefferson about the course of study at the former president's nonsectarian University of Virginia. Jefferson responded in 1824 with details about his college's curriculum.

52 Connecticut legislator J. Wood wrote to Silliman on June 3, 1831, that "by appropriating part [of the bank bonus] to Washington College, they probably picked up some Episcopal and Hartford votes for the appropriation." Cited in Kelly 1974, 497, note 36.

53 Whitehead 1973, 111.

54 The president and fellows of Yale College approved a motion on September 20, 1832, thanking Tappan "for paying the tuition of more than twenty

students in the present and preceding classes, during their whole collegiate course" (Tappan 1870, 78).

55   Elizur Goodrich was a Patriot during the Revolution, Yale graduate, and an experienced attorney who served as secretary of Yale from 1818 until 1846. As a signer of the annuity bond and indenture, Goodrich presumably had an important role in negotiating terms, but there is no record of his involvement. A contemporary biography notes, "While a student, when the British forces took and pillaged the town of New-Haven, he was wounded and taken a prisoner. From 1781 to 1783 he was a tutor in Yale College. He studied law with Charles Chauncey, Esq., afterwards a judge of the superior court; was admitted to the bar in 1783; and immediately commenced practice in New-Haven... In May, 1795, he was a representative from that town in the General Assembly...until December, 1799, when...he became a representative in the Congress of the United States...He was judge of the court of probate...from June, 1802, to June, 1819...In September, 1801, he was appointed Professor of Law in Yale-College; which office he held until 1810, and then resigned it, as interfering too much with other public duties. He has since received from the corporation of that institution the honorary degree of LL.D." (Various n.d., 25).

56   Twining died on December 18, 1832, and his pledge of a loan was not replaced, a fact not noted by Silliman.

57   Sizer, *The Autobiography of Colonel John Trumbull*, 374.

58   Sizer, *The Autobiography of Colonel John Trumbull*, 322–323.

59   Trumbull, Letter to Wyllys Warner, treasurer of Yale College, 1833. The author is grateful to Tanya Pohrt of the Yale University Art Gallery for providing him with several references to Trumbull's letters from 1833 and later, as well as images of the admission tickets.

60   Ibid., 322.

61   Daniel was the son of Jeremiah Wadsworth, who, according to the Connecticut Historical Society, "was one of the founders of the Bank of North America and the Hartford Bank, and was an executive with the Bank of New York and [the] United States Bank. He was involved with some of the earliest manufacturing and insurance partnerships in

Hartford." Daniel later founded the Wadsworth Atheneum. See http://
www.chs.org/finding_aides/finding_aids/wadsworth.html.

62   Trumbull, 284–85.

63   Trumbull, 284.

64   Trumbull's letter is in the Yale University Library.

65   Silliman may have felt no need to copy the texts of Yale's annuity bond and
indenture, since Trumbull had published both in his *Autobiography* (1841).

66   Theodore Sizer quotes from the records of the Yale Corporation: "Voted
that a suitable building be erected on the ground west of the College
Chapel for the exhibition of Colonel Trumbull's paintings…provided
that the total expense of the building does not exceed $3,000" (Trumbull
1953, 375). As noted earlier, Yale eventually spent $5,000 on construc-
tion of the Trumbull Gallery.

67   This was a one-life annuity. Trumbull's beloved wife, Sarah, had died
in 1824.

68   "Dying on time" is a modern actuarial phrase. By 1857, "the ordinary
valuation of human life" was measured scientifically by most life insurance and annuity firms, following the business model of the NYL&T
(founded in 1830), whose president, William Bard, was one of America's
first actuaries.

69   "An assumption that something is true even though it may be untrue"
(*Black's Law Dictionary* 2009).

70   Augur wrote to Benjamin Silliman on October 18, 1836, suggesting that
the Trumbull Gallery acquire the two statues of his work *Jephthah and his
Daughter*, whose tragic story is told in the book of Judges, chapter 11. The
Connecticut Herald reported on November 21, 1837, that the subscription
campaign had raised $3,695 and that more gifts were expected.

71   Quoted in Trumbull 1904, 109.

72   All donors to the Augur campaign received free admission to the Trumbull
Gallery for six months. Donors of $50 received admission for ten years.
A $100 gift entitled the donor to admission for life, and $200 provided a
family ticket for life (Augur 1837).

73   In the Middle Ages, identical wording for two indenture contracts was
drawn up on a single piece of parchment or paper and then cut apart

irregularly in a jagged line. Each party to the contract would sign and exchange one part of the indenture. The "teeth" (dentures) could later be matched up to prove the authenticity of each document.

74 "It is also further Enacted by the Authority aforesd that the sd undertakers & Partners & their successrs be & hereby are further impowered to have accept acquire purchase or otherwise lawfully enter upon Any Lands Tenements & Hereditamts to the use of the sd School…& receiv all such Gifts Legacies bequests *annuities* [emphasis added] Rents issues & profits arising therefrom" (Connecticut 1701).

75 A metaphor links two familiar terms to explain a third new idea, shaping how that new idea—in this case, an *annuity bond*—is used.

76 For the society's annuity campaign in 1919, "(1) It was decided that the annuity bonds should not be designated as Bible Bonds, but as annuity bonds of the American Bible Society. (2) It was decided that the annuity bonds be printed on paper and in typographical style that is conventional for securities of this nature" (Zimmerman 1967, 89).

77 Gilbert Darlington, treasurer of the ABS, warned participants at the fourth national gift annuity conference in 1931 that courts, regulators, and lawmakers would take a close look at a charity's "correspondence and publicity" in deciding tax cases that involved gift annuities. Darlington concluded that the use of terms and phrases such as *interest*, *bond*, and *principal remaining* "should be avoided in all correspondence dealing with annuities." *Rules, Regulations and Reserves in Using Annuity Agreements* (New York: Subcommittee on Annuities [SOA] of the Committee on Financial and Fiduciary Matters [CFFM] of the Federal Council of the Churches of Christ in America [FCCCA], 1931), *Wise Public Giving* series [WPGS] No. 38, 32. Darlington was an ordained Episcopal priest, bank president, and an expert on taxation who served as a CGA member from 1928 to 1972, as chairman of the committee from 1939 to 1959, and as honorary chairman from 1960 to 1980.

Section 3

American Gift Annuities, Marketing, and the Law (1831-1926)

W hat happened in America between the annuity bond contract issued by Yale in 1831 and the first national nonprofit gift annuity conference in 1927?

This section illustrates early American life-income gifts and shows how nonprofit leaders responded to new gift ideas and a changing legal landscape with policies and practices adapted from financial firms, how nonprofits embraced flawed annuity bond investment terminology in their advertisements, and how the American Bible Society conducted a phenomenally successful annuity bond campaign in 1919. ABS generously provided the author with access to its archives, making it possible to publish the details of its early history and extraordinary campaign for the first time.

EARLY ABS GIFT ANNUITIES (1831–48)

Gift proposals for life-income trusts and annuities considered by the American Bible Society in the 1830s and 1840s provide vivid illustrations of the ingenuity of donors and their professional advisors in this formative period of American philanthropy. The gift arrangements are interesting in themselves and are even more important in that the legal and financial issues they raised led the ABS to refine its gift-acceptance policies, resulting in general rules that enabled its gift annuity program to become the world's most successful.

Aware of the historical importance of these gifts, in 1964, Eric M. North, general secretary of the American Bible Society, wrote an account of its "Annuity and Trust Agreements" from 1831 to 1848. He and his staff combed through minutes, reports, and financial records to document the gifts as meticulously as possible. Many of the records had already been lost.[1]

North recognized that gift annuities and life-income trusts had become "of very great benefit to the Society,"[2] but in the 1840s, ABS leaders experienced "occasions of doubt" and "hesitations"[3] about the legal authority to accept such gifts and the financial risks they involved. After accepting several gift annuities and life-income trusts and turning down others, the ABS Board went through an important evolution in policy in less than two years.

On June 4, 1846, the ABS Board decided to put a stop to accepting any more gift annuities: "It is the policy of the Society to pause in this course before any serious consequences result." The course of American philanthropy may have been far different had this policy decision not been challenged.

On February 3, 1848, the board considered whether some gift annuities might be acceptable and decided that "it shall be discretionary with the Board of Managers to accept the stewardship of the property thus entrusted to them." This flexibility begged the question of what considerations ought to guide the board's discretionary judgments.

On March 2, 1848, a select committee chaired by Luther Bradish presented a report "examining the precedents both of

English and American law of the legal right of a corporation to receive funds in trust" and to issue annuities. The *Bradish Report* (appendix IV) persuaded the ABS board to adopt a general rule in favor of accepting and promoting life-income gifts, a decision that "was to be of great value to the Society in its bearing both on trust agreements and on annuity programs."

Because of the *Bradish Report*, ABS "sought such gifts instead of having hesitations about receiving them."

The Bradish Committee structured its report in response to the policy issues raised by life-income gifts that were proposed, accepted, or declined by ABS. As a preamble to examining the report in detail, we will take a brief look at these gifts.

The earliest recorded ABS life-income gift inquiry did not result in a gift. North described a letter dated March 3, 1831, from John Fry of Palatine, New York, asking whether ABS would accept a gift of $1,000 to $1,200 from his estate and make payments at 7 percent to his sister for her life. A member of the legacy committee wrote back to Fry with questions about the sister's age, the payment rate, and when the payments would start, but "no further record is found."

Ten years later, on February 4, 1841, the ABS board voted to accept a gift of $1,000 proposed by Joseph Womersley of Poughkeepsie, New York, "to pay lawful interest thereon during his lifetime" and to use the remainder at his death as an "unconditional donation." The gift was received and recorded in the board minutes on June 3, 1841. North considered this a life-income trust rather than an annuity contract.

On May 6, 1841, the ABS board received a report from its legacy committee, chaired by Peter Augustus Jay, regarding a large proposed gift from the estate of Mr. W. B. Martin of Baltimore. Martin said he would arrange to transfer $18,000 from his estate, to be held by ABS in trust, on condition that ABS pay an annuity of $500 to his surviving wife and $100 to each of his four sisters.

The five annuities would total $900, or 5 percent of the original gift amount.

At issue in the Martin gift proposal was the question of whether ABS had the authority under the laws of New York to accept a testamentary charitable gift in trust and to act as trustee. New York law on charitable trusts in 1841 was among the most restrictive in the United States, nor did the new ABS charter grant the power to issue annuity contracts.

North reported that the legacy committee recommended a counterproposal involving an independent trustee: "The Committee doubted that the Society could legally accept such a trust, but found that the N. Y. Life Insurance and Trust Company[4] could and would accept it, estimating that after paying all the annuities more than $18,000 would remain to the Society."

North wrote that "the committee suggested the bequest be made to the N. Y. Life Insurance Company," but Martin apparently did not complete the gift: "The ultimate outcome of this proposal has not been located."

In 1843, a gift of $500 from Joseph Keith of Enfield, Massachusetts, to the American Bible Society in exchange for a promise to pay him $30 per year for his life has long been celebrated as America's "first charitable gift annuity."[5] In contrast with the extremely well-documented gift-planning process that led to Yale's annuity bond contracts with John Trumbull in 1831 (the contracts were published during his lifetime and documented in Benjamin Silliman's *Reminiscences*), very little is known about the gift arrangements with Joseph Keith.[6]

Surprisingly, North devoted a mere two sentences to the gift annuity with Mr. Keith (not mentioning the donor/annuitant's name) that was accepted by ABS in 1843. North wrote that Keith's annuity was "similar" to Martin's testamentary trust, and he alludes to no specific legal difficulties: "On April 6, 1843, the Board was informed that the Rev. Seth Bliss had reported a similar proposition on a payment of $500. The Board referred it to the Committee on Publication and Finance which had already (Mar. 31) approved it and at 6%."

Whether Keith or John Trumbull—or a donor yet to be discovered—deserves to be recognized as "the first" modern annuitant is an interesting question, but it is not as important as the impact their gifts have had for American philanthropy. In the 1920s, the gift annuity program of the Bible Society would become by far the largest in the United States, and ABS would provide national leadership for nonprofit organizations issuing gift annuities for many decades.

North wrote that when ABS received a gift proposal three years later from Mr. Amasa Lord on behalf of his client Gurdon Miller, "hesitation set in." The proposal was to give ABS $5,000 in exchange for a 7 percent annuity for Miller's life. Minutes of the Committee on Publication and Finance dated May 29, 1846, record their concerns: "Although a precedent had been set by accepting Keith's gift annuity, gifts like these might become too popular: "this disposition may if encouraged, become a favorite one with its [ABS's] friends."

Accepting financial obligations for making payments to annuitants would soon add up: "Ultimately a large debt may thus be incurred, the interest upon which would be burdensome." (Here, the committee assumed that ABS would spend the initial gift amount upon receipt rather than holding it in reserve.)

Even if ABS held the initial gift amount in reserve, the payment rate of 7 percent was higher than could be earned and would deplete the principal, "so that the Society would not only not obtain any benefit from the gift so long as Mr. Miller lived but would become guarantors of the amount [paid to him] without any compensation or advantage."

The strongest objection was the absence of legal authority to issue annuities:

The receiving a certain sum of money and agreeing to pay a yearly interest upon it, is but another name for granting an annuity to the Donor. As this priviledge [*sic*] has been granted by the [NY] Legislature to certain corporations, it is supposed to be denied to those, to whom it has not been given; Now as it has not been granted to this Society, your Committee do not deem it wise or prudent to exercise any priviledges which are not expressly given to us by our Charter.[7]

All things considered, on June 4, 1846, the ABS board approved the committee's negative and far-reaching recommendation: "to decline the present proposal **and all others of like character**" (emphasis added). Mr. Miller was so informed.

Two years later, on January 6, 1848, the ABS board discussed a gift proposal from Mr. Amos Wright of Edmiston, New York, who was said to be "76 years of age and infirm in health." Wright offered to give ABS $2,000 for a gift annuity.

Based on the Miller decision, the board voted to decline the gift, but some members of the board questioned the wisdom of a general policy against accepting gifts from well-intentioned older donors. On February 3, ABS treasurer Edward J. Woolsey[8] introduced a preamble and resolution reopening the possibility of accepting certain gift annuities, using part of the money to purchase a commercial annuity from an approved firm and using the rest toward the ABS mission:

Whereas, cases have occurred and may again occur where individuals in the value of life, are anxious that the property from which they draw their support shall be devoted to the promulgation of God's Holy Word, after their departure; who however from various circumstances deem it prudent not to entrust the performance of their intentions to others but act in a measure as their own Executors, and whereas **there are Institutions organized especially for the purpose of granting annuities** [emphasis added] and which institutions are on account of their permanent character, resorted to by the Courts of Equity of this State as the safest depository of funds which must be invested by such courts, it is hereby

Resolved: that on the application of individuals who are in the decline of life, asking to place their property in the hands of this Board, receiving legal interest of the same during their few remaining days & the principal to revert to the Board of Managers after the decease of the Annuitant—it shall be discretionary with the Board of Managers to accept the stewardship of the property thus entrusted to them— to invest such part of the principal in the aforesaid named corporation as will secure the amount of legal interest to the grantor during his life & apply the remainder of the principal to the distribution of the Word of God.

The next step was to develop policy guidelines for accepting certain gift annuities. ABS Vice President Luther Bradish suggested that a committee of three people be created to bring back a report to the board. President Theodore Frelinghuysen[9] appointed Bradish as chair and Treasurer Edward J. Woolsey and Benjamin L. Swan as members.

The cast was set for producing a landmark in American philanthropy.

THE BRADISH REPORT: ON THE MATTER OF ACCEPTING TRUSTS (1848)

The *Bradish Report* is the earliest example of an American nonprofit organization confronting the question of whether to accept and encourage life-income gifts in the form of charitable trusts and gift annuities. The report, now known as *On the Matter of Accepting Trusts*, provided the basis for a national leadership role for the American Bible Society in charitable gift planning. We will explore it in some detail.

The committee was commissioned on February 3, 1848, and a seven-page document with nearly three dozen legal citations drawn from 1,500 years of history was presented to the ABS board on March 2. Such a far-ranging and tightly argued report could have been completed so quickly only if Chairman Luther Bradish was very familiar with the legal arguments for and against charitable trusts and annuities under the laws of New York.

In fact, whether charitable trusts were valid under New York law was a live issue when Bradish served as speaker of the state assembly and presided over the state senate.[10] Stanley Katz has written that the revised statutes enacted by New York in 1836 "seemed to abolish trusts for charity."[11] A Supreme Court decision in *Vidal v. Girard's Executors* in 1844 restored legal protection for charitable trusts in New York for a brief time, but that protection was soon shattered when the New York Constitution of 1846 abolished the court of chancery.

In February of 1848, as Bradish knew well, New York was struggling to redefine its entire system of the laws of equity governing charitable trusts that formerly were adjudicated in chancery court. The Bradish Committee characterized its task as of "paramount importance"; it aimed to establish a "general rule" in favor of accepting gifts in the form of charitable trusts and gift annuities.[12] Bradish seized the moment to express a legal opinion on behalf of all nonprofit organizations in New York and nonprofits in other American states that were interested in promoting, accepting, and administering life-income gifts.

Beyond the question of legality, there was the practical consideration of whether the benefits of life-income gifts outweigh the financial risks. The ABS board was on record opposing the gift offered by Gurdon Miller, as quoted above: "The Society would not only not obtain any benefit from the gift so long as Mr. Miller lived but would become guarantors of the amount [paid to him] without any compensation or advantage." Why fight for the legal right to accept charitable trusts and annuities if nonprofit organizations like ABS did not understand and appreciate their value?

The challenge for Bradish was to assure the ABS—and others interested in this burning question—that nonprofit organizations not only have the legal right to promote, accept, and administer charitable trusts and gift annuities but also that a well-designed program of fundraising through such gifts would provide important new sources of financing their philanthropic missions. Program design was the key, or, as Bradish wrote, "**there is a right way of doing even right things**" [underlined in the original].

The first objective was to articulate the legal validity for life-income gifts like that offered by Amos Wright. The report makes a flat assertion about the law of gift annuities: if gifts like the one offered by Wright are structured as contracts, "no doubt could for a moment be entertained that it would be entirely lawful" for ABS to enter into such contracts. The report does not comment further on annuity contracts, perhaps because the legal right of nonprofit corporations chartered by the State of New York to enter contracts was firmly established, and ABS was party to many legal contracts in its normal course of business.[13]

However, if life-income gifts like Wright's are considered trusts under New York law, the question becomes extremely complicated: "Perhaps upon no branch of the Law have opinions been more variant, or the Law itself undergone greater changes than that which regards the capacity of Corporations to take and execute Trusts."

Bradish reviewed precedents for charitable trusts in English law from before the introduction of Christianity. In that dark time, "the ancient and extreme doctrine undoubtedly was that a

Corporation could not be a Trustee." The prohibition was relaxed in the case of "Religious corporations and in favor of charitable uses [i.e., trusts]" by the time of Saint Augustine's arrival in the year 597, if not earlier. Bradish claimed that, long before the civil law was introduced around 1138, charitable trusts managed by nonprofit organizations had been "incorporated into the Common Law of England."[14]

In 1601, the English Parliament enacted the Statute of Charitable Uses "in order to remove all doubt" about the legal validity of charitable trusts, and "giving the Courts of Equity jurisdiction over them." Bradish pointed out that modern legal scholarship had documented many existing charitable trusts received by nonprofit organizations in the centuries before 1601. The great statute was "not the enactment of new law" but "merely declaratory of existing law" of "very ancient date," supporting the common practice of life-income trusts managed by nonprofits.

Next, Bradish examined American legal precedents. Not every state had adopted the British Statute of Charitable Uses, but even if a state had not taken positive action, nonprofit corporations in every state benefitted from America's common-law heritage regarding charitable trusts. Bradish cited the then-recent finding of the Supreme Court in *Vidal v. Girard's Executors* (1844)[15] that nonprofit corporations had a legal right under common law pre-dating the statute to accept and administer charitable trusts: "It is now held that where the Corporation has a legal capacity to take and hold Real and Personal Estate, there it may take and hold it upon trust, in the same manner and to the same extent as a Private Person may do."

Finally, Bradish cited half a dozen cases in New York State to show legal precedents in favor of charitable trusts managed by nonprofits, such as the 1828 decision supporting a trust created by the will of Nicholas Anderson, which appointed Saint

George's Church as trustee to support purposes consistent with the church's mission:

> Nicholas Anderson, the Testator gave to St. Georges Church in New York a Legacy of Four thousand Dollars <u>in trust</u> that the same should be put out at interest or vested in Public stocks, and that the income thereof should be paid to his Housekeeper for life; and after her death the Income thereof to be applied to the purchase of a Church Library, the support of a Sabbath School in the church and other church purposes, to which the church contributions may be applied agreeably to the Canons of the Episcopal church.[16]

New York law on testamentary trusts had become more restrictive since the Anderson case.[17] Recognizing the unfavorable treatment of gifts at death to a trust managed by a nonprofit, the committee argued that donors were now motivated to complete gift arrangements while they were alive to remove any doubts about the uses of their gifts. Gift annuities can function as a will substitute:

> This feeling [of wanting to further the mission of ABS by a lifetime gift] is not a little strengthened by the new difficulties which modern legislation presents in regard to testamentary dispositions of Estates generally and especially to the creation by will of valid and effectual trusts. These have given rise to the strong desire in all, as far as may be practicable to execute their own wills in their own life time. It is natural that this should be so.

Bradish observed that gift annuities satisfy the needs of donors as well as nonprofit organizations: "In giving effect therefore to these feelings in the way proposed, the Donor and the Recipient would be benefitted."

Having established the legal authority for accepting and managing gifts in the form of lifetime charitable remainder trusts and gift annuities, Bradish turned to the question of expediency: Would accepting such gifts provide additional financial support for ABS? If so, how should ABS safeguard its interests?

The committee found a flaw in the logic of the board's decision in 1846 "to decline the present proposal [by Gurdon Miller] **and all others of like character**" (emphasis added). ABS need not spend the original gift amount immediately, leaving the organization with no cash to make annuity payments. To do so would be "mismanagement of the funds to be received in the manner proposed." Instead, ABS should invest the entire amount in one of two ways:

1. Purchase an annuity from a "Trust Institution" to make the payments to the annuitant. This was not satisfactory, since ABS would become "a Guarantor of the Annuity and of course of the continued solvency of the Institution issuing it."
2. Self-insure: "The society itself would be the exclusive manager" of the original amount transferred and "would therefore incur no risk except from her own want of wisdom and prudence."

In either case, there would be significant financial benefits for ABS. After the death of the annuitants, "a considerable surplus" of their donations would "still remain" for use toward its mission. Bradish asserted that the financial risks of ABS managing a prudent gift annuity program amount to one-tenth of the risks "now incurred in many of her ordinary and daily operations."

Bradish encouraged the ABS board to imagine its prospective gift annuity donors. These are people with a "deep interest" in the organization's goals and "a strong desire to contribute to their promotion." They were older and had accumulated some money but felt that they still need income from their assets, and the idea of transferring risk to an organization they loved and trusted appealed to them:

> The future may present many cases of aged persons in the possession of wealth from which they are soon to be separated [i.e., by their death] but the use of which during their lives is essential to their comfort, might with a view of relieving themselves from the trouble, the responsibility, and the risk of its management...desire to give that wealth upon the terms proposed.

The Bradish Committee was certain that there would be strong interest in a gift annuity program: "That the confidence reposed in this [American Bible] Society will render such a disposition of funds as that contemplated a favorite one with its friends, if encouraged your Committee do not doubt." ABS could expect "frequent and important donations" through gift annuities.

The report concludes that if ABS could raise money for spreading the word of God through a gift annuity program, it had a moral obligation to do so:

> Shall this Society then in view of the great good she might accomplish both for charitably disposed individuals and in furtherance of her own objects, still shrink from the responsibility of assuming such trusts in the way proposed...If by adopting the course proposed and thus giving exercise and effect to individual benevolence, the means of the Society would be so increased as to enable her to place in the hands of a single additional benighted Pagan or destitute Infidel the living oracles of Light and Life, and thus under the blessing of God become the means of reclaiming from error and bringing to a knowledge of the Truth one additional human soul, how immeasurably would this outweigh all the considerations that even the most shrinking timidity or the

most extreme fastidiousness could possibly suggest against the plan proposed?

The report makes clear that Mr. Woolsey, who recommended against accepting the Miller gift in 1846, had changed his mind and fully supported the new course of action: "The Committee are unanimously of opinion that the Society not only has the right, but that it is her duty to adopt the Plan proposed **as a general rule for her future action**" (emphasis added).

The Amos Wright gift was accepted by the board. The gift contract had not survived, but it appears to have been in the form of an annuity bond. Minutes of the ABS Publications and Finance Committee, dated June 30, 1848, record that ABS issued a bond to Mr. Wright, guaranteeing his payments: "The General Agent stated that he had received $1,000 from Mr. Amos Wright & **had executed a Bond to him** as directed" (emphasis added).

Apparently, the ABS board considered purchasing a commercial annuity to "reinsure" the payment obligation in 1848 but did not do so immediately: "The question of investing a sufficient amount to pay the interest to Mr. Wright during his life time was deferred for the present." It is not known whether the board continued to self-insure the annuity.

The *Bradish Report* provided a sound basis for a robust gift annuity program. Nevertheless, ABS was slow to pursue these gifts. Eric North found that in 1881, ABS reported having six current gift annuity accounts that were received between 1871 and 1876, though "others had been received earlier and had lapsed."[18] North provided a very brief description of how the gifts were structured: "Most of these were agreements only to pay over the income and not a fixed per cent, but in most cases the investment was in Bond & Mortgage @ 7% interest, income paid over half-yearly."[19]

Little documentation has been uncovered about America's gift annuity programs in the last half of the nineteenth century. At a conference in 1930, Paul C. Cassat of Vassar College reported on a survey of "approximately 90 religious and charitable organizations" that "tabulated the replies of 38 church boards and other religious organizations of the Methodist, Baptist, Presbyterian, Congregational, Lutheran, Reformed, and other denominations, as well as undenominational bodies."[20] The survey reported that ABS had been the "pioneer" in issuing gift annuities since the 1850s. The American Baptist Home Missionary Society had begun writing gift annuity agreements in 1861, and another unnamed religious organization began its annuity program in 1870.[21] This may refer to the Methodist Church, which started writing gift annuities in 1872.[22]

THE AMERICAN ECONOMY ROARS

For many reasons, gift annuity programs began to flourish in the 1920s. Just as the Roaring Twenties began, Frank H. Mann, secretary of the American Bible Society, caught a wave of "phenomenal"[23] success: from 1920 through 1930, the ABS issued 4,615 annuity bond contracts with a face value that exceeded $4.3 million.

Historians attribute the dramatic growth in American demand for financial products in the 1920s to several causes, one set of which had to do with economics. Victory in the First World War in 1918 raised the animal spirits of American entrepreneurs. Factories in the United States had not been bombed, as many in Europe had. US manufacturing capacity started high and grew much higher. International consumer demand was strong, which led to the creation of new American jobs in industries such as automobile and steel production.[24] Federal control of railroads and telecommunications was returned to the private sector. Travel and trade restrictions were removed.

Reflecting the robust economy, the US stock market soared. From 1920 to 1928, the Dow Jones stock-price index rose from

$72.20 to $278.65 per share, an increase of 285 percent.[25] The number of people who were capable of giving large gifts to favorite charities increased, as the country's total wealth more than doubled between 1920 and 1929.[26]

As the pace of the postwar American economy accelerated, so did the rate of social change. Most new jobs were in larger cities, which attracted families to leave their farms and small-town retail shops.[27] The urban migration is typified by Nick Carraway, narrator of *The Great Gatsby* (1925), who moves from the Midwest to join "the bond business" in New York City.[28]

Millions of people like Carraway left behind long-standing support systems of community relationships. The need for organized, urban charitable services to replace or supplement informal family and village networks grew significantly during this time. Charitable fundraising campaigns through the YMCA, Red Cross, and Community Chests (later known as the United Way), as well as civic philanthropy through various community foundations, were organized to raise money efficiently to meet increased demands for services.[29]

The creation of new wealth and the dependence on high urban wages stimulated American families to demand financial protection against the death of the primary wage earner. Public-benefit programs, such as social security and unemployment insurance, enacted during the New Deal, were unforeseeable in the 1920s.

Life insurance as the solution to family financial independence and "the anxiety created by the unpredictability of death"[30] was promoted by ads and by sponsored articles in magazines and newspapers, by direct mail and the new technology of radio, and by specially trained, professional-insurance salesmen.[31]

Since the mid-nineteenth century, the US life insurance industry led the world in developing actuarial science to calculate ever more precise insurance premiums, annuity payment rates, and reserve fund requirements. The fruits of actuarial science were continual improvements in business practices, financial controls, and targeted marketing—a risk-management system that contributed to increased profits. Progressive reforms, active regulation by states such as New York and California, and voluntary self-regulation through the American Life Convention helped to boost sales by assuring customers of the security of the life insurance industry. No comparable security system for charitable gift annuities existed before 1927.

From 1919 to 1930, as the ABS campaign exploded, the sale of commercial annuities and of life insurance reached record heights. Year after year, sales of life insurance set new records. As the historian and educator R. Carlyle Buley wrote: "Life insurance sales, which had shown but slight gain in 1918 over the preceding year, spurted amazingly in 1919—a gain from slightly more than five billion dollars in 1918 to more than eight billion in 1919. The question was, would the boom continue?"[32]

Life insurance sales by United States companies for the year [1924] were estimated at $13,500,000,000:

> [The year] 1929 had been the greatest year to date for the purchase of life insurance…[American Life] Convention companies closed the year with $26,511,733,651 of life insurance on their books…more than $100,000,000,000 of life insurance [was] in force, an amount more than double that of all other countries combined.[33]

The sale of commercial annuities, while smaller in volume than life insurance, grew at a much higher rate: annuity premiums increased from $7.9 million in 1915 to $108 million in 1928 and to $510 million in 1935.[34]

MARKETING NONPROFIT ANNUITY BONDS

At the March 1927 Conference on Financial and Fiduciary Matters, Charles White described a gold rush by charities that sought gift annuities:

> Missionary societies, educational institutions and various organizations for philanthropy in this country are increasingly active in securing funds on which annuities are given to the donors. Ten years ago very little publicity was given to this subject and as a result very small amounts were received, until a persistent publicity campaign on annuities was started by the missionary societies of one denomination. The marked increase of receipts of these national societies in four years was registered by the following sums: The basic year, $125,000 was received; the next year, on an expenditure of $600 for publicity, the amount received was $325,000; the third year, with $2,000 spent in advertising, the receipts were $750,000, and the fourth year about $1,100,000.[35]

In the Roaring Twenties, the number of American charities of every kind offering gift annuities grew to an extent that modern readers may find surprising: "Today [1927] there are very few missionary societies, hospitals and other charitable organizations, colleges and theological seminaries, that are not active in securing sums of money on which annuities are paid."[36]

Arthur Ryan of the Bible Society observed that nonprofit organizations were hiring full-time planned-giving staff to promote and manage their gift annuity programs:

> Increased interest in annuities was very manifest and some denominations are now employing full time secretaries to solicit annuities and legacies and other large gifts. The Presbyterian Board of Foreign Missions has just inaugurated this system and other denominations are thinking of doing the same.[37]

Charities that issued annuities in the 1920s borrowed ideas and methods selectively from businesses that sold annuities, life insurance, and pension plans. Far too many nonprofit organizations embraced the then-current opportunities of fundraising through life annuities without clear visions of their long-term obligations for responsible rate setting, accounting, and consumer protection.

The need for a sounder business model is demonstrated most emphatically in the ways in which charities advertised gifts as investment contracts. The extent to which Jay's annuity bond metaphor dominated the thinking of nonprofit organizations is illustrated in their ads. Early in the 1900s, many religious charities, colleges, and other nonprofit organizations promoted gift annuities as financial investments in ways that would be unacceptable today.

Given the consumer demand for family financial security, it is not surprising that nonprofit fundraisers would piggyback on the success of commercial finance. The use of investment terminology, as we've seen, became widely known through Yale's annuity bond with John Trumbull. Jay's annuity bond terminology persisted. The ABS and most other nonprofit organizations in the opening decades of the twentieth century energetically promoted the financial benefits of annuity bonds, focusing on the similarities rather than the differences between a charitable gift annuity and an investment. Gifts poured in, current expenses were low, and wishful thinking minimized the risks of financial obligations.

As an example of annuity bond terminology, in 1905, the monthly magazine of the Baptist Home Mission Society included this advertisement:

A BETTER WAY. The Society will receive your money now, giving a bond for the payment to you during life if you so desire it. Send for our Annuity Plan.[38]

The *Methodist Year Book* for 1918[39] had a typical ad:

LIFE ANNUITY BONDS, prepared under expert legal advice and protected by the investments of the Board, are sold at liberal rates to those who desire to help the Board, but who require an absolutely sure income during life.

An advertisement by the American Sunday-School Union in 1921[40] was more aggressive, even stating (incorrectly, one hopes) that gift annuities "yield a higher income than ordinary bonds."

Are You Looking for a "Safe" Investment?

ASSURED INCOME BONDS

ISSUED BY THE
AMERICAN SUNDAY-SCHOOL UNION
are SAFE and SATISFYING BECAUSE

They are profitable while you live and useful when you are gone.
They are not an experiment, but a long-tried business proposition.
They afford absolute security.
The income is always paid promptly.
They yield a higher income than ordinary bonds.
They never fluctuate or default.
They may be purchased by persons of any age.
They require no medical examination.
They make provision for old age.
They avoid the cost of settling estates.
They make you your own executor.
There are no commissions to pay.
They put money otherwise idle to the best use.
They make a perpetual investment.
Assured Income Bonds create peace of mind.

For further information about the several kinds of **Assured Income Bonds**, write to

JOHN E. STEVENSON, Treasurer
American Sunday-School Union
1816 Chestnut Street   Philadelphia, Pa.

ABS embraced without question the aggressive marketing of annuity bonds as investments. The society's fundamental advertising strategy was set before Frank Mann's arrival. Below is an ad from the Bible Society Record in January 1919.[41]

A SAFE INVESTMENT

The Annuity Plan of the American Bible Society

ADVANTAGES

No anxiety. Good Interest. No unfortunate ventures. Income is fixed, sure and regular. No burden in old age in the care of property. No temptation to spend or invest money unwisely.

Bestows blessings on others. Assists in the translation of God's Holy Word. Shares in the fundamental world-wide work of the American Bible Society.

For rates of interest, form of agreement and other information, apply to William Foulke, Treasurer, American Bible Society, Bible House, Astor Place, New York City

As seen above, ABS gift annuity ads imitated the look of investment bonds, and its gift annuity contracts were "printed on paper and in typographical style that is conventional for securities of this nature."[42]

The annuity bond contract used by the Board of Foreign Missions of the Methodist Episcopal Church was designed to resemble a commercial investment bond:

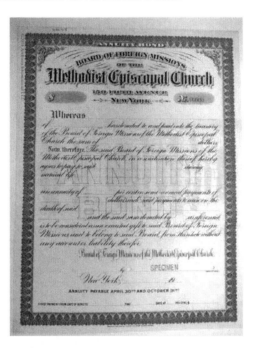

Like many charities, the ABS promoted gift annuities as an alternative to war bonds, as in this ad from 1921.[43]

The most energetic and well-known advocate of annuity bonds as investments—Henry Albert Collins, "The Annuity Man"— was deeply involved with the ABS.

THE ANNUITY MAN: HENRY ALBERT COLLINS

On June 15, 1920, Frank Mann reported to the ABS Ways and Means Committee that he had met with Mr. and Mrs. Henry Albert Collins, "who are devoting their lives to life annuities for religious institutions."[44] A popular author nicknamed "The Annuity Man," Collins incorporated overt sales pitches for gift annuities in his novels, short stories, interviews, lectures, and pamphlets. Collins was so influential, and his marketing strategy so typical of charities in the early 1900s, that it is worth providing a few selections of his work. Readers unfamiliar with how charities used to promote gift annuities might be surprised to see the ways in which they used to operate.

For example, in 1914, a regional Presbyterian school system in Mississippi published a thirty-two-page pamphlet by Collins entitled *After Many Days: A Story*,[45] designed as an extended conversation among four men on a train. A passenger named David Gladden tells how he used part of an inheritance from his father to purchase an "Optional Life Annuity Bond," which "contained the provision that in case my wife or I should ever need the income from this twenty-five thousand dollars, on demand the organization would pay us six per cent. annuity annually."

Gladden suffers a series of financial shocks: his cotton mill fails, boll weevils destroy his crops, his wife requires expensive medical care. After many years, he talks with the organization that had issued his annuity bond and learns he is entitled to receive back payments: "He asked me if we wanted all the earned and unpaid annuity to be paid to us, or whether we wished the accrued amounts to be added to the original twenty-five thousand dollars,

105

and on this sum to draw the annuity as long as Mrs. Gladden or I should live."[46]

Mr. Gladden takes his deferred annuity payments as a lump sum, with which he buys a local bank! He tells his travel companions that after nine years, he has earned $200,000 "because I took my wife's advice and bought a life annuity bond that paid us large annuities after many days."

One of the passengers listening to the story happens to be Dr. M. E. Melvin, superintendent of the Correlated Presbyterian Schools of Mississippi (an actual person whose photo and contact information are printed in the pamphlet), who thanks Gladden for his testimonial and says, "It will be a help to me in securing money on the life annuity plan for our schools and colleges… Thus far we have issued a few Life Annuity Bonds, all Immediate Bonds. We are also ready and willing to issue Optional, Deferred, or Survivorship Life [two-life] Annuity Bonds."

Naturally enough, someone asks Dr. Melvin about his schools, and he gladly provides a full description of their missions and heartwarming anecdotes of poor but deserving students. Mr. Gladden is moved to invest in one of Melvin's annuity bonds.

After Many Days includes applications of gift annuities that are quite sophisticated. There was considerable flexibility for philanthropic planning in the years before state and federal authorities recognized, taxed, and regulated charitable annuities. A passenger wants to help the schools but says all his money is invested in real estate that is mortgaged, "so your plan will not fit my case." On the contrary, the pamphlet claims that Dr. Melvin can accept and sell the property, pay off the mortgage, and provide an annuity based on the sale: "We have taken in trust some real estate at certain valuations, and with the assistance of the owner we have been able to find a purchaser for the property at the price named. Then after paying the indebtedness on the property we issue an annuity bond for the balance of the proceeds."[47]

A fourth passenger asks Dr. Melvin for a private conversation, which leads to an extended summary of the benefits of gift annuities, an application form, and "a sample of a Life Annuity Bond." He, too, is won over and agrees to give an annuity. Who could resist such a deal? "Cast your bread upon the waters," Dr. Melvin says, "and after many days it will come back to you buttered."

Collins concocts a similar story in his novel *Ice-Cream Alley*.[48] A wealthy widow tells the president of "Endeavor College" that she does not trust her two sons to spend an inheritance wisely: "Riches have been a curse to them." After hearing the many benefits of annuity bonds, she agrees to transfer all her securities and her real estate in trust to Central Bank to purchase survivorship gift annuities for herself and her children.

In *His Master's Word*,[49] a pamphlet published by Otterbein College in Ohio, Collins wrote of a concerned husband and father who regrets learning about annuity bond investments so late in his life: "I wish I had understood this life annuity system when I was in the bank because many of our friends asked my advice about making investments and I could have suggested a better use of money than making investments in lands, mortgages, bricks and mortar."[50]

There is no pretense of novelistic license in the misleading claims that Collins made in his booklet for the Methodist Episcopal Church, entitled *Life Annuity Bonds*,[51] which begins with the headline "Add Years to Your Life":

> As people advance in years they are often burdened with the fear that their riches may take wings and fly away.
>
> Competent authorities estimate that in this country alone over a hundred million dollars annually are engulfed in the whirlwind of predatory finance. Much money can be saved by the adoption of the life annuity system. This is a much better way of disposing of money or property than by making

a will...Freedom from the business cares of life and an annual assured income adds years to the span of life. It enables the annuitant to spend the sunset of life in comfort and peace.

The booklet lists seven "Objections to a Will," such as legal costs and uncertainty: "It puts responsibility upon others [i.e., trusting an executor to follow directions] which ought to be borne by oneself." Collins also enumerated twenty-seven benefits of a life-annuity bond, including the following examples:

(3) The fear is removed that the will may be broken, as is frequently the case where there is enough money involved.

(7) As Life Annuity Bonds are nontaxable, they are a preferred investment.

(24) Life Annuity Bonds oftentimes benefit the relatives more than by simply leaving them money which they may lose.

One page of the booklet is a sample annuity bond contract. The piece ends with a strong assurance that gift annuities are more secure than money in a bank:

BOARD OF FOREIGN MISSION BONDS ARE AN ABSOLUTELY SAFE INVESTMENT

During the past 50 years, 2,193 State and private banks have failed in the United States, involving a loss to investors of $110,625,555.69. The Board of Foreign Missions has been in existence for nearly a century and has never failed to pay every dollar of obligation.

Frank Mann found in Henry Albert Collins a kindred spirit of enthusiasm for gift annuities. Their conversation was enormously helpful to Mann as confirmation of the course he had set for the ABS. He had his notes from the meeting with Collins typed and reproduced for the WMC in June of 1920; he then presented committee members with sample marketing materials that Collins had written for other charities:

> He [Mann] submitted for the Committee's information a bound volume of the typewritten notes of the interview and also various annuity material which had been received from agencies suggested by Mr. Collins. The interview was very profitable and furnished a fund of information to the Officers of the Society about annuities.

Here is one last example from 1920[52] of how ABS followed Collins on promoting gift annuities as investments:

SAYING GOOD-BY TO TROUBLE

Investors' Troubles

THOSE who depend for life's comforts and necessities upon the interest of invested capital are never quite free from anxiety. A mortgage or a bond can mature, when the money received by the owner must be quickly reinvested; dividends on stocks unexpectedly shrink and the diminished resources do not suffice; a safe may not endure the heat of a burning building and the valuable securities within may be reduced to worthless ashes. Many such possibilities worry those who live upon the income from investments.

An Investment That Stands

Those who place money in an annuity of the American Bible Society have an investment that does not require a change every few years, of which the income does not shrink, and of which the capital cannot burn up. Money given to the American Bible Society on condition of receiving a fixed annuity for life is kept apart and specially invested throughout the lifetime of the donor. It is as safe as human wisdom can make it.

An Investment That Blesses

Furthermore, this sort of gift to the American Bible Society, besides assuring the donor a fixed income, does a most beneficent work after this income is no longer required. It is used, after the donor has passed away, for God's work of spreading the Holy Scriptures among all nations.

An interesting booklet entitled
Bibles and Bonds
tells the details of this plan of investment. It will be sent upon request.

AMERICAN BIBLE SOCIETY
BIBLE HOUSE, ASTOR PLACE
NEW YORK CITY

American Bible Society,
    Bible House, Astor Place, New York City.
Gentlemen: Please advise me regarding a safe and productive Christian investment, with annuity income for a person _____ years of age.
Name _____ Address _____

A contentious challenge to the aggressive emphasis on annuity bonds as investments would divide the ABS's leadership five years later, when the financial stakes had become enormous. The phenomenal success of its marketing efforts cast a national spotlight on the fairness and accuracy of the ABS advertising campaign. Leaders of the Society rose to the challenge.

THE INTERNATIONAL GIFT ANNUITY CAMPAIGN OF THE AMERICAN BIBLE SOCIETY (1919–30)

In February of 1919, the American Bible Society hired Lieutenant Frank H. Mann[53] as secretary of its new Ways and Means Committee (henceforth "WMC"), reporting to ABS members that he would "give a very large part of his attention to strengthening the resources of the Society" through the direct solicitation of donors. He would aim to reduce its reliance on gifts from religious denominations and church congregations.[54]

Lieutenant Mann hit the ground running. At his first meeting with the committee on February 25, he reported sending fundraising letters to 9,000 Presbyterian ministers and 4,749 ABS donors. He then outlined an ambitious plan for "a financial campaign dealing with individuals, churches, and advertising, with appropriate follow-up system." Members of the committee enthusiastically "authorized the employment of such additional clerical assistance and the purchasing of such supplies as might be necessary" for these efforts.[55] As the ABS evolved toward a national direct-response fundraising organization, Mann depended on top professional advertising consultants, such as Ivy Lee, "the father of public relations,"[56] whom he hired to manage the ABS membership campaign in New York City.[57]

On April 24, 1919, during his third month on the job, Mann reported that four advertising firms had responded to his request for proposals. Two submitted rates for advertising in religious papers, another submitted plans for the creation of a proposed publicity department within the ABS, and the Morse International Agency proposed plans for developing and advertising ABS annuity bonds.[58]

Mann encountered resistance among his colleagues. Members of the WMC were not certain about hiring a professional firm to design and place ABS ads in national religious publications: they approved a trial contract with the Philip Ritter Company "on a month-to-month basis, subject to change or cancellation on thirty days' notice." They rejected the idea of creating a publicity department. Perhaps this struck them as too much like Hollywood for the ABS, though the era of mass-marketing campaigns for health organizations and United Ways was well underway.[59]

The committee also hesitated on the advertising strategies that the Morse Agency and Secretary Mann recommended for a national gift annuity campaign. Gift annuities were not a major source of funding for the ABS prior to 1919.[60] The society had issued gift annuities since 1843, and Judge Bradish had strongly encouraged the society to promote life-income gifts in his report in 1848, but the ABS's annual report in 1881 listed only six annuity agreements under management, with a face value of $21,383. These had been received between 1871 and 1876. The 1899 annual report listed nine annuities, with a value of $60,363.[61] Early in 1919, the ABS had perhaps fifty gift annuities under management. In November of 1920, the ABS estimate for spendable income from terminated annuity contracts was just $15,000, within a total budget of $1,188,600.[62]

The gift annuity advertising motion adopted by the WMC on April 19, 1919, shows something less than enthusiastic consent: "That the suggestions made by the Morse International Agency on... Bible Society Annuity Bonds, be made a subject of further inquiry, and that $1,000 be set aside for this feature of the advertising plan, if the Committee later approve of the details as worked out."

Bringing a 103-year-old international religious organization to cautious agreement on an advertising campaign for life-income gifts was an accomplishment for the young man appointed just three months prior. Even so, it's fair to ask, was Mann moving ahead too quickly?

There is nothing in the minutes for the crucial months of February–April 1919 to indicate that ABS discussed the long-term implications of an international[63] gift annuity program that might commit the ABS to lifelong financial and stewardship relationships with thousands of annuitants over many decades. There is no record that they considered the legal or investment risks. Nor was there recognition at the start of Mann's campaign that the costs of professional staff and administrative services—payable from current budgets—for a massive program with long-term financial benefits could divert resources from fundraising for then-current operations of the society.

In fairness, no one could anticipate how phenomenally successful the annuity bond campaign would become or the challenges that success would bring. By the year 1950, the ABS was managing 13,258 annuity contracts, involving 6,758 annuitants.[64] In 1959, the year George Huggins died, the ABS issued 1,420 gift annuities, the largest number of annuities ABS had issued in any year to that time, with a face value of $1,419,603.[65]

Where could Mann and his colleagues turn for professional guidance? Before the Conferences on Annuities began in 1927, there were no reference books on charitable annuities, no commonly accepted set of best practices, and no consulting firms or peer networks to guide the managers of a rapidly growing deferred-gift program.[66] And few settled federal or state laws and regulations existed for a charitable gift bundled with a life annuity. From 1919 until he left the ABS staff in 1924, Mann and his colleagues would learn by doing.

In June of 1919, his fourth month as financial secretary, Frank Mann was "all-in" for the aggressive promotion of ABS annuity bonds. The WMC minutes of June 19 quoted below recorded the initial elements of the world's most successful and most influential gift annuity campaign, including a few details of the Morse advertising proposal (which, unfortunately, has not been saved) that were amended by the committee or referred to the ABS board for final approval.

PROMOTION OF ANNUITIES:

Secretary Mann submitted a plan for increasing the sale of Annuity Bonds, prepared in accordance with the Committee's request, by the Morse Advertising Agency. This plan, in brief, provides for advertisements in various religious and secular papers calling attention to the Society's Annuity Bonds and urging that persons write for booklets which will be specially prepared for the purpose.

A number of questions were raised in the plan, calling for the Committee's consideration. The following actions were taken:

1. It was decided that the Annuity Bonds should not be designated as Bible Bonds, but as Annuity Bonds of the American Bible Society.

2. It was decided that the Annuity Bonds be printed on paper and in typographical style that is conventional for securities of this nature, and that they be printed in denominations of $50, $100, $500, and $1,000, and in blank form to be filled in.

3. It was decided to recommend to the [ABS] Board, That the rate of interest now employed by the Methodist Church be adopted on the Annuity Bonds of the American Bible Society.[67] It was decided that it was unnecessary to secure the endorsements of banks and leading citizens.

4. It was decided that the wording of the Annuity Bond Certificate be prepared by the General Secretaries.

5. It was decided that the form of application blank, copy for advertisements, copy for circulars, papers to be used, and other similar matters be left with power to the General Secretaries.

6. It was decided that the designation of the annuities as Annuity Bonds of the American Bible Society, the wording of the Bond, and the rate of interest be referred to the Board for action after advice from counsel.

The ABS launched gift annuity advertising and direct-mail activities in late summer of 1919. In January of 1920, Secretary Mann reported that as of "October 1, 1919, $29,600 had been received for annuity bonds."

Mann understood the need to secure financial resources adequate for an extended national campaign and for an administrative system for managing annuity revenues and expenses. Anticipating many more gifts to come, Mann proposed a conservative gift annuity accounting and investment system and a growth-oriented business plan:

1. The annuity funds shall be kept in a separate and distinct account and known as the "Annuity Account."
2. All Annuity principals of living annuitants shall be kept intact and invested and known as "Trust Funds With Life Interest."
3. There shall be established out of funds available by the death of an annuitant, an "Annuity Covering Fund," which shall be kept always at least one and one-half times the amount of Trust Funds With Life Interest.[68] The interest from the Trust Funds With Life Interest and from the Annuity Covering Fund shall be used to pay
   - All annuity expenses.
   - Five per cent on each annuity to be used for advertising and promoting the sale of annuities.
4. Any balance, of interest after paying the above two accounts, shall be put into the general fund of the Society.[69] Any funds made available by the death of annuitants over and above the amount required for maintaining the Annuity Covering Fund, shall be used as directed by the Board or its appropriate Committees.

Members of the WMC were not convinced of the wisdom or practical expediency of approving advertising expenses based on a front-end load equal to 5 percent of the face value of annuity gifts received each year. Instead, the committee approved use of a regular advertising account, with the understanding that the ABS board would make "adjustments" for promotional expenses based on the value of annuity gifts received.

Nothing succeeds like success. On April 20, 1920, Mann reported that from January through March, ABS issued twenty-three gift annuities, with a face value of $47,434. He projected astronomical fundraising results for the coming years. Even these proved too conservative:

If the present rate is maintained, the sales for the year will approximate $200,000, of which between 75 and 85 per cent will be returnable to the Society as net profit…with a moderate effort in promoting the sale of these bonds, it will be easily possible for the Society to raise from $200,000 to $300,000 each year in this way.

In 1921, the ABS received 207 gift annuities, with a face value of $268,856. The face value of annuities grew to $321,021 in 1923 and reached $566,111 in 1925. Under Mann's proposed formula for spending 5 percent of the face value of new contracts, this would have provided an annuity advertising budget of $28,306 in 1926. The actual ABS annuity advertising budget was about half that amount.

Immense success five years out was not apparent to Mann's colleagues in the spring of 1920, when the country was in the midst of a serious economic recession. Mann pleaded for more money in April to advertise gift annuities and to hire additional staff. Senior ABS leaders were beginning to recognize the scope of the opportunity. Members of the committee recommended a generous contingency amount:

> That an amount equivalent to five per cent of each annuity sold be set aside for promotion purposes and that the said amount be taken from annuity funds made available by the death of annuitants; and, in case that is not sufficient, from the General Funds of the Society for an amount not to exceed $10,000 for the year 1920. This money to be used in the discretion of the Executive Officers of the Society for the employment of suitable persons to promote the Campaign[70] and for the appropriate advertising of the bonds.

By September 27, 1920, the ABS had 127 annuity contracts under management, with a face value of $507,394. Seventy-two of these annuities had been funded since January of 1920.

On October 19, 1920, Secretary Mann presented his strategic plan for ABS fundraising efforts, including its fledgling gift annuity program. He proposed that the society should pay extra attention to investment strategies for the annuity reserve funds and that all cash gifts should be invested promptly. He proposed acquiring new annuitants through advertising and sponsored articles in various religious and secular papers and in the ABS's own *Bible Society Record*, by direct mail, by producing specialized booklets on gift annuities, and by ensuring "careful follow up of all inquiries."[71]

Mann also presented an analysis of "the first 1,100 inquiries received in response to the annuity advertising": "This report had to do with sources from which the inquiries had come—the number received from each state and from foreign countries; the number received from men and from women, etc. The bulk of the inquiries have been received as a result of advertising in the various papers."

The WMC duly authorized "to continue the advertising program based on the returns of last year for the sum of $5,000 which is within the provision made in the Budget for 1921. Authorization [is] also given for experimenting with advertisements in popular weekly and monthly papers."

Examples of papers where ABS placed annuity ads include the *Christian Herald, Moody Bible Institute Monthly, Presbyterian Magazine, World Outlook*, and the *Sunday School Times*.[72]

On December 23, 1920, Mann gave the committee a draft letter to be used in a direct-mail gift annuity promotion targeted toward some of the ABS's best donors and most loyal members:

Secretary Mann presented to the [Ways and Means] Committee a circular letter on the double letter-head advertising the Society's annuities and entitled "Two Birds—One Stone." It is proposed in the early months of 1921 to send this letter out to Life Members and during the year to send it out to annuity prospects whose names were gathered from the Society's records and other sources...The Committee expressed its approval.[73]

In January of 1923, Secretary Mann again pleaded "that it was important to carry the largest possible amount of advertising" in religious publications. Members of the committee approved additional annuity ads to be paid through the annuity reserve fund ($4,000), the ABS general-advertising fund ($2,500), and the ABS church-promotion fund ($2,500). The committee considered (but did not approve) ads targeting bankers and attorneys.[74]

Frank Mann resigned as financial secretary in October 1924 to become president of New York Guaranty Mortgage Company. He continued to serve as a volunteer member of the WMC until at least 1930.

After Mann's departure, it became clear that the annuity advertising campaign was not closely supervised. Several of Mann's orders for annuity advertising had been inadvertently continued after he left the ABS staff. The WMC fretted that the $7,500 appropriated for annuity expenses in 1924 had been overspent: $21,044 in annuity expenses were reported.

Mann's successor Arthur C. Ryan first proposed cutting the annuity advertising budget to zero for the remaining months of 1925, but that emotional reaction was temporary. On March 19, 1925, the WMC approved a budget of "not less than $15,000 and if possible $16,000...as the Budget for the Ways and Means part of the annuity program for the year 1925," with money taken from the annuity fund rather than the general operating budget. The minutes of April 23, 1925, reflect that "the new inquiries received and the money received on the annuity basis, would seem to indicate that this advertising has well paid for itself." Nevertheless, "in view of the Budget for the year 1925, the advertising for the remaining nine [sic] months will need to be greatly decreased."

By the time of the first WMC meeting after Mann's resignation, it was clear to all that Mann's gift annuity campaign was succeeding beyond everyone's wildest dreams. The face value of the 342 new gift annuity contracts issued by the ABS between January 1 and November 20, 1924, totaled $413,233. In the first eleven months of 1924, the society had received 1,919 gift annuity inquiries. The committee "was very gratified at this showing."[75]

The results of the annuity bond campaign continued to outstrip all expectations. At the January 1925 meeting, the WMC received a stellar report on the fundraising results from ABS gift annuities in 1924. The year-end volume of inquiries was astounding, resulting in a year-end total of 2,569 inquiries from prospective gift annuity donors, as shown in the table below.

Year	Number of New Inquiries	Number of Sales	Amount of Sales
1923	1,000	312	$321,021
1924	2,569	381	$438,424
Increase 1924	1,569	69	$117,403

The table below shows the results of the ABS gift annuity campaign from 1920 to 1930, as reported in its official history.[76] Some observations:

1. The ABS advertising campaign produced an unprecedented number of gift annuity inquiries: 16,309 over nine years. Considering that the population of the United States in 1920 was 106 million, compared with 322 million in 2017, an equivalent number would be nearly 49,000 inquiries: roughly 5,300 a year, or twenty-one new life-income gift inquiries every working day for nine years!

2. Responding effectively to so many inquiries demanded a huge commitment of staff time and a well-managed administrative system. The ABS was well positioned to

fulfill responses because of its preexisting international, high-volume Bible-sales system.[77]

3. Issuing 4,615 gift annuity contracts based on 16,309 inquiries is an enviably high conversion rate of 28.3 percent.

4. Only nine gifts (0.2 percent) had a face value of $20,000 or more. These nine gifts totaled $343,000 (7.9 percent) of the $4,439,204 received. The face value of the average gift annuity was $961.91. Average gift values were consistent from year to year.

5. The number of gift annuities fell after the market crashed in 1929, but the face value in 1930 was nearly equal to that of the previous year.

| | | | American Bible Society | | | |
| | | | Annuity Income Statistics, 1920-1930 | | | |
Year	Total # New Inquiries	Total # Annuity Bond Issues	Total Amount Received	Average Amount Per Annuity Bond	Annuity Bonds of $20,000 or more
1920		72	$ 158,995.57		
1921		207	$ 268,856.56	$ 1,298.82	1 for $50,000
1922	1,712	218	$ 189,590.00	$ 869.67	
1923	1,000	309	$ 321,021.38	$ 1,038.90	
1924	2,564	385	$ 438,624.25	$ 1,139.28	2 for $30,000
1925	2,033	577	$ 566,111.00	$ 981.13	3 for $20,000 1 for $40,000
1926	2,116	585	$ 520,053.00	$ 888.98	1 for $33,000
1927	2,107	610	$ 560,884.15	$ 919.48	1 for $100,000
1928	1,948	647	$ 533,938.14	$ 825.25	
1929	1,564	534	$ 444,312.57	$ 832.05	
1930	1,265	471	$ 436,817.68	$ 927.43	
Totals	16,309	4,615	$ 4,439,204.30		9 for $343,000

Mann's departure marks the end of the first phase of the ABS's gift annuity campaign. The appointment of Ryan[78] in February 1925 signaled a clear change in direction. Where Mann was a hard-charging, entrepreneurial marketer, Ryan's focus was on sound administration. Mann created a national advertising campaign from scratch. Ryan inherited a thriving gift annuity program, but it had inherent challenges.

Ryan's political and organizational skills were soon tested by a crisis involving the very heart of the ABS gift annuity advertising campaign. His responses to the crisis became fundamentally important in convening the first COA in 1927, and his death shortly after the conference opened the door for a new era of national leadership by Dr. Gilbert S. Darlington.

THE DECIMAL METHOD OF RATE-SETTING

Frank Mann became the first of many ABS staff to serve as a national spokesman for the gift annuity movement, when Dr. Anthony selected him as a member of the Committee on Financial and Fiduciary Matters (hereafter CFFM) that Anthony set up in 1923 for the Home Missions Council.[79] This important committee was soon brought under the national umbrella of the Federal Council of Churches of Christ in America.

Mann left ABS in 1924 to become president of an insurance-based investment company.[80] In 1925, Mann was serving as volunteer treasurer of the CFFM, which invited him to address a national gathering of nonprofit organization "Treasurers, Financial Secretaries, and Others Intimately Connected with the Administration of Funds" on the subject of "The Issuing of Annuities. At What Rates? Under What Contracts?"[81] As the architect of an extremely productive international gift annuity program, Mann shared his practical experience in investing, accounting for, and promoting gift annuities.

Mann offered his fellow treasurers (many of whom were professional bankers, trust officers, and life insurance brokers) the wisdom of shared experience on investing, accounting for, and promoting gift annuities. In describing the most important element of a gift annuity program—how charities should set their payment rates—he found no agreement on methods: "When it comes to matters of rates, no fixed program can be offered. Rates not only vary as between the boards of various [religious] denominations but they even vary as between the boards of the same denomination."

Mann reported that an unusual decimal method was used most frequently for setting annuity payment rates:

> Perhaps the most commonly employed rate for single life annuity and one which might be considered as the average is arrived at by placing a decimal point between the two figures of the age. For instance, a man of 65 years of age would be given 6.5—in other words, the rate is stated by taking 10 per cent of the age of the individual.

This simplistic method enabled a nonprofit such as the First Presbyterian Church in Macomb, Illinois, to publish an advertisement under the headline "Annuity Bonds of This Board" with an uncomplicated rate schedule: "Will produce a large income: 5% at age 50; 6% at age 60; 7% at age 70. Are absolutely safe; have been bought by many. They enable you to support our Holy Cause without diminishing your income. Write us today about this."[82]

Understandably, Mann was at a loss to explain the reasoning behind the decimal method: "How these figures were originally arrived at I have never been able to learn." It is understandable because the decimal method is not a rationale but a simple-minded solution to a very complicated challenge for a nonprofit that issues life annuities: finding the proper balance between attracting financial support for an important charitable mission and the expectations of annuitants for personal financial benefits.

In the short run, offering a seventy-year-old woman a 7 percent annuity for the duration of her life is easy. In the long run, the decimal method is extremely dangerous. The decimal method cannot be applied reasonably to a two-life annuity contract.[83] It does not account for changes in American mortality rates, which were improving dramatically in the first half of the twentieth century. Nor can decimal rates be adjusted in response to economic changes that are reflected in interest rates and investment experience. These were rocked by the Great Depression, the New Deal, and World War II.

Most importantly, the decimal method was inadequate for ensuring long-term benefits for a charity that is taking on the financial risks of life-annuity contracts to raise money for its philanthropic mission. The method provided a simplistic rate structure, while not taking into account a targeted charitable residuum.

The decimal method was one of the principal practices of nonprofit gift annuity programs that were desperately in need of reform. As more and more charities were issuing annuities with little regard for the economic realities of making fixed payments to people for the remainder of their lives, some leaders of national charities became alarmed. Charities that blindly followed the decimal method had no rational defense when prospective donors demanded higher rates.[84] Donors soon found that they could control gift annuity pricing by negotiating among charities for higher annuity payments.

Many colleges and universities continued to use the decimal method for setting gift annuity payment rates well into the 1930s. A survey of ninety-one colleges and universities conducted in 1929 by Paul C. Cassat, comptroller of Vassar College, found that "the decimal plan of providing 10 percent of the age as an annual payment, i.e., 6.3 percent at age 63, seems a popular plan."[85] A more in-depth survey in 1933 of seventy colleges that issued annuities reported that twenty-two used the "decimal plan" to set annuity rates, while thirty-nine said that "each case [was] treated separately."[86]

After the actuarial revolution in nonprofit fundraising, the simple decimal plan for rate setting was replaced by a complex, mathematical, nationalized system expressed through quantifiable, experience-based assumptions. Nonprofit leaders became accustomed to paragraphs like this one, presented by George Huggins at the seventh Conference on Annuities in 1941:

> The basis of these rates has already been outlined; i.e., the Combined Annuity Mortality Table with interest at 3½ percent, with ages set back two years on the female life basis, and calculated in accordance with a formula designed to produce an average residuum of 70 percent of the amount of the original gift, with the scaling down of the rates below age 55 until they reach 2½ percent at age 35, and letting that rate apply at any lower ages. At the higher-age bracket, the rate is held at 7 percent from 80 and upwards...the rates now submitted are on the basis of lower mortality and lower interest rates, both of which are in accordance with the trends which have developed so acutely since the present uniform rates were adopted [in 1934].[87]

NATIONAL PHILANTHROPIC LEADERSHIP BY THE AMERICAN BIBLE SOCIETY

This is an appropriate point to recognize the leadership of the American Bible Society in advancing philanthropy in the United States.[88] Charitable gift planners owe a tremendous debt to ABS and its leaders Frank Mann, Arthur Ryan, Gilbert Darlington, and Charles Baas.

After Mann's departure from ABS in 1924, Arthur Ryan and his colleagues embarked upon an important transitional period of consolidating gains in their annuity program and strengthening the ABS's administrative policies and procedures. There was a new openness to comparing the practices of other charities and a growing sense of responsibility for sharing the successes of the ABS.

To his credit, Ryan scrupulously adhered to the published ABS rate table. On November 19, 1928, the WMC minutes reflect that due to a clerical error, an annuity was issued at a rate "one-tenth of one percent above the published rates." Since an annuity contract had been signed, the committee approved the special rate.

Dr. Anthony selected Ryan as a founding member of the Committee on Gift Annuities (CGA). Ryan died suddenly in June 1927 and was succeeded as ABS financial secretary by George William Brown. The ABS spokesman for gift annuities was clearly Rev. Gilbert Darlington, who would lead the CGA as chairman (1939–59) and honorary chairman (1960–80).[89] It was Darlington who lobbied officials in New York in 1923 and 1925 to recognize the legal validity of gift annuities issued by nonprofit organizations.

The extent to which the ABS gift annuity program under Darlington continued to lead the country is extraordinary. For example, in 1952, George Huggins surveyed fifteen of the larger nonprofit organizations regarding their gift-annuitant mortality experience, gathering data on 26,718.5 life years from 1947 to 1952. Over the same period, the American Bible Society reported its experience with 39,747 life years of gift annuitants.[90] In 1952 the ABS had 15,231 gift annuity agreements in force with a face value of $13,726,441.[91]

For thirty-two years, from the 1927 conference to his retirement as chair of the CGA in 1959, Darlington expertly tracked and made a series of reports on federal and state attempts to understand and regulate gifts to charity that provide fixed payments back for the life of a person.

Charles W. Baas, who succeeded Darlington as both treasurer of the ABS and chair of the CGA, wrote a brief chronicle of the committee in which he credited Darlington as "often the only tax expert available to the Committee" from 1927 to the 1950s: "In partnership with George Huggins, Gilbert Darlington helped lay much of the foundation the Committee is building upon today."[92]

Baas joined the staff of the ABS in 1946 and served as its treasurer for forty-one years. According to the ACGA, Baas was the longest-serving board member of the CGA (forty-five years), presiding as chair from 1959 to 1986—a period that included ten Conferences on Annuities.[93]

The CGA had no professional staff of its own. From 1927 to 1989, it depended entirely upon extensive administrative services provided free of charge by ABS, including financial accounting and reporting, mailings, and a sponsorship database. In October of 1989, the Southern Baptist Annuity Board became the second host of the committee after sixty-two years of ABS support. Mr. Tal Roberts, executive vice president of the Baptist Foundation of Texas, served as chair.[94]

STORM CLOUDS GATHER OVER ANNUITY BONDS

There is not a bright line separating an annuity donor's desire for personal financial benefits and wanting to help other people through a favored charity. The most fundamental question about promoting split-interest gifts remained unanswered when the ABS annuity bond campaign began in 1919. The question was front and center when the Conference on Annuities convened in 1927.[95] It is a live topic among gift planners to this day: Are donors of life-income gifts motivated primarily by personal financial benefits or by a spirit of philanthropy? The answer to that question determines whether a nonprofit's advertising campaign appeals to financial self-interest, to sympathetic caring for others, or to some balance between the two.

The terminology *annuity bond* blurred an important distinction between charitable gifts and an investment structured to provide income for a specified term and then return the principal to its owner, rather than to a nonprofit organization. Two controversies over annuity bonds erupted almost simultaneously: an internal argument within ABS over terminology, and a crucial legislative decision on whether to treat gift annuities as commercial investments under the insurance law of New York.

The minutes of the ABS Ways and Means Committee between 1919 and 1924 record no debate over the propriety of employing commercial advertising firms to promote annuity bonds as if they were investment contracts. In 1925, an argument over financial self-interest versus public-spirited philanthropy was in full bloom within ABS.

The immediate cause was a complaint from a donor. The minutes of the WMC on January 6, 1925, record that an anonymous letter dated December 23, 1924, was critical of the promotional materials of the ABS's annuity bond campaign. The writer raised a "question regarding the nature of this literature." As a result, the ABS's finance committee demanded a review of the "literature used in advertising annuity bonds."

The WMC appointed a four-person subcommittee (including its former employee Frank Mann as a volunteer member) and charged it to "look over the advertising material for annuity bonds to see if there is any basis for the complaint made" and to report back at the next meeting. At that meeting, however, the subcommittee put the question back to the finance committee: What changes did *they* think were needed to make the ABS materials acceptable while still keeping them effective?

On February 19, 1925, Secretary Ryan reported that the WMC passed the following motion: "Resolved that the General Secretary ask each member of the Finance Committee to send in his criticisms of our annuity literature for the benefit of the subcommittee of the Ways and Means Committee appointed to revise this literature."

Ryan inherited from Frank Mann a rapidly growing source of revenue, but it was one that had become politically sensitive. He decided on a time-honored strategy for the incoming manager of a controversial program: he hired the nationally recognized actuary George Augustus Huggins to perform a general audit of the ABS annuity program. It was through his work with the ABS that Huggins gained his knowledge of gift annuities issued by nonprofit organizations.

Change was in the wind in the spring of 1927. In March, Ryan reported to his WMC that he had accepted an invitation to serve on a national Subcommittee on Annuities (SOA) with an important mission: "Further to study the whole question of annuity contracts, rates, publicity, etc., and to call at a later date a meeting of all parties interested in the issuing of annuity bonds, to try to devise ways and means of closer cooperation."[96]

Ryan did *not* report back to ABS that leaders of the Conference on Financial and Fiduciary Matters had discussed the specific question of whether it is appropriate to promote *annuity bonds*. The charge to the new SOA included this very clear policy decision: "That organizations engaged in writing annuity business discontinue use of the word 'bonds.'"[97]

Ryan gave the WMC a lengthy description of the gift annuity conference held on April 29, 1927, beginning with a mention of Huggins: "At this conference a detailed report on annuity rates as determined by objective was made by George A. Huggins of Philadelphia, the actuary who made the detailed study of the ABS's annuities about a year ago."[98]

Ryan carefully summarized the highlights of Huggins's presentation on the "Actuarial Basis of Rates" for the committee. Two points are clear from Ryan's summary: the WMC had not seen Huggins's report before the conference, and Ryan fully intended that ABS should follow the standards of practice recommended by Huggins for gift annuity programs.

> First, that a 70 percent residuum is a reasonable goal to work toward in the issuing of annuities. Second, that the rates of annuities should be determined in conformity with this objective, using [actuary Emory] McClintock's tables with interest on invested funds calculated at 4½ percent. Third, that care should be taken in issuing survivorship annuity bonds not to include more than two persons unless absolutely required by the donor and in all cases, where a survivorship bond is issued, the rate paid should be based upon actuarial tables and not upon the rate of the younger person.

The General Secretary [Ryan] presented to the Committee tables prepared by Mr. Huggins showing comparative rates and other information connected therewith.

Ryan strongly endorsed the findings of the conference, though his reasons were defensive of his own policies and practices, claiming that the "scientific study" produced from Huggins's audit gave ABS bragging rights:

> The General Secretary believes that the cooperation of the ABS representatives in this general conference on annuities was exceedingly valuable for the Society because it called to the attention of the different persons present the fact that the ABS has made a scientific study of this question and is issuing annuity bond agreements on a careful, conservative basis.

Although Ryan reported that both he and Gilbert Darlington had made conference presentations, he did *not* mention that they had aired publicly their disagreement over annuity bond advertising terminology.

To Ryan, promoting gift annuities as bonds remained a live option. He surveyed thirty-one major charities that issued annuities and reported to the April conference that the prevailing terminology included *annuity bond, life annuity bond,* and *annuity bond agreement.* Ryan acknowledged a "more recent tendency" away from the term *annuity bond* to avoid confusing gifts with commercial bonds, "which are documents guaranteeing the return of the principal as well as payment of interest."

While noting that some people had begun to allege that use of the word "bond" was "not quite ethical," Ryan asserted that confusion could be avoided by clearly stating the nature of the gift annuity in the charity's advertising and in the contract, claiming that the term *annuity bond* simply "defines the kind of bond."[99]

Secretary Ryan took the opportunity to question the findings of the Committee on Annuities: "The Committee was not unanimous in its judgment regarding the nomenclature for the form of annuity contract, but the majority was inclined to recommend *annuity agreement.* The minority held to the term annuity bond agreement."

Ryan made clear that he was among the dissenters who argued in favor of annuity bonds: "From his investigations, the writer sees no reason why any of the names quoted above should not be used, providing the essential statements in the document itself are in accord with legal requirements governing such contracts."

Darlington followed Ryan at the conference podium. Darlington had managed gift annuity accounting, investments, and financial reporting since becoming treasurer of the ABS in 1920. He did not share Ryan's certainty on the terminology of annuity bonds. Speaking about his experience with federal and state legislators, including some who were considering whether to tax gift annuities as if they were commercial investments, Darlington observed diplomatically that "there is great need for cooperation in facing this problem fairly and squarely...There are those who think that the wording of annuity contracts or agreements may have an important bearing on this point. Does the phrase 'Annuity Bond Agreement' make it more difficult to meet this situation, and if so, why?"

The public debate between Darlington and Ryan ended abruptly with the death of Ryan on June 22, 1927. There was no official action on the question of *annuity bond* terminology at the second COA, held in November 1928, but the third COA in November 1930 came down strongly opposed to promoting gift annuities as bonds. In his preface to the conference report, Dr. Alfred Williams Anthony wrote about "certain perils," such as misleading terminology:

> The word "Bond" is frequently employed in this connection. Annuity agreements have nothing to do with "bonds" in the ordinary investment and financial sense of that word, for they are not secured by any mortgage upon real estate or other real property. They are bonds only in the sense that they are written contracts which bind two parties.

Darlington became the international spokesman for the ABS on gift annuities. Under his leadership, the ABS formally changed its advertising policy on February 19, 1931.

Some drama was involved. The committee reviewed the advertisements for annuity bonds of the ABS that were "now appearing in 28 periodicals," clearly the largest and most profitable annuity campaign in the United States. ABS Financial Secretary George William Brown read aloud "the paragraph dealing with terminology" that Huggins had delivered at the third COA in November 1930:

> As to the terminology, it is suggested that the term annuity agreements be used, rather than annuity bonds, contract annuities, or conditional gifts. It is also suggested that the return to the donor be referred to always as annuities, rather

than as interest. In a similar vein, it is suggested that the solicitation for funds, to be administered in connection with annuity agreements, be on the basis of featuring the service being rendered by the organization, rather than as an investment; nor should the annuity return be stressed too greatly as the appeal for the gift.[100]

Brown added that during the previous month (January of 1931), at a conference held by the Methodist Episcopal Church, the ABS had been criticized for ads that featured its maximum annuity payment rate of 9 percent. This was a full percentage higher than the maximum the Methodists offered. The ABS highlighted the 9 percent rate in a way that could be misleading to most annuitants, who would, in fact, receive much lower annuity payments.[101]

Members of the ABS Ways and Means Committee voted an approval of historic recommendations to overturn the entire promotional strategy of the ABS:

That the phrase "as high as 9 percent" be modified to avoid any possibility of misinterpretation; that the term "bond" be eliminated; and that the use of terms implying "investment" be discontinued; and that all annuity advertising be in harmony with the highest ethical standards.

The ABS board of managers approved the recommendations in March. At its meeting on May 21, 1931, the committee reviewed new advertisements in which "such phraseology has been used as to conform to the highest standards of annuity advertising."

Now that his own house was in order, Darlington could speak freely to other charities that were issuing annuities. Addressing "The Up-To-Date Legal Situation" at the fourth COA in 1931, Darlington warned that courts, regulators, and lawmakers were taking a close look at charities' "correspondence and publicity" when deciding issues that involved gift annuities.

Darlington urged charities to review and revise their terminology: "The use of such words as *interest, bond,* [and] *principal remaining* should be avoided in all correspondence dealing with annuities."[102] The inappropriate use of *annuity bond* terminology continued to be a concern as late as 1955.[103]

THE NEW YORK INSURANCE LAWS AND GIFT ANNUITIES

Debates over the proper balance between philanthropy and self-interest heated up in the 1920s, as legislators, judges, and regulators sought to understand the nature and policy implications of a charitable gift bundled with a life-annuity contract.

The charitable-gift-annuity movement nearly died in its infancy in 1923, when the New York state superintendent of insurance recommended prohibiting annuity contracts issued by a nonprofit organization unless they followed all the laws and regulations applicable to annuity contracts sold by licensed life insurance companies.

No charitable organization whose success depended on appealing to donors for financial support would want its gift annuity program to be regulated as if their nonprofit were responsible for meeting the expectations of investors seeking to maximize their financial returns. Investment vehicles such as commercial bonds and annuities meet consumer demand with products that are constructed around a single bottom line, with no consideration given to the love of a charitable mission.[104]

New York's approach to regulating gift annuities was held up as a model by the CGA. The principal actuary from the New York Insurance Department made keynote presentations at the sixth COA in 1939 and at the seventh and tenth conferences, in 1941 and 1959, respectively. New York was the only state to be invited to play a leading role in the conference agendas. In his report announcing a new actuarial basis for gift annuity rates in 1927,

George Huggins assumed the 4.5 percent rate of return mandated by New York to calculate the value of annuity contracts. He justified the mortality table selected for his first gift annuity rate table as both the best available and "the standard in the State of New York and many other states" for commercial annuities.

How did New York become America's most influential model for public policies toward gift annuities? It's true that ABS was headquartered in lower Manhattan, the Committee on Gift Annuities was based there, and eight of the first ten Conferences on Annuities were held in New York City, but their location resulted from New York's leading role.

To appreciate the national importance of New York's legalization of gift annuities issued by nonprofit organizations as a model for other states, it is necessary to look at how dominant the New York life insurance industry had become.

In the early 1900s, life insurance companies controlled far larger financial assets than did banks, and they exercised their economic power. Corporate law professor Mark J. Roe wrote:

At the beginning of the twentieth century, the largest American financial institutions were not banks, which today have aggregate assets far exceeding any other type of financial institution, but insurance companies. Insurers were larger than banks by not just a hair; the largest insurance companies were twice as large and were already moving into adjacent financial areas. They were underwriting securities. They were buying bank stock and controlling large banks. They were assembling securities portfolios with the power to control other companies.[105]

The life insurance industry was heavily concentrated in New York City at the time. In 1906, the admitted assets (i.e., legally required reserves) of life insurance companies domiciled in New York State represented 58.1 percent[106] of all US life insurance companies' reserve assets, but that understates the influence of New York. When one adds the assets of out-of-state life insurance companies licensed to do business in New York (and thus subject to New York laws), the total represented 97.5 percent of the assets of all US legal-reserve life insurance companies. Haughton Bell and Harold G. Fraine wrote that New York law had long required out-of-state insurance companies to comply with the state's investment restrictions: "Since its investment laws have consistently been among the strictest in the United States, its laws have had a more important influence than the laws of any other state in marking out the areas in which life insurance funds may be invested."[107]

In the year 1905, the "Big Three" life insurance companies were all headquartered in New York City. The value of their admitted assets had grown by 500 percent in twenty years. They dwarfed the assets of commercial banks:

Company Name	January 1, 1885	January 1, 1905
Mutual	$103,583,301	$440,978,371
Equitable	$57,548,716	$412,438,381
New York Life	$58,941,739	$390,660,260[108]

Without disclosing their financial positions, some life insurance companies were secretly acquiring banks and other companies, actively managing them, and manipulating financial operations for their own self-interests. A series of sensational stories in the national media about "the manipulation of insurance company investment funds through subsidiary trust companies"[109] by the Equitable, at the time "the most conspicuous institution in the whole world of insurance and finance,"[110] outraged many policy owners and stockholders.

Widespread abuses of economic and political power by other large American life insurance companies were uncovered (and reported nationwide in newspapers and magazines) during the Armstrong Committee investigation commissioned by the New York State Legislature in 1905.[111] Reform-minded legislators were particularly focused on preventing life insurance firms from extending their control over other financial services.

New York enacted laws in 1906 that prohibited life insurance companies from investing in common stock—not because of investment risk, but because buying common stock had been the insurance industry's preferred means for acquiring and manipulating other businesses. Legal sanctions against investing their reserve funds in common stocks had the unintentional but very welcome benefit of protecting the life insurance industry from the worst effects of the stock market crash in 1929 and the Great Depression.

The threat of punitive legislation after the Armstrong investigation led to voluntary national reforms that restored consumer confidence in the business of insurance. Life insurance firms around the country came together in 1906 for self-regulation through the American Life Convention, much as nonprofit organizations were to organize in 1927. Model legislation developed by the convention was circulated among the states. The Armstrong hearings demanded the attention of all state insurance commissioners. There was a wide range of legislative responses.[112]

Restoration of public confidence in the conduct of companies issuing annuities enabled strong growth in sales during the Great Depression. Life insurance company revenue from annuity premium payments rose as investors sought to protect their principals while receiving steady incomes:

> Annuity premiums in the principal companies were $7,200,000 in 1920, $33,900,000 in 1925, $82,900,000 in 1930, and $406,800,000 in 1935...The large sums of money received in recent years have been due to (a) the sense of security which is afforded by the life insurance

companies, and (b) the difficulty of investing money at remunerative rates of interest.[113]

Today, the sale of individual annuities by life insurance companies is a very big business. Individual-annuity premiums in 2015 totaled $209 billion, and the value of reserve funds held by life insurance companies for their individual annuity contracts was a colossal $2.3 trillion.[114]

Our national policies regarding the charitable nature of gift annuities were shaped by events in New York in 1923–25. A legal opinion memo by New York's Office of General Counsel traces the authority of the state to regulate gift annuities to a recommendation by the superintendent of insurance in 1923 that would have prohibited nonprofit organizations from issuing gift annuity contracts:

> Prior to 1923, organizations that paid annuities to donors in exchange for charitable contributions were not subject to regulation. To ensure public protection, and as part of legislation that also explicitly brought regulation of annuity contracts and endowment policies under the Insurance Law, then Superintendent Francis R. Stoddard, Jr. proposed prohibiting the practice entirely.[115]

The legal counsel of the governor of New York asked Stoddard to comment on several amendments to the insurance law in 1923. Stoddard noted that there had long been "considerable controversy" over the question of whether commercial annuities sold by life insurance companies were subject to the insurance law.[116] He told Parsons that the main objective of the proposed amendments was "bringing clearly under the Insurance Law and regulating the issuance of all kinds of endowment policies and annuity contracts." Amendment 152 to the New York Insurance Law in 1923 mandated that annuity contracts be regulated within the business of insurance: "Inasmuch as these contracts are issued by insurance companies and are based upon life contingencies the Department believed that the law should be amended in order to remove any doubt as to their being insurance contracts."[117]

Stoddard wrote that initially, he saw no reason for nonprofit organizations issuing gift annuity contracts to be exempt from the insurance law and that his department favored ending the practice:

> Furthermore, at various times it has come to the attention of the Department that certain corporations were issuing annuity contracts to persons who made donations to such corporations upon agreement that the corporation would pay to them a certain income during their lifetime. There seemed to be no regulation or supervision of these contracts or of the corporations issuing the same so that **it appeared desirable that this practice be prohibited** (emphasis added). This would have been the result of the amendments to the above mentioned sections of the law as originally introduced.[118]

The amendments to the law required that after July 1, 1923, no annuity contract could be issued in New York unless it contained certain specified provisions and had been preapproved by the superintendent of insurance. Several of the required provisions in standard business-annuity contracts, such as those relating to a grace period and contestability, were inappropriate for gift annuity contracts issued by nonprofits.[119] Standard gift annuity contracts could not be approved under the new law.

Stoddard's proposal to regulate nonprofit gift annuities as if they were in the business of life insurance was opposed by several nonprofit organizations. Stoddard told the governor's attorney that he had heard from some leaders of nonprofits early in 1923 and had changed his mind about prohibiting gift annuities:

> After the bill was introduced, however, representatives of certain religious and philanthropic corporations which

have, it seems, for some time issued these contracts and have received very large contributions, took the matter up with me, and after going into the question carefully, I decided to amend the bill so it now makes an exception of charitable, religious, missionary, educational and philanthropic corporations conducted without profit, **where such corporations maintain reserves at least equal to their outstanding liabilities** in accordance with McClintock's "Mortality Table among Annuitants." (emphasis added)

Stoddard's rationale for recognizing the legal rights of nonprofit organizations to issue gift annuities is worth quoting at length. Note especially that Stoddard admits to having no previous data on gift annuity programs or evidence of abuses, and that the testimony of the American Bible Society, which had launched its gift annuity campaign in 1919, was crucial in swaying his opinion:

These [nonprofit] corporations have, it seems, been operating for a great many years and have had millions of dollars given to them under agreements to pay to the annuitants an income during their life time. Heretofore they have never been required to maintain reserves but some of them, I believe, have done so voluntarily. There has never been any complaint from annuitant [*sic*] because of the failure of any one of these corporations to carry out their annuity contracts and inasmuch as they will hereafter be required to maintain reserves on all these contracts, there is no reason to believe that there will be any such failure in the future.

While I am not sure that it is altogether wise to allow corporations other than insurance corporations to issue annuity contracts, where such corporations are not under the supervision or regulation of any state department, nevertheless, because of the high standing of the corporations which have been issuing these annuity contracts for some time, such as the American Bible Society and other prominent missionary and philanthropic corporations, and because of the requirement that they maintain the reserves for such contracts which life insurance companies are required to maintain, I believed it advisable at this time to consent to the amendment in favor of such corporations in order to remove the opposition to the bill which I thought very desirable to have passed.

Notwithstanding Stoddard's change of heart, the New York legislature did *not* provide an exception for gift annuities in its insurance law in 1923. Perhaps he gave some assurance to the Bible Society that New York would not enforce its law, since ABS issued a growing number of gift annuity contracts in 1923–24.

In 1925, as the legislature was amending other sections of the law, Gilbert Darlington of the ABS invited George Huggins to join a small coalition of nonprofit organizations to make the case that Superintendent Stoddard was correct—that charitable gift annuities were essentially different from annuity investments sold by commercial firms. This time, Darlington and his colleagues succeeded in convincing New York lawmakers to enact an exception in the law, allowing nonprofit organizations to issue gift annuities.[120]

Darlington opened his presentation at the first Conference on Annuities in 1927 by telling the story of nonprofits lobbying the New York legislature.[121] He told the story again in 1952 to make the point that the CGA was founded to defend the differences between charitable gifts that return life annuities and commercial investments: "By having this statement included in the Insurance Law of New York State, the right of religious and charitable organizations to issue annuities was recognized and approved."[122]

Concerned that this important historical context might be lost or forgotten, Darlington quoted the exemption statement for nonprofit organizations in the New York Insurance Law of 1925 so that it would be preserved in the conference record:

> Annuity contracts issued by charitable, religious, missionary, educational or philanthropic non-stock corporations conducted without profit where such [a] corporation maintains a reserve fund to carry out such contracts at least equal to its contract liabilities calculated in accordance with the provisions of Sections 84 and 85 of this Chapter.

The one requirement for nonprofits under the insurance law of 1925—a very important requirement—was that they must comply with New York's actuarial methods for calculating the "contract liabilities" of their gift annuities. Starting in 1925, nonprofits that issue gift annuities in New York have been required by law to apply standardized actuarial principles to measure the financial obligations involved with their payment rates and the average mortality of their annuitants. They must also prove that they are maintaining a reserve fund adequate to meet their obligations.

The New York Insurance Law of 1925 formalized a legal distinction between commercial annuities and charitable-gift annuities, but for the rest of the United States, the law's initial direct impact remained limited. Donors, their advisors, and annuities-issuing charities in the 1920s had to make decisions in the face of important public-policy uncertainties, such as whether and how a wide range of state and federal laws, judicial rulings, and administrative regulations on commercial financial products applied to gift annuities that were issued by nonprofit organizations.

Huggins understood that his insurance-business model for gift annuities would have profound public-policy implications that would have to be worked out. An effective national plan had to provide a responsible, transparent process for rate setting and for consumer protection that public officials could use to address the inevitable questions that would arise involving income and estate taxes, the adequacy and risk exposure of reserve accounts, the accuracy of marketing claims, the soundness of legal contracts, and other policy issues familiar to commercial-insurance companies.

The first step was to scan the legal horizon to understand current policies. In his report to a CFFM Conference in March of 1927, Huggins said that "I would like to see this committee investigate the existing insurance laws and departmental rulings as to their bearing on the issuance of these annuities."[123]

Huggins recommended a wide-ranging survey of the public-policy landscape: "the laws and rulings pertaining to the income and inheritance taxes—both federal and state, as they may apply to the principal of the annuity gifts or to the income received by the beneficiaries." Just as important, he advocated raising the voluntary standards of gift annuity programs to protect the interests of all concerned:

> Personally, I favor constructive legislation, but I fear destructive legislation, and if we do not conduct the [annuity] business on the highest possible plane, with equitable returns to the donors and absolute protection as to their annuity payments, we are bound to have a reaction in the form of hostile and possibly destructive legislation.

The State of New York opened the door for Huggins's actuarial solution to the central problem of gift annuity rate setting. It did so indirectly by imposing regulations on reserve investments for existing gift annuity contracts. The New York Insurance Law of 1925 did not mandate a process for establishing gift annuity payment rates, but the higher the rates, the greater the amount that must be held in reserve.[124] To comply with the law on gift annuity reserves, nonprofits would need to apply actuarial principles in their rate setting.

New York's principal actuary made this point explicit in 1939:

> The requirement that the [gift] annuity rates shall be non-competitive with those of life companies, does not appear in

these exact words in the law. What the statute does prescribe is that the rate of life income to be paid shall be so computed as to leave with the [charitable] corporation upon the annuitant's death at least one half of the purchase money.

ARE GIFT ANNUITIES LIKE INVESTMENT BONDS OR LIFE INSURANCE?

Another aspect of the New York Insurance Law of 1925 is important in the early history of the Conferences on Annuities: a well-intentioned attempt to redirect gift annuity reserve fund asset allocation by using the law to compel gift annuity fund managers to behave more like life insurance fund managers.

There was good reason for concern. Freedom from legal and regulatory controls in the 1920s and 1930s allowed nonprofit organizations to invest their gift annuity reserve accounts as they chose. Unfortunately, many chose unwisely. Whether an investment strategy for charitable gift annuities is effective depends on what fund managers think they are investing and why.

The prevailing annuity bond business model contributed to some of the mistakes. Corporations issuing a bond will often pledge real estate or equipment as collateral to be liquidated in case of default.[125] Pledging a building as collateral, or promising to use the revenue from student dormitories, is inadequate for a gift annuity reserve fund; nonprofit organizations are extremely unlikely to sell their buildings to make up deficiencies in annuity payments.[126]

The new actuarial model for gift annuities forced nonprofit organizations to rethink the business they were in. Huggins and Darlington believed that charities had to stop acting as if gift annuities were *like bonds*, which followed the rules of the credit-investment markets and start acting as if they were *like life insurance*, a highly regulated, consumer-based business with far different investment considerations.[127]

Darlington asserted at the 1927 COA that compliance with the New York Insurance Law meant investing gift annuity reserve funds in "proper securities" approved for life insurance reserves, though the law applied only to the valuation of gift annuity reserves and not to the nonprofits' choice of investments:

> As long, therefore, as such a reserve is maintained in securities suitable for the investment of funds of life insurance companies of the State of New York a certificate of the Superintendent of Insurance is not necessary...As long, therefore, as the groups mentioned [i.e., nonprofit charitable organizations] maintain their reserve funds in proper securities there is no fear of their being forced to submit to the full authority of the Superintendent of Insurance.[128]

Ryan, Darlington's colleague at the ABS, extended this guidance by asserting that all nonprofits that issued annuities should invest their annuity reserves as required for life insurance companies that operated in the state in which the organizations were incorporated: "It is the belief of your Committee that all funds received on the annuity basis should be invested in securities suitable for insurance companies operating in the state in which the institution is incorporated, and that the full 100 percent of these funds should be held in such investments until the death of the annuitant."[129]

Ryan and Darlington went a step too far. No one had identified a state with a legal requirement that nonprofit organizations must invest their gift annuity reserves as if they were life insurance reserves.[130] Unfortunately, it was also a fact that most leaders of nonprofits that issued gift annuities had no idea what their state laws and regulations said about life insurance reserves or whether the laws of their home states affected charitable gift annuities in any way.[131]

At the second COA in 1928, George Sutherland contradicted Ryan's and Darlington's investment advice, stating, "It is not necessary that these funds should be invested in securities which are legal for [life insurance] trustees in the states where such [an] organization is incorporated." In fact, he said, "a larger income can be secured if the [investment] committees do not limit themselves to legal investments."[132]

After its 1928 conference, the Subcommittee on Annuities recognized that while state laws did not compel charities to invest their annuity reserves as if they were life insurance companies, charities would do well to observe life insurance investment laws voluntarily. Most states followed New York by requiring commercial life insurance companies to invest nearly all their financial-reserve accounts in highly rated fixed-income assets.[133]

At the third COA in 1930, William T. Boult made a presentation entitled "Administration and Investment of Annuity Funds," which became very popular and was published as a separate issue in the *Wise Public Giving* series.[134] Boult argued that gift annuity reserve investments should be "so sound that leading financiers and business men would commend them," and "State Insurance Commissioners, who may possibly call upon us to submit lists of securities, will also be favorably impressed." After reciting the assets acceptable under the New York Insurance Law, Boult provided the prevailing wisdom of the CGA: "There can be no question that we are morally bound, **and may some day be legally bound** in a similar way." (emphasis added)

That day arrived in June of 1939 with the enactment of a new insurance law by the State of New York, which required non-profit organizations that promoted gift annuities in the state to file annual reports on their segregated annuity reserve funds and to qualify for certificates. The New York Insurance Law of 1939 imposed the same investment restrictions on admitted assets for gift annuity reserve funds as for life insurance reserves.[135] Charities that issued gift annuities in New York had a grace period until 1950 to conform their reserve fund investment strategies to the new actuarial business model,[136] while charities that issued annuities in unregulated states remained free to invest their annuity reserves as they chose.

In 1959, the New York insurance commissioner told the Conference on Gift Annuities that the state's limited control over gift annuities had been very successful in protecting the interests of gift annuitants:

> The experiment commenced 20 years ago of limited statutory supervision of gift annuity securities has worked out entirely satisfactorily from the Department's viewpoint. The substantial amounts of annuity funds involved have been adequately safeguarded and I believe that the prestige of the gift annuity societies has thereby been enhanced.[137]

Even within the boundaries of New York's regulatory constraints, investment managers had considerable autonomy in their asset selections. One could follow all the official rules and still make unsuccessful investment choices. As will be discussed in section 4, asset selection and investment strategies for gift annuity reserve funds were prime topics at conferences during the Depression, when the value of "safe" investments, such as mortgages and railroad bonds, plummeted.

Exemption from most provisions of the New York Insurance Law of 1925 was a major victory in the battle to protect the soul of charitable gift annuities. Now that the leading regulator had recognized the special characters of such annuities, nonprofits had to behave accordingly to distinguish their policies and practices from those of commercial annuity firms.

In coming pages, we will see how nonprofits slowly adopted appropriate practices. Not all charitable gift annuity programs were alike, and neither were the public policies imposed by federal and state authorities.

LEGISLATORS CHALLENGED BY GIFT ANNUITIES

For nearly five decades after the modern federal tax code was enacted in 1913, a basic element for gift annuity calculations was missing. American policies on gift annuities were crazy quilts. It was impossible to be certain how federal and state tax laws and regulations would be applied in a donor's specific situation.

After his successful lobbying in New York State, Gilbert Darlington of the Bible Society took responsibility for tracking and reporting to American nonprofits on relevant federal and state tax legislation affecting gift annuities. At the first conference, he reported a major change because of the US Revenue Act of 1926. For many years, in the absence of definitive guidance, people had assumed that payments from gift annuities were tax-free returns of principal until the full amounts transferred to the nonprofit had been received back. That was no longer the case.

Darlington expanded upon the new tax landscape in 1928 by citing a revenue ruling by the Treasury Department on the taxation of gift annuities:

> This Ruling appears to split every annuity to a religious, educational or charitable corporation into two parts: one, the purchase price of the annuity, and two, the amount that is a gift. This means that hereafter it cannot be said that an annuitant can receive back the full amount paid to religious, educational, or charitable corporations without paying an income tax to the Federal Government.[138]

For gift planners, this brought profound changes in the need for professional training and would forever change their relationships with donors:

> The amount of exemption from Federal Income Tax here granted to the annuitant must be figured out very definitely

on the principles laid down by the Treasury Department. This is technical and very precise work. It cannot be attempted by the ordinary annuitant without help and assistance from someone who is familiar with what must be done to get the proper result.

Clarity in policy immediately ran into a harsh reality. The Treasury ruling totally misunderstood how gift annuities work. Its analysis in the ruling confused the annuity payment rate of 5 percent with the investment assumption used in performing the tax calculations, which should have been 4 percent, not 5 percent. Darlington points out the absurdity that if the annuity payment rate was 9 percent, the Treasury apparently would assume a 9 percent annual investment return for tax purposes.

As a direct result of the Treasury ruling, the tax situation at the state level became far more complex. In 1928, just eleven states had their own income taxes. Would the states follow the flawed federal income tax ruling on gift annuities or not?

There may be states that have followed this Ruling of the Treasury Department, but the writer is not aware of them. Whether it is advisable to take up with the different states that have income tax laws as to whether or not they will follow in this matter, is an important question.

Darlington advised waiting to see what individual states would do: "It may be better to wait until specific situations come up that require action."

This was the most prudent course available, given the general lack of information about state laws and no national network of trained public-policy specialists. Tracking state legislation, rulings, and administrative practices placed quite a burden on the fledgling Committee on Annuities. At the third conference in 1930, Darlington's presentation occupied twenty-nine pages of a conference report totaling 104 pages. His comments on

"Taxation of Annuities Under State Laws" testified to the difficulties he encountered:

> It is not always easy to answer a question as to whether an annuity is taxable under the laws of a specific state. This may be because the law as embodied in the Constitution, and/or political code or statutes of the state, is not plain; because the interpretation of the Constitution and/or the statute law by different authorities varies; and/or because for some reason or other the law is not being complied with at the moment.[139]

Federal policies on the tax treatment of gift annuities often were incomplete, misinformed, or misguided. While it is beyond the scope of this book to track the tangled legislative history,[140] two more examples will give evidence of the confused and confusing tax landscape.

In 1953, the Committee on Gift Annuities was unable to persuade the IRS to change an inappropriate formula that taxed annuitants unfairly by undervaluing the charitable residuum, so it approved a legal challenge: "The committee unanimously agreed that the use of the standard annuity table, with interest at 2%, is unjust to the annuitant and rather than accept it the chairman is authorized to take action in the courts to oppose its use for valuing gift annuities for Federal Income Tax purposes."[141]

Darlington complained again about the unfair federal valuation of gift annuities at the ninth conference in 1955: "The Treasury Department is still attempting to value gift annuities solely on the basis of individual annuities without refunds or dividends at a 2-percent interest rate…It appears that the time has come to solve this problem for the future just as soon as we can do so, even if it requires action in the courts."[142]

This valuation problem must have been resolved before the tenth conference in 1959, since it was not mentioned in the report.

A second important question was raised when the US Treasury Department issued a private letter ruling on September 9, 1955, regarding the tax treatment of a gift of appreciated property through a gift annuity, and then it announced on November 10, 1955, that it was reconsidering its position, as cited by Darlington:

> The Revenue Service has under reconsideration the tax consequences of the transfer of property and securities to charitable organizations for an annuity contract and the proper method for reporting these transactions for Federal income tax purposes. It is contemplated that a Revenue Ruling will be issued in the near future on this subject.

At the tenth COA in December of 1959, Charles Baas noted that no such revenue ruling had appeared: "To the best of my knowledge we are still in the near future." An expert on the tax implications of gift annuities reported to the ninth COA in 1955 that untangling the strands of federal law was not a task for amateurs:

> From the first modern tax law until the present day, the tax problems of annuitants have proven particularly difficult to solve…The Internal Revenue Code of 1954 changes much of the law relating to annuities…Like its predecessors, however, the new law's coverage of the charitable annuitant's problems is incomplete and, as a result, reference to and reliance upon judicial decisions and Treasury Department regulations and rulings is often necessary.[143]

Thanks to decades of advocacy by Gilbert Darlington, George Huggins, and others representing nonprofit organizations, the Committee on Gift Annuities was able to publish a reliable manual for federal-tax calculations entitled *Tax Implications of an Annuity Gift* (the "Green Book") in August of 1961.[144] The committee produced a series of these manuals for use in the painstaking work of calculating tax implications by hand, until gift-planning software in the 1980s automated the process.[145]

The Tax Reform Act of 1969, which introduced substantial changes for charitable-remainder trusts and pooled-income funds, made only minor changes in gift annuities.[146]

The public-policy debate on the proper balance between philanthropy and self-interest boiled over in the 1990s during an expensive and protracted class-action lawsuit that centered on the annuity rate-setting process created by Huggins for the COA. Attorneys for the plaintiffs alleged (among many other charges) that all nonprofit charities using the voluntary rates recommended by CGA were engaging in price-fixing to lower payments to gift annuitants and retain more money for their organizations. The plaintiffs sought triple damages (that is, repaying annuitants three times the amounts of their original gifts) in what the attorneys claimed was a "billion-dollar lawsuit."[147]

Nonprofits lost one legal battle after another. The case was resolved by a Supreme Court ruling involving the ABS[148] and unanimous enactment of three federal laws: the Philanthropy Protection Act of 1995,[149] the Antitrust Relief Act of 1995,[150] and the Charitable Donation Antitrust Immunity Act of 1997.[151]

In the end, the Texas lawsuits were settled by invoking the fundamental distinction between commercial annuity investments and charitable gifts articulated by George Huggins in 1927. The stated purpose of the Philanthropy Protection Act is "to facilitate contributions to charitable organizations by codifying certain exemptions from the Federal securities laws."

We turn now to the introduction of actuarial science to American fundraising, and the creation of technical and political processes for incorporating Huggins's major ideas.

Notes

1   North 1964. North was unable to find documentation for many early life-income gifts, noting that "it seems impossible to produce a summary

of funds received as trusts terminable on death of an annuitant, as the records seem not be available or not kept in a manner in which this can easily be determined."

2   As of December 31, 1990, "there were 11,929 living beneficiaries of American Bible Society annuities and trusts" (Bell 1991, 29).

3   Quotations not otherwise identified are from North's essay on "Annuities and Trust Agreements."

4   As discussed above, the New York Life Insurance and Trust Company was the first American life insurance firm led by an actuary. Peter Augustus Jay was a founding board member of NYLIT in 1830.

5   See, for example, Schoenhals 1992 and Bell 1991: "Thus Joseph Keith became both donor and beneficiary of the first charitable gift annuity."

6   "Regrettably, we lack further information about Mr. Keith. His lifespan, his family, his business career, even his subsequent involvement in Bible Society activities remain a mystery" (Bell 1991, 6). The ABS gift annuity contract with Keith has not been located.

7   ABS received its charter from New York in 1841: "After some difficulty the legislature of the state of New York finally passed an act in 1841 incorporating the American Bible Society" (Dwight 1916, 122).

8   Edward John Woolsey (1803–73) was a member of an important American merchant family tracing back to the 1620s.

9   Theodore Frelinghuysen (1787–1862) served as attorney general of New Jersey (1817–29), US senator from New Jersey (1829–35), mayor of Newark, NJ (1837), president of New York University (1839–50), candidate for US vice president (1844) and president of Rutgers College (1850–62). He served as president of ABS from 1846 to his death in 1862.

10   Luther Bradish (1783–1863) was a powerful legislator who served as lieutenant governor of New York, presiding over the state senate (1839–42); as a member of the New York State Assembly (1827–30 and 1835–38); and as speaker of the Assembly in 1838. He ran unsuccessfully for governor of New York in 1842 and served as assistant US treasurer (1842–44), after which he retired from politics to devote his life to nonprofit organizations. At the time of his report in 1848 he was first vice president of the ABS and was elected president in 1862 but died the next year. He served

as president of the Historical Society of New York from 1850 to 1863. See Johnson (1929, 1957).

11   Katz 1985, 67.

12   Quotations not otherwise identified are from the *Bradish Report.*

13   The New York Insurance Law did not define annuity contracts as being subject to insurance regulations until 1923 and did not mention annuities issued by nonprofit organizations until 1925.

14   On the evolution of church law and common law on charitable trusts, see for example, Shael Herman, "The Canonical Conception of the Trust" and other essays in Helmholz 1998; Bean, "The Origin and Development of Uses" (1968, 104–79); Jordan 1959; and Jones 1969.

15   Vidal v. Girard's Executors 1844, 205. In the Vidal case, the court upheld a charitable bequest from the estate of banker Stephen Girard, one of the wealthiest people in American history. Girard died in 1831. In his will, Girard intended to create and endow a school in Philadelphia through a trust funded with $2 million—an enormous sum in 1831 and by far the largest bequest to an American charity up to that time. Girard was a widower with no children of his own. A group of his relatives in France filed a challenge in the Circuit Court of the United States for the Eastern District of Philadelphia claiming (among other things) that since Pennsylvania had not adopted the Statute of Charitable Uses, the gift should be disallowed and the $2 million distributed to them. Diligent legal historians reported that some fifty chancery court cases involving charitable trusts were decided in favor of charity long before the Statute of Charitable Uses was enacted by Parliament in 1601. The circuit court found in Girard's favor; the relatives appealed to the Supreme Court and were represented by Daniel Webster. The US Supreme Court found in Vidal that "charity is one of those objects for which a court of equity has at all times interfered to make good that, which at law was an illegal or informal gift."

16   In the Matter of Howe, etc., Executor, and Anderson, Deceased, 1828. Also cited above in the brief history of charitable trusts and annuities.

17   "In 1829 the New York legislature in a statutory revision of all its laws codified the law of uses and trusts. The new statute permitted four types

of trusts, but did not mention the charitable kind. Throughout the nineteenth century, New York Courts interpreted the statute strictly, which meant in practice that a testator could not give his property to a charitable trust in a manner that would withstand judicial scrutiny" (Fishman 1985, 627).

18   North 1966.

19   After more than six decades of restrictive legislation, New York finally sanctioned the legal validity of testamentary charitable trusts through the far-reaching Tilden Act (1893) in order to save a large gift from the estate of former governor Samuel Tilden: "The new law not only restored the charitable trust as a legal instrument of philanthropy in New York State to make it easier to give money, but also made it possible to leave a bequest undefined and to put the trustees in charge of redefining its goals for each generation" (Zunz 2012, 11–17). His bequest through the Tilden Trust helped found the New York Public Library.

20   I have not found similar survey results for Jewish, Catholic, and other non-Protestant religious denominations. I strongly suspect that gift planning in many communities has escaped documentation.

21   See Cassat 1931, 35–50.

22   "We and our predecessors [in the Methodist Church] have been issuing gift annuities for 83 years" (H. Burnham Kirkland, "State Supervision of Gift Annuities," in Various 1955, 15). A survey of thirty-five colleges related to the Methodist Church in the fall of 1929 found that thirty-two colleges had gift annuity programs. In total, 640 annuity contracts had been issued since 1920. The face value of 851 existing annuity contracts was $6.2 million. The value of annuity reserve funds was $5.6 million, and college endowments totaled $31.5 million (Reeves 1932).

23   Charles Lincoln White, executive secretary of the American Baptist Home Mission Society, announced at a March 1927 conference of financial professionals that "the American Bible Society has had a phenomenal call for its annuity bonds and in seven years has increased its funds from this source from practically nothing to in one year more than $600,000." From "Annuities," in Various 1927a, 87.

24 Average US wages were higher relative to prewar levels, but inflation in the cost of food and other goods and periodic spikes in unemployment resulted in a series of major labor strikes in the 1920s.

25 Such 2009, accessed October 5, 2009. James Grant (2014) points out that a depression in 1920–21 involved severe downturns in the economy and the stock market before each recovered strongly en route to record levels.

26 History.com 2014, accessed October 18, 2014. Eric Burns (2015) describes many aspects of America's economic boom and its various impacts on social life.

27 "For the first time, more Americans lived in cities than on farms" (from "The Roaring Twenties," Ibid.). Akron, Ohio, (the author's hometown) was one of the fastest-growing cities in the United States; families were drawn to the Rubber City by tire makers such as Firestone, Goodyear, and B. F. Goodrich.

28 Written by F. Scott Fitzgerald (1925), *Gatsby* dramatizes the changing values of urban America during the Jazz Age.

29 After all these years, the best history of American fundraising was written by Scott M. Cutlip, originally published in 1965: *Fund Raising in the United States: Its Role in America's Philanthropy* (reprinted 1990). Bremner (1960; rev. 1988) remains invaluable. Olivier Zunz (2012) makes many good observations on American fundraising from the late nineteenth century to the present, particularly on the rise of "mass philanthropy" at the turn of the twentieth century. His focus is on "the ways the philanthropic system has intersected with government and influenced policy in the United States for more than a century" (xii). *Philanthropy in America: A Comprehensive Historical Encyclopedia* (Burlingame 2004) has many useful entries. None of these books mention gift annuities or charitable-remainder trusts.

30 Murphy 2010, 137.

31 "At the heart of the whole [life insurance] movement are two concepts from which many others flow: (1) life insurance is a vital and unique opportunity for every person who has financial plans, and (2) selling life insurance is an art which can be taught" (Stalson 1942, 576). Stalson highlights the year 1916 as the breakthrough for modern marketing: "The

year 1916 has claim to special notice in life marketing annals; it was, so to speak, the culmination year of a long period of awakening to life insurance selling and sales management on a higher plane."

32   Buley 1953, 563.

33   Buley 1953, 625, 680.

34   Stalson 1942, 879. Similar growth in annuity sales is reported in Table Cj727-732 (n.d.).

35   Charles L. White, "Annuities," in White 1927, 86. White was selected to chair the first COA in April 1927.

36   White 1927b, 86.

37   Minutes of the ABS Ways and Means Committee, March 31, 1927.

38   "A Better Way" 1905, 400.

39   "Life Annuity Bonds" 1919, 156.

40   "Assured Income Bonds" 1921, 1090.

41   "A Safe Investment" 1919, 31.

42   Minutes of the ABS Ways and Means Committee, June 1919. The ad appeared in "A Safe and Productive Investment" (1919, 186).

43   "Millions in Liberty Bonds Stolen" 1921, 1080.

44   The author and his wife put their money where their heart was: "the Secretary [Mann] reported that Mr. and Mrs. Collins are proposing to purchase an [ABS] annuity bond of between $500 and $1500."

45   Published by Collins (1914).

46   This creative annuity payment arrangement is modeled on a once-popular deferred-dividend insurance plan known as a tontine. See Ransom 1987, 379–90.

47   The ABS took gifts of real estate in exchange for annuities a step further than Collins. At the first COA in 1927, Arthur C. Ryan, general secretary of ABS, incorporated the society's real estate gift-acceptance policy in his presentation: "Other property, including stocks and real estate, which is satisfactory to the Finance Committee of the board concerned may be accepted under a trust agreement to pay the donor or donors thereof the actual net income on such property, when and as accrued, with the understanding that the Society shall have the right to sell such property, and that when such property is sold

the society will issue a single or a survivorship annuity agreement for the net proceeds received from the sale of such property at the rate of income paid to annuitants at the age of the donor or donors of such property at the time the sale of the property has been affected [*sic*]" (from Ryan 1927, 25).

48   Collins 1918.

49   Collins 1920.

50   Collins quotes several satisfied annuitants in an article for the *Christian Philanthropist*, the "official paper of the National Benevolent Association of the Christian Church." One testifies that "wife and I began giving on the annuity plan in 1899. We consider it the safest and best investment a person can make." Reprinted under the caption (Collins 1916, 688).

51   Collins 1916.

52   *Bible Society Record* 65, no. 5 (May 1920).

53   According to "A New Officer at the Bible House" (1919), Frank Mann was one of ten children and was orphaned at age two. He was raised by his uncle, William Hodges Mann, "a lawyer, judge, and senator, and governor of Virginia." He attended Hoge Military Academy and Hampden Sydney College. Mann served in a US Army field artillery unit during World War I from 1914 to 1918 and was promoted to first lieutenant. He was not ordained as a minister, but he was an elder and an active volunteer with the Fifth Avenue Presbyterian Church in New York City when he was selected for the staff of the ABS.

54   "The most important aspect of financial promotion and cultivation during this period, 1901–1930, concerned the Society's direct approach to individuals and denominational organizations." In Zimmerman 1967, 1. Creation of the WMC was approved by the ABS board on March 2, 1916. The committee became much more effective with the hiring of Mann as financial secretary after a long national search.

55   In March of 1919, Mann proposed to develop a list of seventy-five thousand or more prospective donors to be solicited "by means of letters, circulars, and such other means of approach as could be devised."

56   Ivy Lee was a Georgia native and son of a Methodist minister who received a bachelor's degree in economics from Princeton in 1898. He

served major corporate clients, such as the Pennsylvania Railroad and Standard Oil, as well as guiding the public relations of the American Red Cross during the First World War. Lee served as a board member of the ABS and was a member of the WMC when it selected Mann. For his bio, see: http://en.wikipedia.org/wiki/Ivy_Lee. There is an excellent account of Lee's "saturation publicity campaign" for the Red Cross in Cutlip 1965, 1990, 127–33.

57   "Mr. Mann presented a program for a membership campaign in New York City...Mr. Mann suggested that the campaign might best be conducted under the direction of a good Advertising Agency and that Mr. Ivy Lee's organization was willing to handle the campaign for the sum of $500." The ABS WMC approved the hiring of Lee at its meeting on January 5, 1920.

58   Originally founded in 1849 as the S. M. Pettengill Company, the Morse International Agency specialized in newspaper advertising. In the 1920s, the company was located at 449 Fourth Avenue in New York City.

59   See esp. "The Coming of Mass Philanthropy," in Zunz 2012, 44–75.

60   "The Society issued annuity agreements as early as 1843; however, the first systematic cultivation of this means of income was first undertaken in 1919 under the leadership and direction of Secretary Mann" (Zimmerman 1967, 88).

61   Cited by North (1966, 19).

62   Gifts from churches were estimated at $290,000 for 1921, and gifts from individuals at $70,000. The largest income item was the sale of Bibles and related materials: $450,000. WMC minutes dated November 11, 1920.

63   The minutes of the WMC for July 21, 1922, record that the ABS had issued annuities to people in thirty-eight states and the District of Columbia, China, Cuba, and the Netherlands. On February 19, 1925, the committee discussed a complaint from the Canadian Bible Society on the ABS's issuing of gift annuities to Canadian citizens. The committee decided the American society would no longer respond to gift inquiries from Canadians but would refer them to their own national society.

64   ABS annuity reserve accounts in 1950 totaled $11,743,211. In 1949, 265 annuitants had died, providing a charitable residuum of $621,805 toward the mission of the society. From Bell 1991?, 18.

65   "Annuity agreements have exceeded one million dollars annually in 14 of the last 15 years" (WMC minutes, February 18, 1960).

66   Mann attended a conference in March of 1922 "called by the Home Missions Council of various boards and organizations making use of the annuity plan," but he reported that "no Findings have been presented and there was nothing of unusual significance discussed that needs to be presented to the Committee." The primary outcome of this conference was a working relationship between Mann and Anthony.

67   The ABS offered significantly higher payment rates than the Methodist Episcopal Church, including a maximum rate of 9 percent for annuitants at ages eighty and over, compared with 8 percent by the Methodists. The ABS lowered its annuity rates in 1931, as recommended by the CGA.

68   The Covering Fund was based on the face value of existing annuity contracts, not the present value as determined by an actuary.

69   Note that this system precludes any donor restrictions on the ultimate use of a gift.

70   The hiring of paid callers was a failed experiment that was terminated within a year. The ABS annuity campaign was conducted by direct mail and advertisements.

71   Noticeably absent from the annuity campaign plan are gift officers making personal visits.

72   The ABS later expanded its reach beyond religious publications. For example, *Forbes* magazine was listed as a source of annuity gifts in the minutes of February 18, 1960.

73   The willingness of ABS leaders to invest in annuity advertising soon led some of their colleagues to request a share of the budget. In December of 1920, two Home Agency secretaries asked that they be given money to promote gift annuities. The WMC agreed to provide 5 percent of the face value of gift annuities received to the Home Agency budgets "in cases where the Agency Secretary has been directly involved in the securing of the annuity either by having initiated it, or having given essential aid in securing it." On March 24, 1921, the WMC voted to incorporate the annuity promotion allowance for home secretaries in the regular budget process.

74   "The attention of the committee was called to the fact that Trust Companies and lawyers have very little knowledge of the annuity operations of the various missionary boards. Secretary Mann stated that it is his belief that prospective annuitants frequently consult their attorneys or banks in regard to these matters…he recommended…that he be authorized to suggest to the Foreign Missions Conference and the Home Missions Conference that some arrangement be made for advertising annuity bonds of these various boards in the technical papers reaching bankers and lawyers—the expense to be borne jointly by the several boards cooperating. It seemed best to the Committee that this should not be undertaken" (Minutes of April 23, 1923).

75   Minutes of November 21, 1924.

76   Zimmerman 1967, 94. The numbers for 1924 are slightly different than reported in January of 1925.

77   In 1919, the ABS headquarters building/warehouse known as Bible House occupied the entire block of Ninth Street between Third and Fourth Avenues in Manhattan.

78   Arthur Clayton Ryan was born in Grandview, Iowa, in 1879; he graduated from Iowa's Grinnell College in 1909 and from Oberlin Theological Seminary in 1911. He served as secretary for the Levant Agency of the ABS, based in Constantinople, from 1920 to 1924, and was responsible for producing and circulating the Bible among various European and Middle Eastern countries (ABS news release February 10, 1925; also see ABS July 1927, 111–12).

79   Dr. Anthony was appointed executive secretary of the Home Missions Council in 1918. The council was a nondenominational, Christian evangelical organization encouraging cooperation, tolerance of differences, and inclusiveness among American churches and nonprofit organizations (see Anthony 1918).

80   Mann was president of the Union Guaranty Mortgage Company, "organized under the Insurance Law of the State of New York…to make loans secured by mortgages on real property which it sold to its customers with a guaranty" (see https://casetext.com/case/in-re-union-guarantee-mortgage-co-2, downloaded October 20, 2014).

81   Frank H. Mann, "Annuities," in Mann 1925, 21–27. In 1929, Mann succeeded Dr. Alfred Williams Anthony as chairman of the CFFM.

82   First Presbyterian Church 1922.

83   "Perhaps the greatest difficulty has arisen in the case of two-life rates, for if one has been accustomed to consider that the continuance of the annuity to a second beneficiary is not a matter of great importance, it becomes difficult to get used to the fact that it may involve a material reduction in the rate if properly calculated" (Huggins 1928?, 28–29).

84   Paul Cassat noted that almost one-third of colleges he surveyed did not report their maximum gift annuity payment rates: "It is likely that in several of these instances much higher rates are granted under pressure, and covered by some such remark as 'No definite schedule published,' or 'Each case treated on its merits.'" A new member of the Committee on Annuities, Cassat expressed the hope that "as time goes on, we will see much less of this sort of thing. We can all help the annuity cause by rapping hard this unfair competition in rates" (see Cassat 1931).

85   Cassat 1931, 37. For example, in 1927 Boston University launched an annuity bond program "the unique feature of which is that they pay interest on a basis equal to ten per cent of the age of the annuitant when the bond is issued" (*Journal of Education* 1927, 48).

86   Table 10, "Bases Used by 70 Colleges and Universities in Determining Their Schedule of Annuity Rates," in Wellck 1933.

87   Huggins, "Rates for Gift-annuity Agreements," in Various 1941, 24.

88   For a full account of the many ways ABS has provided international religious leadership since 1816, see Fea (2016).

89   Rev. Gilbert S. B. Darlington was a graduate of Columbia University (BA 1912; his PhD studies were interrupted by service as a navy chaplain during WWI) and General Theological Seminary (1914) and received an honorary DD from Dickinson College (1945). Darlington was treasurer of the American Bible Society from 1920 to 1957. He was president and chairman of the board of Harbor State Bank, chaplain general of the Naval Order of the United States, and an Episcopal priest. Darlington served as a volunteer member of the Committee on Gift Annuities from 1928 to 1972 and as honorary chairman until 1980.

90   Huggins 1955, 31–34.

91   Huggins, "Rates, Mortality Experience, and Reserves," in Various 1952, 106.

92   Baas 1991, 73. Baas described Darlington as a Renaissance man who served as president and chairman of Harbor State Bank, director of the Pan American Trust Company, and chaplain general of the Naval Order of the United States, among many other accomplishments.

93   ACGA 2006, 1. Baas was born in 1920 in Atlantic City and earned degrees from Rutgers University, New York University, and Wagner College. His colleagues insisted on adding Baas's biography to the roster of "Prime Movers" in his *History*, including these comments: "Charley Baas' name is synonymous with the Committee on Gift Annuities for an entire generation of planned giving officers, treasurers, business officers and others who work for charitable organizations throughout the United States...Charley Baas has led, sustained and nurtured the Committee for 45 years. There will never be another like him."

94   Baas 1991, 93.

95   The charge to the SOA in March 1927 included, "This committee should be guided in its study by an early determination as to what is the primary motive in the writing of annuity contracts" (CFFM 1927b, 152).

96   WMC minutes dated March 31, 1927.

97   CFFM 1927b, 5.

98   The minutes of the WMC of the ABS for May 19, 1927, reported that at a "special conference on annuities" on April 29, "a detailed report on annuity rates as determined by objective was made by Mr. George A. Huggins of Philadelphia, the actuary who made the detailed study of the American Bible Society's annuities about a year ago."

99   Ryan 1927, 19. Referring to comments like Ryan's, Ernest Hall reported at the second COA in 1928 that "it has been the policy of our Board [Foreign Missions of the Presbyterian Church in the USA] to avoid using the term 'Bond,' because in the usually accepted sense of the term it is not a bond." From "Printing and Advertising," *Conditional Gifts Annuity Agreements* (1928), 24.

100   Huggins 1931, 13.

101   At the second COA held in November of 1928, Ernest Hall of the Board of Foreign Missions of the Presbyterian Church in the USA specifically

criticized the ethics of the headline "As High as 9 percent," arguing that this was "the maximum rate which a few old people get. It is attractive but is misleading, and people who reply to such an advertisement are likely to be disappointed and indignant when they find out what they can actually get…Advertisements put out by religious societies are scrutinized by experts and should conform to the highest ethical standards" (Hall, "Printing and Advertising," in Various 1929b, 24).

102   Darlington, introduction to Various 1931b, 32.

103   "As to terminology, some of us call what we sell 'gift annuities.' Some of us call them annuity bonds, while some call our contract a conditional gift" (John Rosengrant, "Correct Terminology in Promoting Annuity Gifts," in Various 1955, 22).

104   For-profit enterprises organized around social impact (a "double bottom line") appeared many years later (see Monitor Institute 2016, retrieved January 9, 2016).

105   Roe 1993, 639.

106   H. Bell 1952, 46.

107   H. Bell 1952, 46.

108   Adapted North (1954, 211). Cited by David Moss and Eugene Kintgen (2009, 16). The largest US commercial bank (National City Bank, founded as the City Bank of New York and known today as Citibank) had $155 million in assets in 1900 (Roe 1993, 659). National City Bank was a major supplier of cash for banks around the United States before the Federal Reserve was created in 1913 (Lowenstein 2015, 14).

109   Buley 1953, 200.

110   Buley 1953, 199.

111   The context, hearings, and aftereffects of the Armstrong investigation are analyzed in R. Carlyle Buley's (1953) magisterial two-volume history.

112   "The effects of the Armstrong investigation did not reach the states in force until 1907. The year began with a flood of gubernatorial recommendations and insurance bills" (Buley 1953, 300).

113   Hunter 1937, 508.

114   "During 2015, Americans deposited $209 billion in individual annuities, down 16 percent from 2014…Individual annuity owners received $51

billion in benefit payments, leaving $2.3 trillion in individual annuity reserves at year-end 2015" ("Annuities" in American Council of Life Insurers [2016, 74]). The numbers cited for individual annuity contracts do not include the far larger market for group pension and retirement plans, most of which are also annuity contracts.

115   NYS Office of General Counsel 2008.

116   New York had considered companies issuing annuity contracts as life insurance companies since 1909, but firms such as Metropolitan Life challenged the validity of New York's insurance law for characterizing the purchase of an annuity as payment of a "premium" (see *Columbia Law Review* 1921, 294).

117   Parker 1928, 8.

118   Stoddard 1923.

119   "Standard provisions for annuities and pure endowment contracts," in Parker 1928, 153–56.

120   "The amendment by ch. 525 of 1925 excluded from the definition of 'Insurance,' only the life insurance of annuity contracts issued by charitable, religious, missionary or philanthropic corporations, which are non-stock and conducted without profit, where such corporations maintain statutory reserves." Editor's note: Parker, *Insurance Law of 1909*, 8. Robert F. Sharpe Jr. has written extensively on the relationships between gift annuities and investments. See Sharpe (2008) and Horner (1997).

121   See Darlington's presentation "Legislation and Taxation" from the first COA in Various 1927a, 27–28. Darlington also informed the 1927 conference that the state of California had enacted a law that required charities issuing annuities to "establish and maintain a reserve fund based on McClintock's Table of Mortality among Annuitants with interest at 3½ percent" and to "show the reasonably commensurate value of the benefits created."

122   Darlington 1952, 110.

123   The motion approved by the FFM Conference instructed its new SOA "to ascertain and advise as to the legislation in the United States and the various states regarding annuities."

124   Dubuar 1939, 9.

125   For a list of physical assets that may be pledged in support of corporate bonds, see Ganguin (2005, 225).

126   At the second conference in 1928, George Sutherland warned that it was unacceptable to finance annuity payments from current operations or from "income-producing dormitories" ("Investments," in Various 1929b, 37). At the fourth conference in 1931, Ernest F. Hall reported that "it has been discovered that some organizations do not have sufficient reserve funds, and that what they have are so tied up that it would be impossible to realize on them in case of necessity. Such is true of some colleges which have put their annuity gifts into campus buildings" ("The Trend Toward Uniformity" in Various 1931b, 9).

127   For an interesting analysis of the investing environment and historical asset allocation for life insurance firms, see Society of Actuaries (2002).

128   Darlington, "Legislation and Taxation," in Various 1927a, 27–28.

129   Ryan 1927, 26.

130   Ryan himself admitted that "so far as the Committee was able to learn, no other states [other than New York and California] have legislation governing such annuities."

131   A 1930 survey of charities that issued annuities reported that only two of twenty charities followed legislation in their home states related to gift annuities. The committee chair noted that "the survey showed that a good many organizations are not familiar with the laws even of their own state governing reserves and the method by which those reserves must be determined" (Hall, "Unfinished Tasks and Future Activities of the Committee," in Various 1930, 103).

132   George F. Sutherland, "Investments," in Various 1929b, 37–38.

133   For the composition of life insurance company portfolios for the years 2010–2014, see NAIC (2014, downloaded May 9, 2017).

134   Originally published in Various, 3rd Conference (1930, 81–100). Published separately as *Administration and Investment of Annuity Funds* (1931), WPGS no. 35.

135   "Annuity funds must be invested generally in the types of securities permitted domestic life companies...The law does not allow a domestic life company to purchase common stocks" (Various 1939, 10, "The

Regulation and Supervision of the Issuance of Annuity Agreements by a Charitable Society"). Minutes of the Committee on Gift Annuities show that Huggins met with Charles Dubuar and other New York officials to provide comments on a draft of the new law. The committee cooperated with New York in implementing the provisions of the 1939 law with respect to gift annuity reserve funds, including convening a special meeting with Dubuar and New York Deputy Superintendent of Insurance R. Harris on October 19, 1939, to provide nonprofits an opportunity for comment on any changes.

136   Charities that issued gift annuities in New York could maintain unqualified assets in their annuity reserve funds rather than sell them at a loss, but after January 1, 1940, they were not permitted to make new investments in assets that were not admitted in New York.

137   "State Regulation of Gift Annuity Funds," in Various 1959, 60. Over time, New York has increased its restrictions and oversight. See http://www.dfs.ny.gov/insurance/life/char_rsve_impt_2016.pdf.

138   "Legislation and Taxation," in Various 1929b, 8.

139   "Taxation and Legislation: Recent Developments," in Various 1930, 54.

140   For a full account of developments in federal tax laws regarding gift annuities up to the mid-1960s, see Desmond (1967). For current laws, see Minton (2017).

141   Minutes of the Committee on Annuities, March 3, 1933.

142   Darlington, "Address of Welcome," Various 1955, 4.

143   Ralph L. Concannon, "Charitable Annuities and the New Tax Law," Various 1955, 39.

144   The "Green Book" was so named because of its cover. The booklets were updated as needed with current IRS tables. They provided instructions and illustrations to aid in hand-calculating tax data. Sales of this and similar booklets on CRTs and PIFs would become a significant source of income for the CGA.

145   Planned giving software firms founded in the 1980s include PhilanthroTec (1983), Crescendo (1984), and PG Calc (1985).

146   "I am happy to report that, except for the bargain sale implications [i.e., pro rata treatment of capital gains], the new law was not aimed

at the Charitable Gift Annuity" (Dr. Roland C. Matthies, "Tax Reform Legislation," in Various 1971, 29). Dr. Matthies, chairman of the Committee on Gift Annuities and president of Wittenberg College, testified at the Senate Finance Committee hearings on the Tax Reform Act of 1969.

147   US senator Kay Bailey Hutchison (R-TX) wrote that "the lawyers ask for the return of all charitable annuity donations plus treble damages—damages that would have to be paid from endowments or unrelated donations." Her statement accompanied the introduction on June 28, 1995, of a Senate bill entitled the Charitable Giving Protection Act of 1995.

148   American Bible Society v. Richie, 522 US 1011, 118 S. Ct. 596, 139 L.Ed.2d 486 (1997).

149   H.R. 2519, P.L. 104-62.

150   H.R. 2525, P.L. 104-63.

151   H.R. 1902, P.L. 105-26.

Section 4

___

George Huggins and the Conferences on Gift Annuities (1927–59)

THE INTRODUCTION OF ACTUARIAL SCIENCE INTO AMERICAN FUNDRAISING

We know the precise point in time when the rationale and fundamental elements of actuarial science were first proposed for American fundraising.

On the morning of April 29, 1927, forty-eight people—representing ten national Protestant Christian denominations (Baptists, Congregationalists, Methodists, Presbyterians, and others); six Bible and tract societies; three colleges; the YMCA and YWCA; two actuaries; a management consultant; and the Bank of New York and Trust Company—gathered in the modest boardroom of the Federal Council of the Churches of Christ in America (henceforth "FCCCA") at 105 East Twenty-Second Street, just east of Park Avenue in New York City.

Invited to this emergency meeting only a month earlier, they came together to head off an impending financial crisis: charitable gift annuities were a major source of their revenues, and that revenue was threatened. The convener of the meeting warned that charities that issued annuities needed to change their ways of doing business, "lest financial weaknesses develop, disaster follow and heavy reproach ensue, damaging to all parties concerned and to the interests which they represented."[1] Those interests were, of course, extremely important: educating young scholars, providing a haven from tough streets, saving souls in the United States and abroad, and more. The quality of many people's lives was at stake.

George Augustus Huggins. Photo taken on December 23, 1955, and provided by Michael Mudry and Molly Hill of Hay-Huggins, Inc.

A large man who "would be viewed as a candidate for an offensive tackle spot on the football team"[2] if he had been an undergraduate took the stage for the opening presentation. Born in Nevis, British West Indies (which, today, is half of the independent two-island nation Saint Kitts and Nevis), where he had lived until the age of twelve, the speaker had a formal style that showed evidence of his British roots even after thirty-five years in the United States.

For many people in the room, George Augustus Huggins needed no introduction; he was the nation's leading consulting actuary for clerical-pension plans. After working in the actuarial department of the Fidelity Mutual Life Insurance Company of Philadelphia from 1902 to 1911, he founded his own actuarial firm of Huggins and Company[3] in Philadelphia and assisted in establishing actuarially sound retirement plans for businesses, states, cities, professional associations, religious denominations, and colleges nationwide.

Huggins began his presentation by stating an ambitious intention: "As a basis for the consideration of the subject of annuities, offered to donors by the various organizations, **we show schedules illustrating the fundamental principles that underlie the whole subject**" (emphasis added).

Huggins's "Actuarial Basis of Rates" (appendix V) was the first presentation at the first conference. This foundational document is quite short, barely four pages of narrative devoted to introducing seven schedules.

Before diving into a deep analysis of the presentation, let's review the objectives for the concluding section.

The heart of this section explores how George Huggins adapted actuarial methods for use by American philanthropy in 1927, and then provided intellectual leadership through ten national conferences on gift annuities before his death in 1959. Huggins was one of only two speakers to present at all ten conferences.[4] The rich historical territory of the conference reports has been virtually unexplored until now.

Contemporary managers of gift annuity programs realized the enduring practical value of the conference reports, which were "circulated quite widely."[5] They provided unique and accessible guidance for applying the new actuarial principles in the face of extremely challenging conditions. The reports show steady progress over time in constructing best professional practices for nonprofit organizations, thus documenting the historical development of a major source of funding for America's nonprofit sector.

At the second conference in 1928, Huggins noted that his presentation would "take up the discussion at the point where it... left off" in 1927. The preface to the fourth conference reported that "these conferences, while dealing with the same essential matters, are related to each other as a continuing, progressive series, and the booklets which follow, each its conference, are similarly related."[6]

Many of the reports went out of print as long ago as 1952,[7] but in 2014, the ACGA made the conference publications available online as a service to researchers.[8] They provide a window on a rapidly changing America and are indispensable records of the world's oldest continuous series of charitable fundraising conferences.

Huggins gave American nonprofits techniques for evaluating and using mortality tables and investment assumptions to manage unavoidable risks: the unknowable length of a life and the uncertainties of investment performance. He introduced a national system for setting responsible annuity rates and maintaining adequate reserve funds. With Gilbert Darlington, he constructed a political process leading to gradual acceptance of actuarial principles by nonprofits and to support from federal and state authorities for effective public policies on gift annuities and other life-income gifts.

Huggins showed how to develop adequate answers to questions such as these: Can a gift annuitant rely on receiving payments throughout a life that may last for decades? How should a nonprofit organization manage the risks of a volatile economy and the uncertain lengths of annuitant lives, meet its payment obligations, and have enough money remaining for its charitable mission to make an annuity program worthwhile?

The answers involved collections of mortality data over time, expert analysis of economic trends and investment projections, and a political process for setting gift annuity payment rates grounded in actuarial science. In his presentation that April morning in 1927, Huggins succinctly illustrated the use of data on annuitant-mortality experience, the idea of present value, the similarities and differences between life-income gifts to charity and commercial investments, the process of developing investment projections, the rationale for setting a target for the charitable residuum, the importance and limitations of statistical norms, and the probabilistic reasoning behind his recommended national schedule of annuity payment rates.[9]

The world of charitable gift planning would never be the same.

The actuarial revolution in charitable gift planning was not limited to gift annuities. Anyone today who enters a beneficiary's date of birth in a computer program to calculate the benefits of a charitable-remainder trust, pooled-income fund, or retained-life estate is using the actuarial system Huggins introduced in 1927.[10]

Measuring the value of fixed payments for the uncertain term of a person's life during times of rapid change presented quite a challenge. The tumult of the era from the Depression and the New Deal to World War II and the period of postwar recovery, alongside the continual improvements in the longevity of gift annuitants, compelled Huggins to accommodate new data and expand upon his reasoning at each of the Conferences on Annuities.

The scope and rapidity of economic and demographic changes are demonstrated in two charts (appendices VI and VII) illustrating the evolution of gift-annuitant-mortality data, economic analyses/investment projections, and factors involved in calculating payment rates from 1927 to 1959.

WHY A NATIONAL RISK-MANAGEMENT SYSTEM WAS NEEDED

The New York Insurance Law of 1925 enabled nonprofit organizations to issue gift annuities so long as they maintained actuarially sound reserve funds. Taking advantage of that legal blessing involved a series of related questions: Did nonprofits maintain segregated gift annuity reserve funds? Were the levels of their reserve funds adequate, considering their contractual payment rates, the ages of their annuitants, appropriate mortality projections, and investment assumptions? If not, what corrective actions were needed to bring gift annuity programs into compliance with the law?

The most terrible fiduciary failure is default—a nonprofit failing to make its legally required payments to annuitants who trusted the charity and depended on its promise of lifetime payments. Reliable data is not available on the number of charitable annuity program payment defaults and bankruptcies in the decades before World War II, but they did occur. Conference speakers occasionally noted failed programs (without naming the organizations) as a warning to other nonprofits:

> About this time an institution with a long line of graduates collapsed financially. Its annuity funds went into the wreckage and the annuitants suffered disappointment and hardship.[11]

> Not long ago a certain small college went bankrupt and was unable to continue paying its annuitants…Of course, no organization expects to fail, but failure is a possibility, and the protection of annuitants in case of failure should be very carefully considered in advance. [12]

> It is no secret that some religious societies and colleges defaulted in their annuity payments in the years of the depression, because they did not have adequate reserve funds.[13]

Scanning the practices of American gift annuity programs with the eyes of an experienced actuary, Huggins saw a train wreck in the works. Out of enthusiasm, inexperience, or greed, a considerable number of programs lacked sound business concepts and effective methods for avoiding unnecessary risks and managing necessary risks.

Huggins summed up twelve "danger points" for a gift annuity conference held in 1931,[14] a snapshot of the country's gift annuity programs at that time. Here are the points, along with a selection from Huggins's comments on each:

1. **High annuity rates.** When rates are too high, "it is entirely possible for an annuitant, even though rather advanced in age at the time the annuity is entered upon, to live out the period required to exhaust the entire principal sum of the gift."

2. **Competition in annuity rates.** When nonprofits compete for gifts by negotiating with prospective donors to provide payment rates that are a bit higher than those offered by another charitable organization, that changes "the psychology of the givers":

   Where the appeal of the cause is great, the donor is willing to make an absolute gift to the cause and, incidentally, take a modest income on the gift. If, however, cupidity as to annuity rates is aroused in the minds of donors, they will shop for higher rates and make gifts to the organization which offers the highest rate.

   Huggins warned that competition among charities in the form of raising payment rates to attract donors "might well bring about the end of the whole [gift annuity] movement."[15]

3. **High expense rates.** "An annuity department should stand on its own feet; that is, it should bear its share of the administrative and promotional expenses."

4. **Issuing annuity agreements on two or more lives.** "There is, perhaps, more bad practice today in the matter of rates where more than one life is involved than in any other phase of this work." Some nonprofits paid annuity rates based on the older life in a two-life or even three-life contract.

5. **Improper accounting.** "Correct accounting practices in regard to annuity agreements should take into account the amounts of the gifts; the amounts of the annuity payments; the interest earned on the balances in the funds; the expenses chargeable against such funds; the investment losses and gains, if any." If not, "administrators are not in possession of the real facts and the donors will soon become aware of that, lose confidence in the organization and withdraw their support."

6. **Use of funds, which are not strictly available for that purpose, for meeting the excess of annuity payments over the interest earnings.** Some nonprofits "keep intact the principal of annuity gifts until the principal is released by the death of the annuitant." If investment earnings are not sufficient to make the required payments, "in some cases this rate is charged as an item in the administrative expense" of the general budget, which is a bad practice involving "the use of funds given or dedicated for some other purpose."

7. **The use of annuity gift funds for the purposes of the organization before they are properly released.** "This is an extremely unwise and dangerous practice, and one without any justification whatsoever."

8. **Unwise investment policies.** Other speakers at the conference addressed the topic of investment allocation, so Huggins gave general advice: "The greatest care should be exercised in the selection of the investments, because not only must the principal be preserved, but the success of the

annuity department will, to a considerable extent, depend upon favorable interest earnings."

9. **Ill-advised advertising.** "I would class as ill-advised advertising, appeals for gifts on the basis of the annuity returns, and that it was a good investment as such. The appeal should be to support the work of the particular organization by gifts, the rate of return through the annuity being only incidental." Huggins disliked referring to gift annuities as "bonds": "Personally, I do not think the word 'bond' should be used in connection with annuity agreements…Any reference to investments should be featured as investments in the work of the organization rather than investments from the standpoint of financial returns."

10. **Acceptance of assets as consideration for annuity agreements.** Huggins warned nonprofits against accepting gifts of real estate for an annuity: "With the present conditions in the real estate market, an organization that made it known that it would accept real estate, and particularly farms, as consideration for annuity agreements would probably soon find itself in the real estate management business with an active but harassed Farm Management Department."

11. **Lack of number of annuitant lives for proper averages.** When a nonprofit issues a small number of gift annuities, "the results will most likely be unsatisfactory, because the number of lives involved is not sufficient to give the proper distribution of risks necessary to furnish the required averages."

12. **Lack of observation of regulatory legislation.** Nonprofits must comply with state laws: "Those who are charged with the task of securing and administering annuity agreements, should inform themselves as to these regulations and observe them, both in letter and in spirit, otherwise their policies

will not be consistent with the high plane upon which the work of these organizations should be conducted; and, further, they will find themselves in difficulties with the state officials, with the result that penalties will be inflicted and more drastic regulatory legislation enacted."

Huggins knew that unless there was an intervention in the practices of some nonprofits issuing annuities, poor consequences would follow. There would be more defaults, with bad publicity, criminal penalties, and lives ruined by the loss of income. More commonly than defaults, both donors and nonprofits would be sorely disappointed with the amount of financial support left over for charitable purposes by annuities. And if high nonprofit annuity payments began "encroaching on the field of the insurance companies...State insurance officials and legislatures" would act: "The annuity agreement business would, most probably, be legislated out of existence. As a matter of fact, this almost happened several years ago [referring here to the New York Insurance Laws of 1923 and 1925], and it was only by the narrowest margin that this disaster was averted."[16]

Avoiding *danger points* was within the control of nonprofit organizations that wanted to change. Certainly, not every nonprofit was fully aware of the dangers in 1927. Those who were better informed may not have accepted the need for costly and time-consuming improvements in gift administration.

Three external national shocks soon focused the attention of every commercial and nonprofit organization issuing legally binding life-annuity contracts:

1. The Great Depression struck the industrialized world in the fall of 1929 and continued for a dozen years, decimating the US stock market and vaporizing millions of jobs.

2. The yield on fixed-income investments—which made up a very high portion of a typical annuity reserve account,

even before the stock market crashed in 1929—fell further and longer from 1920 to 1946 than in any previous time in American history.[17]

3. Life expectancies in the United States improved dramatically. Year after year, new national mortality tables had to be developed. In 1931 alone, Huggins's conference report discussed the strengths and weaknesses of *eight* different mortality tables for setting gift annuity payment rates.

A remarkably small group of volunteer leaders intervened to head off the worst consequences of the Depression. There is no indication of widespread defaults in gift annuity programs in the reports of the Conferences on Annuities.

FOUNDING OF THE COMMITTEE ON GIFT ANNUITIES

One month before the April conference, Huggins had alarmed a national audience of bankers, insurance executives, attorneys, nonprofit executives, and other leaders in the booming field of financial services.[18]

Speaking on "Proper Handling of Annuities and Creation of Committee on Annuities," he reported the results of his research on the practices of sixteen national nonprofits, focusing particularly on high annuity payment rates: "In the matter of rates the situation borders on chaos." Annuity rates offered to people at the age of eighty ranged from 6 percent to 10 percent. Many charities paid the same high rates, whether one, two, or more lives were covered.[19]

Participants at the March conference, entitled "Cooperation in Fiduciary Service," were generally sympathetic to charities raising money through gift annuities and were willing to help improve their standards of practice:

We regard this second conference, like its predecessor [held in 1925], of striking significance for it has brought together men and women of such diverse occupations who have demonstrated their unity of interests, bankers, trust officers, lawyers, life insurance representatives, college presidents, officers of social, educational, philanthropic and religious organizations, denominational and interdenominational. We have counselled together as to how we might further the interests of humanity, by our common service.[20]

Greater donor confidence in the safety, efficiency, and ethics of charitable gift administration would lead directly to more productive fundraising. Dr. Alfred Williams Anthony, chair of the CFFM and organizer of the conference, intended that the committee would introduce advanced technical knowledge to nonprofit organizations:

[The committee] brings together men who have wisdom and "know how"; it reports measures and methods so that all who will may compare notes and find the best; it correlates movements for the sake of unity and strength; it enlists and makes known to each other the natural allies in the field of finance...Lawyers, bankers and insurance underwriters are our natural allies.[21]

The Committee on Financial and Fiduciary Matters reported audacious accomplishments for the year 1926:

1. The Bank of New York and Trust Company ("the oldest financial institution in the City of New York") published a series of five display advertisements in each of "five of the greatest newspapers in New York," encouraging donors to make charitable gifts through their estate plans.
2. The Equitable Life Assurance Society designated the week of December 13–18, 1926, as Bequest Week: "A period

in which to educate all its agents—nearly 10,000 in number, scattered all over this country—in soliciting life insurance which should ultimately benefit educational and missionary objects." The company printed and distributed forty-seven thousand copies of a Bequest Week pamphlet that led to favorable press coverage in Portland, Oregon; Seattle, Washington; Kentucky; Boston, Massachusetts, and other major outlets.

3. The committee published five titles in its highly influential *Wise Public Giving* series.

4. In 1925 and 1926, Dr. Anthony encouraged close cooperation in charitable gift planning in his presentations to the annual meetings of the Trust Company Division of the American Bankers Association.

5. The committee developed and promoted a standardized charitable-trust agreement, including provisions for charitable-remainder trusts, entitled *The Uniform Trust for Public Uses*, which "has already come into use in five states in our country."

6. The committee convened a national conference of trust banks, insurance underwriters, and charitable organizations in Atlantic City on February 16–18, 1925, and held regional meetings in Saint Louis, Minneapolis, Montclair (NJ), Chicago, and New York City. Anthony announced that a second national conference would be convened in Atlantic City on March 22–24, 1927. This 1927 conference in Atlantic City commissioned the Committee on Gift Annuities, with far-reaching importance for American philanthropy.

Many of the businessmen involved with the CFFM were volunteer leaders of their own churches, colleges, and other philanthropic organizations. Cooperation with charitable organizations to raise their fiduciary standards served the broader interests of the financial community. The success of charities issuing annuities would create new business opportunities in providing financial services to those charities.

This enlightened spirit of cooperation set the stage for a like spirit among participants at the Conference on Annuities the following month and provided the foundation for a culture of sharing successful practices. Professional gift planners are extraordinarily generous in giving their best ideas to one another.

Thanks to the farsighted vision of Dr. Anthony, the consensus among business and professional participants was that the threat demanding attention was not a marginal loss of market share to charitable donors but the real possibility that unsafe fiduciary practices by nonprofits issuing annuities could lead to highly publicized defaults or bankruptcies. Calamities like these would reduce or eliminate highly valued charitable services. They might even shake consumer confidence in the much larger market for annuity investments.

In 1926, Anthony wrote that the overriding goal of CFFM was to provide a persuasive case for giving to nonprofit organizations based on the sound business practices that donors expect:

> We are recognizing, therefore, a variety of methods, because there are a variety of circumstances in which people are placed, and we must bear in mind that men [and women] who have had judgment and perseverance and self-denial sufficient to accumulate property, and those who having inherited it have shown ability adequate to the administration and the preservation of the same, are not men [and women] who can be hoodwinked, cajoled or jollied into charitable impulses. They will think and act for themselves. But they will respond to the plans which wise people, looking even farther than they, may propose, if those plans be accompanied with a manifest indication of good sense and good purposes.

In Anthony's vision, donors respond enthusiastically when presented with technically strong and legally sanctioned gift opportunities with clearly understood benefits that meet a donor's needs:

> We must make it easy for possessors of wealth to give… [and] we must do some clear thinking in anticipation of their wishes, so that when they are ready to act we may be at hand with the proper methods, instruments and agencies which will make it easy for them to give and at the same time will surround all of their benefactions with such safeguards, legal[,] fiduciary and social, as will make their giving safe and wise…without trying to urge, cajole or coerce anyone into using one method as against another, but to help each to find and adopt the method which best fits his own financial and personal needs and conditions.[22]

Successful nonprofit marketing strategies sell solutions, not gift vehicles. He provided a classic characterization of the role of a charitable gift planner: "It is our task and our conscious undertaking, thoughtfully to consider, adequately to foresee, patiently to state and repeat and graciously to urge the ways of wisdom and generosity."[23]

Nonprofit organizations weigh and consider suggested practices and use those they feel are best suited to their operations. Nonprofit leaders must first understand, then accept and adopt, new business ideas and methods. The application of probability theory to gift annuities involved profound changes in worldview, as well as substantially increased burdens of gift administration. Fundamental changes in American philanthropy were made possible over time through education and voluntary acceptance.

Dr. Anthony encouraged general acceptance of "standards of handling and administering [charitable] funds," including "standardized methods to be worked out in regard to annuities, the contracts, the memorials, the investments and the set-up of funds." Anthony characterized the challenge of general acceptance of standards for gift planning as fundamentally "psychological and spiritual." He expanded on the meaning of this at a CFFM conference presentation in 1931: "A mere device which is constructed in such a manner as quite plainly fits it for producing a desired result, will not work in this field unless those who are to use it like it and are willing to come into, or come under its operation."[24]

Philanthropic strategies so all-encompassing and universally appealing required recognition and acceptance of a deep common cause among donors, charities, and financial-service corporations:

> It must be the sweep of inclusiveness in the realm of understanding and coordination of effort around all of those who are active in the field of finance—around the trust companies, which are the depositories and trustees of funds, around the life insurance underwriters...and around the legal profession...This cooperation is reasonable and is becoming recognized, not in a day, but nevertheless with a speed which is gratifying and almost astonishing.

Reflecting on his twelve years of leadership (1919–31) with the CFFM and the Home Missions Council, Anthony felt that his strategy of improving the practices of charitable organizations through sound advice presented through gentle persuasion had created a new American system of cooperation in gift planning:

> It is possible and doubtless profitable for charitable organizations, in smaller or in larger groups, to secure the expert advice of statistical organizations, of technical, promotional agencies, of experts in taxation and in finance, and of other skilled agencies which may serve them all when the results of the service are distributed, assimilated and adopted by each group.

At the 1927 CFFM conference, George Huggins proposed forming a "strong committee" on gift annuities. He persuaded Dr. Anthony and other conference leaders that the new committee should "make an immediate study of rates and...call a conference of interested parties on this matter at the earliest possible date" in order to "prepare what might be called an ideal plan of conducting the annuity business, including a proposed set of ideal rates."[25]

Anthony was convinced that fundamental changes were needed immediately. In his preface to the first COA report, he wrote:

As rates have differed, as methods of soliciting and handling the annuity business have varied...it has become highly important, almost imperative, that some common standards and uniform methods should be agreed upon, lest financial weaknesses develop, disaster follow and heavy reproach ensue, damaging to all parties concerned and to the interests which they represented. [26]

The CFFM commissioned a Subcommittee on Annuities with the following charge:

On Annuities, to study and recommend the proper range of rates, the form of contracts, the amount and type of reserve funds and the nomenclature to be used, to ascertain and advise as to the legislation in the United States and the various states regarding annuities, their taxability, etc. **This committee is requested to make an immediate study of the matter of rates and to call a conference of interested parties on this matter at the earliest possible date** (emphasis added). This committee should be guided in its study by an early determination as to what is the primary motive in the writing of annuity contracts.[27]

Anthony selected six members to join the Subcommittee on Annuities, including two professional actuaries and four highly experienced leaders from international Baptist, Episcopal, Methodist, and Presbyterian organizations, chosen because they "had been making studies of subjects connected with annuities for years." Since the subcommittee was sponsored by the Federal Council of Churches, Anthony was bound to limit membership to Protestant organizations affiliated with FCCCA:

- **Chairman—Dr. Charles L. White**, executive secretary, American Baptist Home Mission Society. White was a graduate of Brown University (class of 1887) and Bowdoin College (DD 1902) who had served as president of Colby College in Maine from 1901 to 1908. The Home Mission Society was founded in 1832 and had issued charitable annuities since 1861.

- **Secretary—Alfred Williams Anthony**, chairman, the Committee on Financial and Fiduciary Matters (CFFM) of the Federal Council of the Churches of Christ in America. A descendant of Roger Williams, founder of Rhode Island, Anthony was a graduate of Brown University (BA 1883; AM 1886) and Cobb Divinity School (1885), and a professor of divinity at Bates College. Anthony appointed the six members of the new Subcommittee on Annuities, served as an ex officio member, and edited and published the conference proceedings until his death in 1939.

- **Ernest F. Hall**, secretary, Department of Annuities, Board of Missions, Presbyterian Church in the United States. Hall served as a member of the subcommittee from 1927 to 1941 and as chairman from 1930 to 1939.

- **George A. Huggins**, consulting actuary. A graduate of Bethel Military Academy, Virginia (1897), and the University of Pennsylvania (1902), Huggins succeeded Anthony as chair of the Committee on Financial and

Fiduciary Matters. Huggins was a devoted member of the Episcopal Church and served as actuary for many national Protestant church-pension funds.

- **Edward W. Marshall**, associate actuary, Provident Mutual Life Insurance Company of Philadelphia. Marshall became a fellow of the Actuarial Society of America in 1914 at the age of twenty-five and later served as the society's president. Marshall joined Provident in 1911, the year Huggins left to start his own actuarial firm, and had a distinguished professional career.

- **Arthur C. Ryan**, general secretary, American Bible Society. Ryan was a graduate of Iowa College (1908) and Oberlin Theological Seminary (1911). As discussed above, ABS issued its first gift annuity in 1843, and its well-publicized and highly successful international gift annuity campaign, which began in 1919, encouraged many other nonprofit organizations to offer gift annuities.

- **George F. Sutherland**, treasurer, Board of Foreign Missions, Methodist Episcopal Church. Dr. Sutherland served as a subcommittee member from 1927 to 1952.

This small group of volunteers got to work organizing an emergency conference in New York City on April 29. Nothing is known about when and where the subcommittee first met. The group must have begun organizing the conference immediately—discussing Huggins's mandates for a national plan, putting together an agenda, mailing invitations to nonprofits affiliated with the Council of Churches, preparing presentations. The conference was held in the boardroom of the FCCCA headquarters.

The subcommittee invited five speakers to address its first conference in 1927, but only Huggins and two speakers from the American Bible Society (George Darlington and Arthur Ryan) delivered their presentations, totaling twenty-seven pages in the conference report. "Free and protracted discussion" of Huggins's proposals lasted all afternoon.[28] The first national conference on annuities was the first to run out of time.

Presentations on marketing ("promotion methods") by committee members George Sutherland and Ernest Hall added sixteen pages to the report. At this and nine subsequent conferences through 1959, participants received presentation handouts. A printed conference report with the presentations, rate charts, findings, and the results of votes was distributed at no charge to participants and made available for purchase by other interested readers some months after each conference.

The first conference report in 1927 was clearly a product of the Council of Churches. Dr. Alfred Williams Anthony wrote the preface and is credited for editing the report. The FCCCA is identified as the sponsor of the Subcommittee on Annuities, and Anthony published the report as number 18 in the FCCCA's *Wise Public Giving* series, providing the Conference on Annuities a well-established channel to reach a national community of nonprofit organizations.[29]

The 1927 conference was not intended to be the first in a series that would continue through 2018 and beyond. The findings committee reported that a vote was taken near the end of the day to hold another conference the next year, primarily to help nonprofit organizations raise more money through effective marketing of gift annuities.[30]

Promotional methods were on the agenda for a second conference, but that was not the sole or most important topic. Reforming annuity payment rates and developing best practices were at the top of the list:

VOTED that in view of the wide variations in annuity rates now granted by religious, educational and charitable organizations, this conference, representing thirty-five organizations, expresses its strong conviction that it is advisable to bring about a standard in rates and uniformity in practice.[31]

The big question in 1927 was this: Could anyone persuade thousands of independent and cash-poor organizations—churches, synagogues, colleges, foster homes, day-care centers, hospitals and clinics, Red Cross chapters, YWCAs, and many others—to adopt a common, sustainable business model for their gift annuity programs in time to avoid a national scandal?

Nonprofit leaders had a lot of work to do in rethinking the fundamentals of their gift annuity programs, organized through a political process for determining best practices and a national rate table. No one at the time could have known that the work of the Subcommittee on Annuities would last so long or that a small group of representatives would evolve into a national professional association of charitable gift planners.

This unincorporated group was the sole national public-policy voice of nonprofit organizations promoting and administering gifts through charitable gift annuities, charitable-remainder trusts, and pooled income funds over the next sixty years.[32]

Many of the participants at the 1927 conference returned for the next conference in 1928. Eight more conferences on gift annuities were held at irregular intervals through 1959. After each conference, a report on proceedings was published in the *Wise Public Giving* series (henceforth WPGS). The number of participants grew, and the range of charitable organizations broadened well beyond the original base of Protestant Christian charities.[33]

The CFFM was the sponsor of the Subcommittee on Annuities from 1927 until the Federal Council of Churches in Christ was succeeded by the National Council of Churches in 1951. That the conferences were sponsored by the Council of Churches enabled actuarial ideas to be spread quickly among its many missions, colleges, and social-welfare organizations, the largest national association of religious organizations.

Dr. Anthony's evangelical, collegial vision continued long after his death and was much in evidence at the Conference on Wills,

Annuities, and Special Gifts convened by the National Council of Churches in 1952, attended by 387 participants:

> One of the most rewarding aspects of the conference was the feeling of fellowship which was manifest among the delegates. Apparently the fund raising personnel of the churches, church boards, church colleges and universities and Christian social institutions greatly enjoy the privilege of counseling together about their common problems.[34]

The reach of this Protestant church-based association was limited. Several decades passed before its leaders addressed the lack of inclusiveness.

HOW INCLUSIVE WAS THE NATIONAL MOVEMENT?

Jewish and Catholic nonprofits issued gift annuities, but I have found no documentation from this period.[35] A lingering anti-Catholic bias among national Protestant organizations that began in the 1830s was slowly dissipating by the 1930s.[36] The Committee on Gift Annuities made intermittent attempts to include non-Protestant organizations in some of its activities. When the committee became independent of the Council of Churches, its new constitution included a statement on freedom from religious constraints: "The Committee will cooperate with the National Council of the Churches of Christ in the United States of America, but it is entirely free to draw its members from other groups who are not members of the National Council."[37]

Religious organizations (including denominational colleges) provided more than 90 percent of the participants at the tenth COA in 1959. Conference sessions opened and closed with a Protestant prayer, as they had done since 1927. As far as can be determined from the roster, no representatives from Jewish or

Catholic organizations participated in the COA in 1955 or 1959. However, at the fourteenth COA in 1971, a speaker reported that among six hundred sponsors of the committee were "church and denominational agencies representing Protestant, Evangelical, Catholic and Jewish groups throughout the nation."[38]

Women were underrepresented from the start and were missing from committee leadership for many years. All seven founding members of the Committee on Gift Annuities were male. Not one of the presenters at the first ten conferences was female.

A woman was selected for the influential Findings Committee in 1927: Ava B. Blank, secretary for endowment, National Board of the YWCA. Gertrude Van Vleck Bruyn, field secretary for Mount Holyoke College, was selected for the findings committee at the second conference.[39] Four women participated in the first conference among a total of forty-seven registrants. Subsequent conference reports did not print a roster of attendees until the eighth conference in 1946, which fifteen women and forty-seven men attended. Henrietta Gibson from the Woman's Division of Christian Services of the Board of Missions of the Methodist Church was the only female member of the resolutions committee at the ninth conference in 1955. At the tenth conference in 1959, there were just nine women and 144 men.[40]

The first female member of the committee was Lulu M. Sehl, secretary of the Annuity and Legal Department of the Salvation Army, who served from 1959 to 1968. Ms. Sehl was the forty-first person selected for the committee.[41] Laurie W. Valentine, trust counsel and chief operating officer of the Kentucky Baptist Foundation, became the first woman to head the ACGA in April of 2017.

Despite underrepresentation in its early years, committee research, rate setting, best practices, publications, and advocacy benefitted all American nonprofits.

A CONSULTANT'S PROPOSAL FOR THE GIFT ANNUITY "BUSINESS"

In constructing a national proposal for gift annuities issued by nonprofit organizations, Huggins did not work from whole cloth. The rapid design and construction of his rate table between the financial conference in March 1927 and the gift annuity conference in April was possible because Huggins was a leading actuarial consultant for life insurance companies and pension plans. He could share his professional knowledge of mortality and investment-return assumptions with confidence that they met generally accepted standards for the heavily regulated American life insurance industry, whose business model employed actuarial-risk-management techniques developed in the nineteenth century.

Given his record of leadership in the business world, it is not surprising that Huggins was a game changer for nonprofits. He was a pioneer in alerting major US corporations and national religious organizations to the need for actuarial audits of their pension funds.[42] In 1927, he was a well-respected expert on determining the accrued costs and projected benefits of annuity obligations.[43] He developed a thriving professional career as an actuary, maintaining a detailed awareness of how major-insurance firms and other businesses were managing longevity and financial risks in their pension and annuity programs.

As a consulting actuary on pensions, Huggins provided advice on all aspects of defined-benefit programs, including plan design, contracts, investments, participant communications, and administration. He guided insurance-company clients in "the design, pricing, experience rating, valuation, administration, and communication" of life insurance and annuity programs.[44]

The business model for charitable gift planning followed the lead of financial services. A new order of complexity had been introduced into American fundraising in the mid-1800s, when the Bible Society, the Methodist Church, and other nonprofit organizations began to issue legally binding contracts to make fixed payments for an unknowable number of years, based on the lives of one or more annuitants. Nonprofits accepted general financial obligations to make annual payments that were more expensive than the original principal could earn.

Nonprofits imitated commercial annuity contracts through the 1920s without adopting business-management ideas and actuarial techniques. It now seems an inevitable consequence of Trumbull's annuity bond contract with Yale that nonprofits intending to raise money through a gift annuity program would need a satisfactory measure of annuitants' lives to manage longevity and investment risks.

Demand grew for specially trained professionals to explain how gift annuities worked. They were people who could manage annuity programs that would apply statistics and probabilistic reasoning to mortality experience and long-term investment performance, and who could track and incorporate numerous changes in federal and state laws and regulations.

Like the firms whose insurance, annuity, and pension products were based on financial commitments for people's lives, charities that issued gift annuities were slow to recognize the need for professional standards of practice. Ninety-six years passed between Trumbull's annuity bond and the development of a national system grounded in actuarial science.

Huggins and other members of the CGA may not have appreciated the challenges inherent in changing core practices of American philanthropy through education and the voluntary acceptance of new ideas and methods by disparate nonprofit organizations. His presentations at the second and third conferences were brief and were focused on reminding people what he had presented in 1927.

The Great Depression that began in 1929 compelled the entire nation to seek answers for coping with a broken economy. Interest in applying actuarial science to charitable annuities intensified. At the fourth conference, held in 1931, three of the presenters were professional actuaries.

HUGGINS'S ACTUARIAL BASIS OF RATES[45]

We will now take a close look at the document that introduced into American philanthropy a systematic approach to risk management based on actuarial principles.

Huggins presented his report in the form of recommendations by the Subcommittee on Annuities (thus the wording of his first sentence: "**we** show schedules"), though it is clear from the statistical data and technical explanations that Huggins was the originator. Given the speed of travel and communications in 1927, there was little opportunity for members in New York and Philadelphia to collaborate on multiple drafts. There must have been at least one meeting of the subcommittee for members to receive and comment on Huggins's recommendations and voice their approval.

Huggins introduced three "fundamental principles" for life annuities, each illustrated by "schedules" or charts:

1. Understanding the impact of investment performance for rate setting and managing annuity reserve funds (schedule A).
2. Estimating annuitant mortality, as longevity experience increased over time (schedule B).
3. Setting a specific target for the charitable residuum, since raising money for philanthropic purposes through a substantial residuum is "the object of issuing these annuity agreements." About half of his report consisted of specific recommendations on the investment and mortality assumptions needed to develop gift annuity payment rates aimed at realizing a residuum target of 70 percent of the

original amount transferred to the nonprofit when a gift annuity is funded.

Schedules C through G all deal with gift annuity payment rates. Three charts containing "Proposed Standard Annuity Rates" were developed after the conference and added to a report that was printed and distributed some months later.

We will briefly examine each of Huggins's schedules and then analyze his three fundamental principles in greater depth.

Schedule A   Study of period required to exhaust principal of $1,000 by interest annuity payments at various rates and periods for exhausting principal sum together with interest earnings on balances at 4½% compounded annually.

Huggins opened by illustrating the magic of compound interest. Schedule A shows how earnings from the investment of a gift annuity reserve fund extend an organization's capacity for making annuity payments. In fact, earnings on investments are fundamentally important for life-income contracts.

For an example, Huggins showed that with no earnings, a payment rate of 7 percent will exhaust the original principal in just over fourteen years, but if the fund earns 4.5 percent annually, the principal will last for more than twenty-three years. The last nine years of this annuitant's payments are made entirely from investment earnings.

Huggins began with schedule A to show "how necessary it is that the funds should be held back of annuity gifts, invested in securities that are not only safe, but which produce a good rate of interest."[46] He would not have had to stress these points if most nonprofits already maintained segregated annuity reserve funds. In the years ahead, conference speakers would often emphasize the importance of maintaining a segregated gift annuity reserve fund, from which we know the lack of adequate reserve funds continued to be a concern.[47]

Schedule B Complete Expectation of Life: Comparison of Years shown by various Tables of Mortality

Schedule B introduces one of Huggins's grand themes: "the effect of the introduction of the life element": "One can readily see, therefore, that the average duration of the lives of the members of a group to whom we promise annuity payments during lifetime, is a very vital matter…In our calculation of annuity rates, the basic table of mortality used is a matter of considerable importance."

By 1927, it was clear to professional actuaries that a significant shift in average longevity was underway. Huggins reported that "we may, therefore, look forward to increasingly lower death rates among annuitant lives and therefore longer average periods of life."

No gift-annuitant mortality table existed in 1927, which compelled Huggins to depend on "the experience of others." Schedule B compares selected data from four mortality tables constructed by British and American life insurance companies and a classic mortality table from the general population of the City of Carlisle in England, with Huggins's annotations on the populations included in each table and the historical periods during which their mortality data was collected. Two tables were constructed from commercial annuitant experience ("McClintock's Annuitants" and "British Offices Annuitants"), two from life insurance experience, and one from a general population.

Huggins notes that "McClintock" was published in 1899 but does not comment on the fact that it was based on mortality experience gathered before 1892 and that most of the annuity contracts were on European annuitant lives.[48] The best available annuitant-mortality table had obvious shortcomings.

196

The "British Offices Annuitants" 1900–1920 table was constructed using the mortality experience of "forty-nine insurance offices (chiefly British) among life annuitants during the period 1900 to 1920 inclusive." Both the British annuitant table and McClintock's table showed separate data for male and female lives.

For further comparison and contrast with commercial-annuitant data, Huggins provided selected data from two life insurance mortality tables: American Men Ultimate, based on insurance contracts issued between 1900 and 1915, and American Experience Table of Mortality, based on twenty years of experience of the Mutual Life Insurance Company of New York, which "has been adopted as the standard for the Valuation of Insurance Contracts in many States."

His fifth example is one of the earliest general-population mortality tables: the *Carlisle Table of Mortality*, "a historic table based on the mortality experience among the population of two parishes of the City of Carlisle from 1779 to 1787."

Huggins draws several observations from comparing the findings from these tables: women were living longer than men; people who bought life annuities lived longer than people who bought life insurance (a process known as self-selection); and more recent mortality tables showed people living longer, a trend which he expected to continue, though no one could have known the extent of the longevity revolution then underway.

Huggins's use of historical perspective in analyzing gift-annuitant-mortality data in subsequent conference reports is explored below.

Schedule C   Comparative Annuity Rates Payable: Calculated on basis of McClintock's Table of Mortality Among Annuitants (Male) with Interest at 4½% compounded annually. Rates varying according to average residuum ranging from 0% to 100%.

This schedule introduced the calculation of payment rates based on a specific charitable residuum. Assuming an annualized investment return of 4.5 percent, Huggins showed the rates for annuitants age thirty to eighty that produced charitable residua ranging from 0 percent to 100 percent.

It is interesting that Huggins showed rates for annuitants up to age eighty and that his rate charts after the 1927 conference ended with age seventy-six. This may have been because of the relatively short life expectancies of Americans in the 1920s. It is also true that Huggins and his colleagues did not have adequate national data on the ages of gift annuitants at the time of their gifts. The most thorough gift annuity survey of colleges and universities to its point in time (1933) did not ask about the ages of annuitants at the times of their first gifts.[49]

In 1952, when gift annuitants were living longer on average than in 1927, Huggins surveyed fifteen larger gift annuity programs and reported that among 1,559 annuitants, 156 (10 percent) were age eighty-one or older at the times of their first gifts.[50] By comparison, with the 2013 ACGA gift annuity survey, 38 percent of immediate-payment gift annuitants were age eighty-one or older at the times of their gifts.[51] Largely as a result of the 1952 survey, Huggins's annuity rates charts went up to ninety years of age, beginning with the ninth COA in 1955.

Note that in schedule C, Huggins assumed no cap for payment rates at older ages and that his highest rate was 10.5 percent for a single annuitant, aged eighty. Rate caps of 9 percent for a single life, aged seventy-six and older, and 7.9 percent for two lives, aged eighty and older, were voted by conference participants and incorporated into charts A, B, and C.

Schedule D   Comparative Rates of Interest paid on Annuities by various boards and Agencies.

Huggins first reported on his survey of sixteen national gift annuity programs in March of 1927, when he wrote that "in the matter of rates the situation borders on chaos."[52] Schedule D shows the range of payment rates provided by each nonprofit organization for annuitants ages thirty to eighty-plus. Some nonprofits were willing to pay 10 percent to a single annuitant, aged eighty, while others capped their rates at 6 percent. Many paid the same high rate, whether one, two, or more lives were covered.

Such huge differences in rates have huge consequences for annuitants and for charities alike. Here is my example: an eighty-year-old woman who makes a gift of $25,000 to Charity #1 at 10 percent will receive a $2,500 annuity for life, while the same gift to Charity #2 at 6 percent provides only a $1,500 annuity. Over ten years, she will receive $10,000 less from her gift to Charity #2.[53] It is likely that Charity #1 will attract a greater number of gifts, while Charity #2 will realize a larger residual amount from each gift.

Schedule E   Gradation of Interest Rates Paid [followed by] Comparative study of Net rates payable according to the McClintock Table of Mortality Among Annuitants with interest at 4½% compounded annually with average residuum as shown; and with gross rates paid by representative Insurance Companies to Male Annuitants with interest payments annually at the end of each year.

The first part of schedule E puts the gift annuity rates offered by each national organization in low-to-high order. This organization of the data highlights the extreme range of rates. For example, for an annuitant at age thirty, the rates range from 3 percent to 6 percent, and for an annuitant at age eighty, the range is from 6 percent to 10 percent.

The second part of Schedule E provides six commercial annuity rates issued by life insurance companies. With no charitable residuum, one would expect commercial rates to be significantly higher than those provided by nonprofits. That was true for older annuitants; nonprofits generally offered about half of the 20 percent annuity rate available to commercial annuitants, aged eighty-plus.

Nonprofits were accepting much greater risks in their payments to younger annuitants, relative to commercial rates. The highest commercial rate for a thirty-year-old annuitant was 5.7 percent. Surprisingly, the United Lutheran Church in America, Board of Ministerial Relief, offered 5.9 percent, and the National Bible Institute (unaffiliated with the American Bible Society) offered 6.0 percent.[54]

The fact that a nonprofit charity would pay a thirty-year-old annuitant a 6 percent life annuity astonished an experienced actuary like Huggins, whose clients included many of America's largest insurance and pension-plan companies.

Looking at gift annuity rates in 1927 from the perspective of 2017 puts three basic assumptions in stark contrast. Two assumptions lead to lower modern rates: (1) on average, today's annuitants live much longer, and (2) the assumed net-investment return in 1927 was much higher: 4.5 percent versus today's 3.25 percent. On the other hand, Huggins's target for the charitable residuum was 70 percent versus 50 percent today, which would produce higher rates today than in 1927.

Suppose we calculate a 6 percent annuity for a thirty-year-old annuitant using current assumptions. With the 2017 ACGA net-return assumption of 3.25 percent,[55] the annuity account would be exhausted when the annuitant is aged fifty-four. On average, payments would continue for another twenty-eight years, based on today's mortality experience. Assuming that the original amount transferred is $100,000, the issuing nonprofit would suffer a net loss of $261,793. The loss would be greater if a recession hit in the early years of the annuity contract or if the annuitant lived longer than expected.

Huggins knew that in 1927, no commercial organization could survive—and under the laws of New York and California, none would not be allowed to operate—while burdened with the level of risk involved with payment rates offered to younger annuitants by some nonprofits at the time.

Schedule F   Comparative Rates of Interest, Calculated on basis of McClintock's Table of Mortality Among Annuitants with interest at 4½% compounded annually, with 70% residuum.

Huggins's judgment about the rates payable to older annuitants was much different from the rates suitable for younger annuitants. One might expect that an actuarially justified gift annuity rate schedule might lower the prevailing rates paid by nonprofits to older annuitants. Surprisingly, Huggins's maximum rate was *higher* than offered by any nonprofit in his survey sample, where payment rates ranged from 6 percent to 10 percent.

In schedule E, Huggins showed that two nonprofits offered a top payment rate of 10 percent for annuitants aged eighty-plus, while in schedule F, Huggins calculated that to realize an average charitable residuum of 70 percent for a single male life at age eighty-plus, the gift annuity payment rate would be 10.5 percent.

While his rates for the oldest cohort of gift annuitants are significantly lower than commercial annuity rates offered by life insurance firms (which ranged from 19.2 percent to 21.2 percent for an annuitant aged eighty-plus), a 10.5 percent gift annuity was beyond the pale for leaders of nonprofit organizations.

Although technically consistent with his mortality and investment assumptions, his aggressive-rate recommendation was the only one substantially modified by conference participants, who capped the maximum annuity rate at 9 percent for annuitants aged seventy-six and over.

Note also that schedule F broke out separate gift annuity payment rates for male and female annuitants, while all rate tables after 1927 have been unisex. Huggins commented on the main reason for a unisex table at the second conference. The reason was to simplify the rate-setting calculations by eliminating a gender-based element:

> When you take into consideration that in the two-life cases, the actual ages and sexes of both lives must be used in determining the amount of reserves to be maintained back of the annuity agreements, you can readily see the large number of factors that must be calculated.

For reasons of simplicity, the CGA has always tabulated gift-annuitant data by sex but has never gathered and analyzed gift-annuitant income, race, health, occupation, or other demographic factors that are routinely examined by the commercial life insurance industry.[56]

Schedule G   Comparative Annuity Rates Payable, Calculated on basis of McClintock's Table of Mortality Among Annuitants with interest at 4½% compounded annually.

Schedule G is the first American rate table for gift annuities. It presented single-life gift annuity payment rate recommendations based on gender. Huggins's one-life rates were based on a male life, since that was "the standard in the State of New York and many other States." His two-life rates were based on a male life and a female life of equal ages and on a male life with females who are five, ten, and fifteen years younger.

Since 1927, a uniform table of maximum suggested gift annuity payment rates has been calculated for voluntary use by nonprofit organizations based on Huggins's fundamental assumptions: a target for the charitable residuum, average expected mortality for given ages and projected investment performance.[57]

We should take a minute to reflect on what is not in Huggins's original rates report. There were no maximum rate caps and adjustments for older or younger annuitants; these would be added by conference participants. There was no loading of administrative and investment expenses in the rate-setting process until the ninth COA in 1955. Survey reports on gift-annuitant data by Paul Cassat (1930) and Arthur A. Wellck (1933) did not include mortality data. Huggins was intimately familiar with the ABS, but an individual organization's program, like an individual life, is subject to idiosyncrasies. It was not until a mortality survey of Protestant organizations in 1934 that fitting standard-annuitant mortality tables to reflect gift-annuitant-mortality experience was possible.

At the administrative offices of ACGA in Smyrna, Georgia, is an original 1927 conference report labeled "Office Copy" and signed by Gilbert Darlington (appendix V). Loosely inserted in this fragile report are three undated charts produced by George Huggins at some point after the conference. There is no reference to these charts in his "Actuarial Basis of Rates":

Chart A   Proposed Standard Annuity Rates

Chart B   Proposed Standard Annuity Rates, Compared with those paid by several organizations

Chart C   Proposed Standard Annuity Rates: Joint Life and Survivorship Annuities on Two Lives

The *Report of Committees on Findings* from the 1927 conference report does not specify the age at which the cap will be applied. After the conference, Huggins provided hand-drawn charts A and B, illustrating payment rates at various ages for a unisex single-life gift annuity, and he capped the maximum payment rate at 9 percent for a single annuitant aged seventy-six or older. Chart C capped the two-life rate at 7.9 percent for annuitants aged eighty and older.

All three charts with the amended payment rates were printed on two pages that were slipped into the published 1927 conference report. Huggins does not refer to the existence of these new charts in his conference presentation, but they are referenced in the *Findings*. A new, unisex, single-life-annuity rate table was published in the report of the Second Conference on Annuities and labeled "Standard Rates Approved April 29, 1927."

Best Practices for Gift Annuities

Having set forth his fundamental principles on investing gift annuity reserves, measuring annuitant mortality, and setting a residuum target, Huggins concluded "Actuarial Basis of Rates" with five recommendations intended to realize the "ideal plan of conducting the annuity business" he had called for in March. Most importantly, he recommended a target of 70 percent for the charitable residuum. Each of the recommendations was preceded by the wording "the Committee recommends":

> An average of 70% as a residuum, that is reasonable in its returns, both to the donors and the organizations, and at the same time consistent with the objects of the annuity gifts.

> That the rate of interest assumed in the [annuity rate] calculations be 4½%.

> That the table of mortality adopted as a basis for the calculations for the annuities on a single life be the McClintock Table of Mortality among Male Annuitants, which is the standard in the State of New York and many other States [for commercial annuities].

> That the table of mortality adopted as the basis for the calculations for the Joint Life and Survivorship annuities where there are two beneficiaries be the McClintock Table of Mortality among Annuitants—male and female.

That annuities be not issued involving the continuance of the payments to more than two lives unless absolutely required by the donor. In such case the rate of the annuity payments should be less than the rate payable to any combination of two of the three or more lives.

The introduction of national norms for gift annuity rates based on complex statistical data generated by professional specialists, along with related administrative practices aimed at producing consistent results among diverse nonprofit organizations, must have come as a shock to many conference participants hearing all this for the first time.

The implications of Huggins's plan were profound. They were also completely foreign to most charities' practices. Annuity donors were showering charities with money. The decimal method, with exceptions for higher rates if demanded, appeared easy, inexpensive, and successful. In the absence of independent monitoring and regulation, nonprofit gift annuity programs were free to market, administer, and invest as they chose.

It is small wonder that two presentations that were prepared for the conference were set aside so that participants could discuss the meaning of Huggins's technical schedules and his recommendations for best practices and a uniform table of maximum payment rates.

In "Actuarial Basis of Rates," Huggins identified the three core principles for gift annuity rate setting and ongoing program management: setting a residuum target, measuring gift-annuitant mortality, and adopting reasonable investment-return assumptions. He made nonprofits aware of the relationships among these elements and demonstrated how to recognize and adapt to new experiences over time. He continuously refined his recommended maximum annuity rates in recognition of changing economic forces, federal and state legislation, and steadily improving information about American gift annuity experiences.

The process of gift annuity rate setting demands careful judgment by leaders of nonprofit organizations, who must weigh projected improvements in annuitant longevity, future investment earnings, investment and administrative expenses, caps on payment rates at older ages, whether donors will find payment rates attractive, and whether key organizational decision makers believe that the benefits of a gift annuity program outweigh its costs.

Huggins functioned as a one-person rates committee for thirty-two years. Conference participants debated Huggins's proposed investment assumptions and recommended payment rates with vigor. With notable exceptions, American nonprofit organizations followed his lead. Prime examples of conference-participant modifications and independent actions are the rate cap imposed at the very first conference, the delayed implementation of his substantially revised set of assumptions at the start of World War II (Huggins turned out to be right), and the postponed action right after the war, in case the economy improved faster than Huggins had predicted (the optimism of conference participants was justified).

The rates recommendations that Huggins presented for consideration at the Conferences on Gift Annuities are now worked out by eight volunteer members of the ACGA Rates Committee. Professional actuarial services in 2017 were provided by the firm that Huggins created and were approved by a twenty-five-member ACGA board.[58]

The "Report of Committee on Findings" in the conference report adds nine specific recommendations to the five Huggins made in "Actuarial Basis of Rates," most drawn from Arthur Ryan's presentation, "Administrative Policy."

Questions about the process of writing, explaining, amending, and accepting America's first standards of practice for gift annuities are quite interesting, but we have precious little information about how the fourteen motions appeared in the form approved by the conference. The "Findings" section of the conference report has a very brief mention about the process: "The report of the Committee on Findings was the basis of discussion of the afternoon session and was finally adopted unanimously by the conference in the following votes, which thereby become an approved standard for the annuity business of co-operating organizations."

The "Findings" report claims unanimous support for the committee's recommendations. The preface by Alfred Williams Anthony is more nuanced: "Free and protracted discussion led to practical unanimity in the conclusions arrived at, respecting the desirability of standard rates and uniform methods."

The first finding affirmed the idea of national standards for rate-setting and program administration:

1. VOTED that in view of the wide variations in annuity rates now granted by religious, educational and charitable organizations, this conference, representing thirty-five organizations, expresses its strong conviction that it is advisable to bring about a standard in rates and uniformity in practice.

None of the participants had the authority to commit their nonprofit organizations to adopting a new table of gift annuity payment rates and standards of practice. The subcommittee neither had nor sought authority to direct the actions of any independent nonprofit organization. The recommended standards were voluntary, as Dr. Anthony intended so wisely. Policy development in a brand-new association is effective only when the people involved understand a proposal, like it on its merits, and adopt it in their own practices.

Dr. Anthony articulated the SOA's hopes for universal acceptance of national rates and standards in his preface: "It is earnestly hoped by the Committee, and it was the desire voiced in the Conference, that all bodies doing an annuity business should conform in rates and methods, as soon as practicable to the standards herein approved."

The new committee had quite a job on its hands in educating less-experienced nonprofits and resolving disputes among organizations that had issued annuities for five decades and more. The official public stance of the committee was that many nonprofits embraced the new rate table immediately. Huggins later admitted that in 1927, "We did not get many organizations to adopt these rates since they preferred to stick to their own higher ones."[59] The committee did not survey its sponsors in these ten conferences to see how many followed its rate recommendations.

Even today, a few nonprofits do not observe the maximum-annuity rates suggested by the ACGA. In five national surveys between 1994 and 2013, 95 percent to 97 percent of nonprofits participating in the survey reported that they "always or usually follow the ACGA maximum rates."[60]

The 1927 conference accepted Huggins's 70 percent residuum target but imposed a cap on payment rates for older annuitants, voting that "the maximum rate paid be 9%" and that no nonprofit should use a rate schedule producing less than a 70 percent residuum.

Conference participants voted approval of Huggins's other recommendations: the 4.5 percent investment return assumption, use of McClintock's mortality tables, and discouraging contracts involving more than two annuitant lives. They added five standards of practice (emphasis added):

That **administrative expense** in connection with Annuity Agreements should be charged to the Annuity Agreement Account. [Note that an expense assumption was not included as a factor in the national rate calculations until 1955.]

That a **separate account** should be set up with each annuitant.

That **periodical reserve valuations** to insure the maintenance of legal reserves required by the state where the organization is incorporated should be taken.

That **Annuity Funds should be segregated**; with separate bookkeeping accounts and securities earmarked.

That all Annuity Funds should be **invested in sound, income-producing, high-grade securities**. [Recommendations for investment allocations are a major topic below.]

These continue to be held up as voluntary best practices by ACGA.[61] One other recommendation by the conference proved difficult to implement: "That the matter of drafting a suggested **standard form of contract** be referred to the Standing Committee on Annuities. This Committee to draw up such a form and report at a later conference." (emphasis added)

Nonprofit organizations agreed on many things, but the subcommittee was not able to develop a broadly accepted national prototype for gift annuity contracts. Several attempts were made over the years, but none resulted in approval. There are many possible explanations for this. The laws of each state respecting gift annuities were unclear and conflicting. Each nonprofit organization developed its own annuity contract forms, which varied considerably across the country.

Gift annuities were not always paid for life but, instead, could be terminated upon an annuitant reaching a certain age or getting married. For example, wording for a testamentary gift annuity is included in a 1924 reference book, prefaced by these remarks:

These forms are submitted merely as suggestions. On account of the diversity between the various states, and the shifting of the viewpoints of some of the courts, even in this day and generation no form that will fit every situation and every state can be devised.

7. Annuity Provision. Said gift shall be subject to an annuity of _____ per year, to be paid on the _____ day of _____ of each year to _____, until such time as said _____ shall die (or become of age, or marry, etc.).[62]

In the absence of legislation standardizing their annuity programs, and before best practices were recommended by the CGA, each charity determined the number of annuitants it would allow to be named in a single agreement. One-life agreements were most common, but some allowed three or more lives for one gift, in near-total disregard of the financial implications. Charles White warned at the third COA in 1930, "It is reported that one organization has entered into a contract for five or six lives, which probably any insurance company would hesitate to do."

Nonprofits took different approaches to basic concepts. For example, Arthur Ryan continued to argue in favor of annuity bonds. Ryan also attempted to expand the appropriation of other forms of commercial annuity contracts for use with gift annuities, highlighting very interesting ideas: two-life contracts with one rate for an older annuitant and a lower rate for a younger survivor; a contract with a flexible deferred annuity payment start date that has only recently become accepted; a deferred-annuity contract that became standardized in the 1930s; and a term-of-years annuity contract. The Findings Committee asked the SOA to study these ideas and report back to a future conference.

After the conference, the subcommittee took additional actions. Two dealt with financing the conference report and recovering other expenses:

That the proceedings of the conference when printed be sold to all organizations desiring copies for not less than $1.00 in order to help defray the preliminary costs of procuring the materials and other incidental expenses of the conference.

That organizations represented by individuals present be asked to contribute toward underwriting the balance of the costs of the conference.

Committee members expressed the general sense that more could be accomplished if there were another conference on gift annuities, particularly emphasizing marketing: "In the judgment of those present it would be wise to have another meeting concerning annuities giving special attention to promotion methods."

It is noteworthy that following up on this first conference, members of the SOA imagined that the most important topic would be marketing. They seemed to take for granted that the new actuarial system would find its way to general acceptance on its obvious merits. The challenge was more fundamental: How would a small, brand-new volunteer committee with no paid staff and virtually no budget encourage nonprofit organizations across the United States to discard many of their current practices and accept a technically complex system for gift annuities that would be costly and time-consuming to administer?

Within a few years, Huggins's voluntary system of best practices provided professional credibility for charities that followed his recommendations. Driving acceptance of his system was the increasingly critical opposition to the common strategy of marketing gift annuities as "bonds." Darlington and the Committee on Annuities depended upon Huggins's financial-security system to assure public officials of the integrity of charitable gift annuity programs during a time of rapidly evolving state and federal tax legislation and regulatory policies.

Perhaps the most important forces driving general acceptance of national standards were two of Huggins's fundamental principles: (1) the steady lengthening of annuitant lives and (2) the economic depression, which challenged nonprofit annuity fund managers looking for safe and productive investments. Each principle is examined below.

What Makes Annuities Charitable? A Residuum Target

We now turn to the first of three fundamental principles in "Actuarial Basis of Rates": setting a target for the charitable residuum. Huggins, the professional technician, focused attention on the spirit of philanthropy. How much of the original amount transferred to a charitable organization for a gift annuity will be available to change and save lives?

When nonprofits agreed to set rates with a common residuum target in mind, people became free to support the missions they cared about most. The annuity rate tables developed in 1927 were set by charitable objectives, not by the investment market.

Nonprofits were looking at gift annuities "from the wrong angle." Huggins wrote:

> That is, rather from the standpoint of what we would like to give or the least amount that can reasonably be given, and yet obtain subscriptions [gifts]…We ought to approach it from the other angle, namely—what residuum on the average do we desire to have ultimately released from the original gift—65 percent, 70 percent, 75 percent or 80 percent or whatever it may be. We ought to know either what average residuum our rates will produce, but better still the rates that can be allowed in order to produce the desired average residuum.[63]

Huggins stressed the fundamental differences between charitable gift annuities and annuity investments, which have no philanthropic element:

> In determining the basis, we must keep in mind the object of issuing these annuity agreements. It must be distinctly kept in mind that these organizations are not selling annuities as

they are commonly sold by commercial insurance companies. They are simply offering to their constituents a means by which gifts may be made to the organizations, retaining for the donors a life interest in the funds.[64]

Throughout his life, Huggins coached nonprofits to focus on the charitable purpose, noting in his last conference report in 1959 that "we must keep in mind that we are not in the gift annuity business just to sell annuities. We are in the business of getting gift money for the cause we represent."[65]

The charitable residuum is the whole point of gift annuities. While the legal responsibility to provide lifetime payments to annuitants is fundamentally important and appropriately regulated by law, that is just the start—it is simply a baseline requirement.

Huggins insisted that charities can and should know exactly how much a gift annuity means to them financially. The money provided by donors for charitable purposes must be protected just as rigorously as corporate profits are sought through the sale of financial products. If nonprofits want to be compensated for the time and expense involved in the professional management of a gift annuity program, they need to be efficient in controlling the costs associated with marketing and administration, and they must find adequate investment returns to protect the value of the charitable residuum that will support their philanthropic missions.

In the 1920s, competing for donors by negotiating the annuity payment rate was all too common. Nonprofits that were willing to negotiate gift annuity rates allowed self-interested investors to create a market, thus losing sight of the charitable purpose.[66] At the second COA in 1928, Huggins warned that offering higher payment rates as an incentive to attract gifts would bring charitable annuities into competition with commercial annuities:

As we approach the condition, where the residuum is reduced and approaches the vanishing point, the organizations will find themselves encroaching upon the territory of the commercial insurance companies that sell annuities. Their rates are so calculated that the principal and interest will, on the average, and in the aggregate be exhausted in meeting the annuity payments.[67]

Huggins urged nonprofits to recognize that unjustifiably high rates were "disastrous." Charities "would be fortunate indeed to break even without taking into account administrative costs." As he wrote:

In other words, they would be rendering a service to their annuitants without any compensation whatsoever…It is not the purpose of annuity agreements, issued by religious, charitable and educational organizations, to render annuity service free of cost—the purpose is to raise funds to carry on the work of the organization issuing the agreement. The higher the annuity rates allowed, the less will be the gain to the organization; the lower the rates, the greater the gain.[68]

Charles L. White, executive secretary of the American Baptist Home Mission Society (ABHMS), warned of the consequences of irresponsible annuity payment rates at a second gathering of financial professionals in March of 1927:

The rates vary, and some of them are probably dangerously near to those paid by insurance companies. I fear there may be a rude awakening by some organizations, if they continue to pay the rates now in vogue, which are sometimes increased in order to attract certain sums of money. Very careful consideration should be given to this question of rates, for if some conspicuous agency granting annuities should fail to keep its contracts, the conservative annuity contracts of other groups [including his own ABHMS, which had issued annuities for many decades] would be called in question and confidence would be quickly destroyed…Some agencies…it is feared, have sown to the wind and may reap the whirlwind, if not the desert.[69]

There was little room for doubt that Huggins's residuum target, which was approved by the conference, produced a charitable gift. On average, 70 percent of the original amount would be available to the issuing charity when an annuitant died. Huggins described the target as "reasonable in its returns, both to the donors and the organizations, and at the same time consistent with the objects of the annuity gifts."[70]

In time, having a broadly accepted national residuum target derived by standardized calculations eliminated competition among virtually all charities[71] that previously had been willing to attract donors by negotiating higher payment rates than those offered by other nonprofits.

This is one of Huggins's most important contributions. Through his actuarially determined charitable residuum target, he fulfilled America's need for a hybrid conceptual model of gifts, clearly motivated by love for a charitable mission bundled with a secure life-annuity contract that protected the interests of annuitants as well as the issuing charities.

No one looking for a good financial deal would be attracted by an investment prospectus illustrating a life annuity in which 70 percent of the original principal was allocated to the issuing charity rather than to the donor's payments. Only a donor who intends to support the philanthropic mission of a charity would agree to such an arrangement.

Nineteen years later, in 1946, facing increased gift-annuitant longevity and a steady decline in investment returns, Huggins recommended reducing the residuum target to 50 percent:

In the rates proposed, it is our thought that the organizations should share some of the losses under these adverse

215

conditions that have developed. We are, therefore, proposing a set of rates with a 50 percent residuum as contrasted with the 70 percent residuum which has been the basis of our rates to date.

Uncertainties over the postwar economy caused the conference to take no action on rate setting in 1946. Huggins's recommendation was adopted at the next conference in 1955. The residuum target remains 50 percent today.

Note that Huggins's rate calculations did not address the impact of inflation on the buying power of the residuum, which was based on 70 percent of the original dollar amount. ACGA first introduced a minimum present-value calculation to its rate-setting process in 2012. This reduces the suggested rates at younger ages.

Accommodating Enormous Changes in Mortality Experience

George Huggins's great passion and professional expertise was the study of mortality. A fundamental risk for an organization issuing a life-annuity contract is that an annuitant may live longer than expected and therefore receive more payments. Because of longevity risk, "the average duration of the lives of the members of a group to whom we promise annuity payments during lifetime." Huggins wrote in 1927 that this "is a very vital matter."[72]

Developing accurate data on annuitant longevity requires a statistical solution based on experience: "No one can predict the future lifetime of an individual, but we do know a great deal about groups of individuals, as a result of statistical studies, based upon the actual experience among similar groups in the past."[73]

The role of a professional actuary is to measure longevity risk so that the risk can be managed: "It does not take an actuary or a statistician to tell us that in the general population there is a steady trend toward lengthening of life, but it does take the actuary or the statistician to make studies that aid us in **determining to what extent** the lives are being lengthened"[74] (emphasis added).

Huggins knew as well as anyone in America that increases in longevity meant greater risks for nonprofits that issue gift annuities, thus sharpening the possibility that annuitants would outlive their expected payments and exhaust the charitable residuum. For example, at the ninth COA in 1955, Huggins reached back in time to the Northampton mortality table of 1785 to demonstrate that the value of a life annuity had increased 92 percent for an eighty-year-old. This near-doubling of the cost to a nonprofit issuing an annuity "is not due to the increase in the cost of living but to the increase in the periods of living."[75]

At the beginning of his pioneering career, reliable data on mortality rates was scarce. When he presented his national gift annuity rate table in 1927, no one had collected data on the lives of American gift annuitants. There were no databases other than those produced for life insurance and commercial annuities. What could nonprofits do?

> In the light of not having our own experience, we must turn to the experiences of others. Here we find that the experience of others has been studied, tabulated and put in shape for our use in the form of tables showing the rates of mortality among various groups according to the actual mortality experience among those groups.[76]

The pattern of his reporting was set at the first conference in 1927, where Huggins compared data and gave "brief histories and explanations" of five mortality tables. In his conference reports from 1927 to 1959, Huggins depended heavily on historical data and comparison of mortality tables over time. As the quality of gift-annuitant-mortality data improved, Huggins taught nonprofit organizations about the virtues and faults of several dozen mortality tables, with examples ranging from a table published in ancient Rome to each new set of modern data.

Huggins helped the leaders of American nonprofit organizations to grasp the practical implications of a world-changing new reality: a continuous and unprecedented lengthening of average lives from 1900 to 1960.[77]

That populations are aging is not news to us. What was surprising at the time was the scope of change and its speed. Huggins and his professional peers lived through and left a record of their responses to monumental changes in longevity.

Peter Laslett, a leading historian of mortality rates, observed that for all recorded history, the average length of human lives was a gently sloping plateau until a wrenching shift toward greater longevity began around the year 1900 in all industrialized countries. Rapidly improving life expectancies curved sharply upward, resulting in the oldest human populations Earth has ever seen.[78]

Demand for mortality information exploded as people began to realize the implications of a longer-lived American population for pension systems, life insurance, and annuities. The scientific understanding of annuitant mortality evolved rapidly between 1927 and 1959. Actuaries published a series of new US-based mortality tables to keep up, as Huggins wrote at the 1946 conference: "In recent years there have been material increases in the longevity of our population...The life insurance companies which issue annuities have had to abandon mortality table after mortality table as their experience showed lowering mortality among their annuitant lives."

It is a big deal and an enormous amount of work to throw out an experience-based mortality table and create an entirely new one, yet it happened quite often during these years.[79] The reality of longer annuitant lives was already apparent to Huggins when he was forced to use the old McClintock table in 1927. He changed the mortality table at the heart of his gift annuity rate recommendations four times in twenty-eight years: in 1931, 1934, 1946, and 1959.[80]

The extent of the changes in American gift-annuitant life expectancy can be shown by comparing mortality tables that were the best available in their times. According to "Emory McClintock's Annuitant's Table" (1899), the average sixty-year-old male had an average life expectancy of 14.65 years. According to the "American Annuitants Table" (1955), a male aged sixty had a life expectancy of 19.57 years.[81]

That is a vast difference in longevity risk for a nonprofit issuing a life annuity, as demonstrated by John Trumbull's experience. When the president of Yale signed an annuity contract with Trumbull in 1831, Yale expected Trumbull, then aged seventy-six, to live for six years, in which case Yale would send him twenty-four payments of $250 per quarter, for a total of $6,000. Trumbull lived for more than eleven years. The college dutifully made forty-five payments totaling $11,250.

If the country's gift annuity rates in 1959 had been based on the average life expectancies in the McClintock Table, it is likely that the reserve funds of many nonprofit organizations would be exhausted.

Through his work with ABS, and more broadly with the Committee on Gift Annuities, Huggins learned about nonprofit gift-annuitant mortality experience. When he discovered that gift annuitants were living even longer than commercial annuitants, he adjusted the standard annuitant mortality tables. Standard tables should be considered "yardsticks against which to measure the actual [gift annuitant] experience as currently observed," and then modified as needed to fit the available data "to conform as nearly as possible to our own experience as a basis for calculating rates and setting up and maintaining reserves."[82]

For example, in 1946, Huggins reported that "the latest table, the 1937 Standard, is already proving inadequate." To accommodate current experience, that table "has to be modified by setting back the ages one or two years."

Investing Gift Annuity Reserves

The first principle Huggins illustrated in "Actuarial Basis of Rates" was the extent to which the value of a charitable residuum depends on the investment performance of a reserve fund over the life of a gift annuity contract.

Financial results for a gift annuity program are determined by actual investment experience, but assumptions about future investment returns must be used for two purposes: (1) in the rate-setting calculations for new gifts and (2) in the periodic valuation of reserve funds required to secure annuity payment obligations.

Investment return assumptions are often different for the two purposes. For example, in 1928, George Huggins used a 4.5 percent return assumption to calculate suggested payment rates for new gift annuity contracts. That same year, the New York Insurance Department mandated a 4 percent assumed return for valuing commercial annuity and gift annuity reserve funds. California required the use of a 3.5 percent return.

For a nonprofit organization to stay on track toward the targeted residuum, the basic goal of a gift annuity fund asset manager is to earn the average annual return assumed for the reserve fund.[83] Designing and evaluating an asset-allocation strategy based on investment experience and future-return assumptions is a fundamentally important management responsibility. The risk that an annuitant's account will be exhausted because of poor returns is assumed by the organization issuing the gift annuity contract. A nonprofit that provides unsustainably high annuity payments is betting its reputation and perhaps its survival on the likelihood of above-normal investment returns throughout the lives of its annuitants.

Like the businesses of life insurance, pensions, and commercial annuity contracts, nonprofit annuity programs became attuned to changes in economic conditions that determine whether and how an investment manager can find the returns needed to meet fixed payment obligations for the lives of individuals while conserving capital.[84] Investment horizons for life insurance and annuity programs are relatively long-term, because cash-flow requirements over time are predictable; when a contract is issued, projected payments are determined for the average expected life of the covered person.[85]

Under normal conditions, financial reserves can be managed effectively using statistical norms derived from past investment experience. The decades from 1927 to 1959 challenged the judgment of nonprofit leaders with a high degree of difficulty. Increasing annuitant longevity changed the norms expressed through a series of new mortality tables, while drastic changes in the economy forced continual reappraisal of earnings expectations and the selection of appropriate investments.

Blind dependence on preconceived ideas rather than being open to fresh investment strategies would have been disastrous. Asset-allocation solutions were very different in each of three distinct economic cycles between 1927 and 1959. As the industrialized world of the Roaring Twenties collapsed into the Great Depression and World War II, conference speakers drawn from the world of finance helped nonprofit managers to cope with a broken economy by maintaining actuarially sound rates and reasonable investment-return assumptions.

The job of analyzing conditions that affect future returns and suggesting model investment portfolios for the benefit of annuity conference participants was filled by a succession of well-qualified economists, bankers, and business professors. Conference speakers often shared valuable wisdom gained through bitter experience. No one predicted the stock market crash, the Depression, or the length of a long, slow decline in yields on fixed-income investments. Most financial experts were surprised that the federal government succeeded in keeping the yields on US and corporate bonds extremely low through the end of World War II.

Today's gift annuity fund managers can learn from economic history that conditions were far worse for our predecessors. It is true that since 2007, managers have struggled with extremely low interest rates. The Great Recession forced interest rates even lower than during the Great Depression. However, the Federal Reserve began raising interest rates at the end of 2015. If rates had declined for as long a period as they did beginning in 1920, it would be 2027 before the Fed acted to raise rates.

Good times returned after the end of WWII with the reprivatization of investment markets and a "great bear market" in bonds (lower prices, higher yields) from 1947 to the tenth conference in 1959. The economic boom of the postwar period became the strongest in US history, reawakening an appetite for stocks and introducing fear of inflation. In the 1950s, gift annuity managers began to focus on total return in addition to the current yields from bonds, mortgages, and other fixed-income investments.

MORTALITY, ECONOMIC CONDITIONS, AND INVESTMENT-RETURN PROJECTIONS AT THE CONFERENCES ON GIFT ANNUITIES

The concluding section of this book follows two major topics through each of the ten conferences on gift annuities held during George Huggins's lifetime:

1. **Gift annuity rates reports**, in which Huggins incorporated current economic and mortality data. At every national gift annuity conference from 1927 to the present, there have been reports on annuity payment rates. Huggins's presentations on mortality experience, his rates recommendations, and conference actions are summarized in appendix VI: Gift Annuity Rates Chart, 1927–59 (Single Life).

2. **Economic projections and investment guidance** by bankers and economists for use by gift annuity fund managers.

The Roaring Twenties (1927–29)

The first two conferences featured rapid growth in gift annuity programs, a lively debate over whether common stocks were appropriate for gift annuity reserve funds, and general confidence in the long-term exuberance of the American economy. In 1927 and 1928, events had not yet compelled Huggins and the COA to develop a dynamic process of fitting a standardized national-rate table to a deteriorating economy and rapidly increasing annuitant longevity.

Organizers of the **first conference (April 29, 1927)**[86] did not schedule speakers on the economy. Behind the scenes, monetary deflation in the mid-1920s was boosting the attractiveness of fixed annuities.[87] Two representatives of the American Bible Society made important remarks on gift administration, legal and investment issues, and ethical considerations bound up with gift annuity reserve accounts.

Having presented all the fundamental principles of gift annuities at the first conference, Huggins introduced no new mortality data or actuarial assumptions until the fourth conference in 1931. At the **second conference (November 9, 1928),**[88] Huggins presented a three-page report, with no charts or graphs, referring to his presentation the previous year "in order that we may take up the discussion at the point where it was left off." He clearly assumed the 1927 conference report was readily available to anyone interested: "It is well to read the first seven resolutions which were presented to the Conference by the Committee on Findings, and adopted unanimously by the Conference." The committee had not surveyed nonprofits issuing gift annuities to see whether they adopted his rate recommendations, though he knew that "some organizations have modified their practices, and changed their rates in conformity with these principles."

Specific investment strategies for gift annuity reserve accounts were first discussed at the second conference by George Sutherland.[89] In 1928, there were far fewer investment asset choices than today, but Sutherland reported that "investment opportunities exist in such number and variety as never before." Professional investment advice for nonprofits was not as readily available or as trustworthy then as now.

He and many subsequent conference speakers provided specific advice on asset classes. For example, Sutherland pointed out that mortgage investments in Manhattan offered a "guaranteed" return of 5 percent, and that similar mortgages in Brooklyn, Queens, and Westchester were yielding 5.5 percent:

> In New York City and vicinity, the best type of investment with the largest return at the present time are mortgages guaranteed by one of the long established and responsible Bond and Mortgage Companies. These companies give a guarantee both as to principal, interest and title of the property mortgaged.

The return assumption Huggins had used in 1927 to calculate annuity rates was 4.5 percent, well below then-current yields to provide a margin of safety.[90] Sutherland drew an optimistic conclusion: "Investments need constant attention and expert advice, but this on the whole is not an especially difficult undertaking. We might all wish that it was as easy to get money on the annuity plan as it is to find proper investments for the funds when they are secured."

Sutherland recommended a diversified portfolio of bonds: "We all feel that a goodly percentage of bonds of high grade should become a part of all invested funds of this nature." In addition to real estate mortgage-backed bonds, his recommended asset classes included railroad and public-utility bonds: "Of late years public utility bonds have been as attractive from an investment standpoint as practically any securities that can be purchased." He said he rarely invested in industrial bonds and avoided the low yield on government bonds.

Sutherland's two-and-a-half-page presentation provided some important advice, but the ease of finding adequate returns in 1928 would change drastically after the market crashed in 1929. By comparison, the investment presentation at the third conference, in 1930, was by far the longest of the ten conferences: twenty pages filled with specific investment information. The next longest was eight pages; most were five pages or fewer.

Since the next COA was held a full year after the stock market crash reflecting the Great Depression, to get a fuller picture of investment advice given to nonprofit organizations during the Roaring Twenties, we will look at a presentation by Leland Rex Robinson at the **Conference on Financial and Fiduciary Matters** (March 19–21, 1929) organized by the Federal Council of the Churches of Christ in America, sponsor of the Subcommittee on Annuities.[91]

Robinson presented much excellent advice addressed to managers of charitable funds like endowments, not specifically annuity reserve accounts. He said that those entrusted with investing funds have a "serious responsibility" that is "a dynamic and not a static problem":

Its intricacies can no longer be resolved by rule of thumb methods, by preconceived ideas, or by a slavish following of antiquated legal standards set for so-called "trustee investments."

He did not trust the officers of American savings banks, who "are chosen more for their respectability, family connections and age than for either business ability or knowledge of investments," but spoke with favor of colleges that are "entering into consultation with investment houses for investment analysis and advice... to develop an efficient management of funds."

Robinson made perceptive remarks on the business and credit (interest rate) cycles affecting stocks and bonds and warned of the possibility of "severe set-backs," though he stressed that adding stocks to a portfolio should not be a matter of timing the market, which is "speculation" rather than "investment." Robinson was an advocate for common stocks, which provide "some protection against loss in the purchasing power of the principal through rapidly rising price levels." He predicted that stocks would benefit from America's current "era of far-reaching expansion...[and] common stocks will prove over the next two or three decades the most profitable investment."

Robinson provided conference participants with an asset allocation model based on that for "private estates and trusts" used by the Brooklyn Trust Company:

Bonds and mortgages:	57 percent
Preferred stocks:	10 percent
Common stocks:	30½ percent
Miscellaneous:	2½ percent

Optimism about the economy and the performance of common stocks in the years ahead was a mistake; seven months later, stock markets in the United States and the entire industrialized world crashed. Few people foresaw the economic cataclysm ahead.

The Great Depression and World War II (1930–46)

The six conference reports between 1930 and 1946 are seasoned with emotionally fraught comments by national leaders struggling to act reasonably in the face of tremendous shocks that wracked the economies of the United States and every industrialized nation. In 1933, 11 million Americans were unemployed, more than 25 percent of the workforce—the equivalent of roughly 40 million unemployed workers today.[92]

A frightful crash in the US stock market illustrates the bleak investment landscape: the Dow Jones Industrial Average plunged from 381.17 on September 3, 1929, to 41.22 on July 8, 1932.[93] The stock-price average did not regain its 1929 value until the mid-1950s.

Looking ahead to our recent experience, we see that the Great Recession that began in 2007 reinforced the lesson that severe losses in the early years of an annuity contract and an extended low fixed-income-rate environment may cause individual annuity accounts to exhaust the original principal of a gift (or "run dry"), while the overall financial health of the annuity program may remain excellent because other annuitants died early or a nonprofit's reserve fund benefitted from periods of higher equity-investment returns.

From 1929 until 1946, very few people advocated investing gift annuity reserves in common stocks, but fixed-income assets provided little relief for anxious investment managers. For nearly two decades, there was an agonizing slide in American interest rates that severely tested the national model. Firm federal monetary controls during World War II continued a long, steady decline in interest rates that began in 1920 and extended past the end of the war. Interest rates earned by life insurance companies fell from 5.8 percent in 1923 to 2.88 percent in 1947, a decline of 50 percent.[94]

The national gift annuity rate table adopted in 1927 suggested a 7.6 percent payment rate for a single annuitant, aged seventy. As the return on acceptable investments shriveled, the recommended gift annuity rate for a seventy-year-old dropped to 6.7 percent in 1931, 6.2 percent in 1934, and 5.5 percent in 1939. Years after the 1939 conference, despite the roaring postwar American economy, there was no increase in the 5.5 percent recommended payment rate for seventy-year-old annuitants from 1939 to 1965. Two factors worked against raising rates: increasing gift-annuitant longevity and the lowering of the residuum target from 70 percent to 50 percent, which Huggins recommended in 1946 and the committee adopted in 1955.

It was not until the high inflation of the 1980s that the recommended rate for seventy-year-old annuitants exceeded the 7.6 percent rate that was adopted in 1927, rising to its all-time high of 7.8 percent.

Year	Annuity rate (%) for age 70 (one life)[95]
1927	7.6
1931	6.7
1934	6.2
1939	5.5
1965	5.7
1983	7.8
2017	5.1

Nonprofit annuity program managers have felt the pain our predecessors experienced from low interest rates. Thanks to the Great Recession, the suggested payment rate for seventy-year-old annuitants adopted in 2012 and reaffirmed through 2017 is at an all-time low of 5.1 percent.

A good number of today's managers remember double-digit inflation and interest rates as high as 18 percent for utility bonds in 1979–81, which explains the 7.8 percent payment rate for annuitants age seventy in 1983.[96] The gift annuity rate for those ninety and older reached a record high of 14 percent in 1980 before declining to 12 percent in 1992.[97]

At the **third conference (November 17, 1930),**[98] William Boult noted that "depreciation in market values of stocks of fifty per cent, and more, has occurred within the last fourteen months," but for nonprofits who adopted the CGA's life insurance-based investment model and followed its advice on observing restrictions against common stocks, their gift annuity reserve funds were invested in fixed-income assets, and earnings from bonds had enjoyed a temporary bounce upward.[99]

There is not a sense of panic in the 1930 conference report, but there is clearly a defensive attitude in that two presentations encouraged nonprofits to avoid financial risks by transferring annuity payment obligations to commercial annuity investments. Charles White, first chair of the CGA, presented a paper based on the recent experience of the American Baptist Home Mission Society, which promoted gift annuities that were "unbundled" to realize immediate outright gifts of cash. Noting that the committee was aware of $43 million in existing gift annuity contracts, and that nonprofits had issued contracts with a face value of $6 million in the previous year, White encouraged nonprofits to consider selling the life interests to insurance companies and spending the amount left over: "If these annuities should be reinsured, a great sum would be available at once to pay debts, to avert the abandonment of key enterprises whose continued life hangs in the balance, and to maintain strongly the present work during a period of world depression."

Dr. Alfred Williams Anthony, chair of the parent Committee on Financial and Fiduciary Matters, also took a defensive position, presenting "Cautions and Restraints" on the perils of gift annuity programs. He sharply objected to the idea of "reinsuring" gift annuities:

> Charitable bodies have in some cases begun to reinsure their risks with life insurance companies, but if reinsurance of annuity risks is practiced by a charitable body, then it

lays itself open to several challenges: (1) Has it not entered into partnership with insurance companies? (2) At least may it not, in the eyes of the law, be regarded technically as an agent of insurance companies? (3) Will prospective annuitants welcome the idea of having at least a portion of their funds, which they mean to designate to charity, shared with a commercial insurance company? (4) Will not the psychology of giving be yet further confused if at any turn it appears to involve a commercial transaction with outside parties? (5) If prospective annuitants know that insurance companies, on a commercial basis, can pay much larger annuity rates because their rates are relatively smaller, will not a good share of the annuity business be diverted to the insurance companies?

This is one of a very few examples of direct editorial criticism of a conference presentation. Dr. Anthony's case seems to have been persuasive. A 1933 survey report by Arthur A. Wellck (summarized below) found that "not a single college or university reported that it had transferred its risk to a life insurance company."[100]

As mentioned earlier, William T. Boult gave a detailed conference presentation entitled "Administration and Investment of Annuity Funds" that was published separately for the use of gift annuity fund managers.[101] Boult covered quite a lot of ground. He encouraged lowering risk in fixed-income securities by staggered maturities, geographic diversification, and asset allocation (emphasis added):

1. A "small proportion" of **US, state and municipal government bonds and foreign country bonds** because of low yields.
2. A "large proportion of **first mortgage railroad bonds, junior issues of the strongest companies, and equipment trust certificates.**" (Boult believed railroad bonds to be

safe because they were "protected by the fundamental economic need of transportation. They are less affected in times of depression than industrials. Under government regulation the railroads are permitted to earn a reasonable return on their investment.")

3. **Public-utility bonds**: Light and power companies are best, since they are "a fundamental industry, usually protected by long term franchises. They are less affected in times of depression because of their classification among the absolute necessities of life." Water and natural gas were less attractive.

4. **Industrial bonds** "should be limited to the largest companies of fundamental industries, such as steel, food, etc., where the management, condition of the property, capital structure, dividend record and earnings over a period of years are favorable."

5. **Guaranteed real estate mortgages**: Avoid farm mortgages. "We recommend guaranteed first mortgages on improved real estate, provided the guarantee is that of a financially strong and well managed corporation." Described the benefits of a guarantee, says current yields in the City of New York were 5½ percent.

6. **Preferred stocks** "should represent a very small percentage, if any, of the entire investments."

7. **Common stocks**: "In general, investments in common stocks should be shunned. Slightly more than a year ago this sort of investment was strongly encouraged by some financial experts. The experience of common stock holders, however, in the last year, very plainly shows the wide fluctuation to which this form of investment is subjected. The first class of security to be hurt in any business depression is common stocks. **Depreciation in market values of stocks of fifty per cent, and more, has occurred**

within the last fourteen months. Dividends have been widely cut or omitted." (emphasis added) Banks in New York State and life insurance companies in most states are not permitted to buy common stocks.

Boult provided this asset-allocation chart for gift annuity reserve funds:

Suggested Percentages for Diversification

Asset type	%
Government bonds	10
Railroad bonds	25
Public-utility bonds	25
Industrial bonds	5
Guaranteed mortgages on improved real estate	30
Preferred stocks	5
	100

A **major national conference on gift annuities organized by the Methodist Church on January 6–7, 1931,** presented survey results involving eighty-eight gift annuity programs as of June of 1930: "The reported rate of earnings on investments for annuity funds varies from 4½% to 7%."[102] The period for this range of returns was not specified.

Francis M. Knight, vice president of the Investment Department of Continental Illinois Bank and Trust Company, delivered an important report on annuity reserve fund investments.[103] Knight stressed "safety, yield, and marketability": safety first, because as good stewards, investment managers are accountable to annuitants for their life payments and to donors for protecting the charitable residuum. He provided much good advice on diversification:

It is through intelligent diversification of your investments that you obtain the correct combination of safety, yield and marketability for your account. Diversification recognizes that every form of investment presents some element of risk, very small in some cases, but present nevertheless. It seeks, not to eliminate risk, which is impossible, but to reduce it to a minimum.

Through intelligent diversification, "over a period of time you will obtain an average yield, which is all that you can reasonably expect." Knight's asset allocation model was a diversified bond fund: "30–40% utility, 20–30% railroad and 10–20% each of industrial, real estate and foreign government."

Knight reported that the "guaranteed" mortgages and real estate bonds recommended as an easy solution by George Sutherland at the COA in 1928 ran into serious trouble by January of 1931: "The number of people now owning farms, who never intended to be farmers, is a clear demonstration of how conditions that cause one of a certain kind of security to default will have a serious effect on all securities of that type…there have recently been serious difficulties with a great many real estate bonds."

The **fourth conference**,[104] held in March 1931, was a turning point. Huggins and the COA realized that uniform national processes for rate-setting and administration had become lifeboats for nonprofits battered by falling interest rates, increasing longevity, greater demand for services, and fewer capable donors.

Just four months after the third COA, the committee convened an urgent new conference to prevent a "disaster" with "consequences of great harm" for "all philanthropic causes." The failure of one gift annuity program might destroy trust in all nonprofits:

In the issuing of annuity agreements sound economic and actuarial principles must be followed and legal requirements in all the states and in the nation must be strictly observed.

If disaster were to befall any religious, educational or other charitable organization in the use of the annuity method of financing its enterprises, or if scandals of any nature were to arise because of lack of integrity, or because of failure to observe legal requirements, consequences of great harm would reach far and would insure all philanthropic causes.[105]

Surprisingly, the 1931 conference did not focus on finding adequate investment assets for gift annuity reserve funds. A presenter observed that "this has been done ably during the various conferences of this group."[106] Panic over the inability to find safe, productive investments would erupt at the fifth conference in 1934 and grow steadily more intense through the Second World War.

The focus in 1931 was on actuarial science. There were four conference presentations; three were by professional actuaries, and there was a brief update by Gilbert Darlington on legal developments. This remains the only COA at which three actuaries made presentations: Huggins and K. B. Piper on rates and Edward Marshall on actuarial valuation of gift annuity reserve funds.

There was no presentation on the investment outlook, despite the economic recession. Ernest Hall, chair of the Subcommittee on Annuities, devoted most of his opening presentation to annuity rates and reserve funds, with a brief mention of legislation and an even briefer glance at projected earnings: "The mortality trend is to greater longevity. The trend of income from investments appears to be toward lower levels. The trend of legislation is to increased safety."

Huggins focused almost exclusively on "the mortality experienced among annuitant lives," reviewing his 1927 report on the *Actuarial Basis of Rates* before explaining the rationale for comparing three new mortality tables:

The general trend is towards lower death rates among annuitant lives, or, expressed in other words, greater longevity, or longer periods of expectation of life. Therefore, in considering the question of uniform rates for annuity agreements, we must first consider the newest tables of mortality among annuitant lives and compare them with tables previously in existence and in use.[107]

The Canadian Annuity Table, published in 1927, was interesting but based on British lives. The Combined Annuity Table, published in 1930, was based on group life insurance policies, including younger workers. The American Annuitants Table was based on older people who had purchased commercial annuities from twenty-five American and six Canadian life insurance companies before 1927. In his exhibit A, Huggins compared annuity rates using the three new tables, the old McClintock table, and the aging British Annuitants Table.

Huggins recommended using the American Annuitants Table as the basis for calculating new gift annuity rates. Actuaries Piper and Marshall concurred, with Marshall noting that New York and Massachusetts had adopted that table because "it is based on more modern annuity conditions."

Piper recommended adding an expense load of 0.5 percent to cover the costs of promotion and administration: "It follows that with investments yielding 5%, not more than 4½% is actually available to provide annuity payments." Huggins would incorporate an expense load in his rates calculations in 1946, though his recommended changes were not adopted until 1955.

There were only incidental comments on investment returns at the fourth COA. Huggins lowered his investment assumption to 4 percent in exhibit A of his presentation, but kept the 4.5 percent assumption from his 1927 report when calculating recommended rates. Piper was more optimistic, using a 5 percent return for his calculations: "The gift may be invested in relatively long term securities and the society is therefore assured of maintaining approximately the current yield. Let us assume that it is possible for the present to realize 5% interest on sound investments."[108]

Edward W. Marshall was less optimistic, warning that nonprofit annuity fund managers faced strong headwinds: it was harder to earn a safe return, and gift annuitants were living longer lives.

Present trends of interest rates and mortality among annuitants suggest that, all other things being equal, the residual gains to be realized on annuities in the near future may average substantially less than those obtained in the last decade or two.[109]

Before the next COA, a major survey report on gift annuity programs documented the fact that higher education had jumped on the bandwagon. Written by Arthur A. Wellck with the cooperation of the National Committee on Standard Reports for Institutions of Higher Education, *The Annuity Agreements of Colleges and Universities* is a landmark piece of research on annuity administration, investment, and risk management, among other topics.[110]

Wellck surveyed 296 of the largest colleges and universities in 1933 and found that 153 of them were offering gift annuities. Most of their contracts were issued between 1924 and 1929.

Of the 153 gift annuity programs, 82 colleges and universities completed an extensive questionnaire on their annuity programs: the number and kinds of annuity agreements, investment policies and practices, and risk management, among other topics. Mr. Wellck reported that the 82 institutions had 1,738 gift annuity agreements in force during the academic year 1931–32, with a face value of $16,291,360. He estimated that if all 153 colleges and universities that reported issuing annuities had participated in the full survey, the value of existing annuity contracts "would reach and probably exceed $35,000,000." This is roughly equal to $625 million in 2017 dollars.[111]

Wellck reported that colleges and universities issuing annuities were all over the lot in determining the schedules of their annuity rates. Only two colleges reported using a published mortality table, and of those with any plan at all for measuring life expectancies, the greatest number (twenty-two) used the "decimal plan" and paid an annuity rate equal to 10 percent of the annuitant's age.

When asked what percentage of the original gift was projected to remain upon the death of the annuitant (the charitable residuum), thirty-six colleges reported that they did not use such an estimate in their calculations. Seventeen reported that they expected 100 percent of the gift to remain, while three reported that they expected the amount remaining for the college to be zero. Of these, Wellck observed that "three institutions seem to be writing annuity agreements with no hope or intention of benefiting directly from the practice."

The main reason for convening a **fifth Conference on Annuities**[112] **on November 20, 1934,** was that payment rate tables based on a return assumption of 4.5 percent, which had been used since Huggins's first table in 1927, had become much too high:

> The conference was called because of the urgent request which the committee had received from many organizations desiring a uniform schedule of annuity rates which should be more in accordance with the objective of an average residuum of 70%, which was impossible to obtain by using the prevailing schedules of rates because of the low income on safely invested securities.[113]

Reviewing the return assumption, a committee member acknowledged that "investment earnings have decreased to a serious degree, and no one dare foretell the date or extent of their restoration."[114]

John H. Gross, treasurer of the Presbyterian Board of Pensions, confirmed the difficulty of achieving the generally assumed return: "It is expected that wherever possible these funds shall be invested to return an average net income of not less than 4% per annum...The task has become increasingly difficult in these days of exceedingly low interest rates."[115]

After five years of economic depression, Gross delivered the most pessimistic conference remarks yet on many investment types (emphasis added):

> Normally the bulk of the [asset] list should consist of **high-grade bonds**...It seems impossible to be certain that bonds which are high-grade today will continue to maintain that status. There appears to be an element of risk in every investment...It is probably no exaggeration to say that some of the very finest **bonds** may be in danger of selling within the next several years five or ten per cent lower than their present price.

> There is a fear concerning all **utility securities** today...[there may be a buying opportunity because of] political agitation against privately owned utilities...the present picture is far from reassuring as to bonds of utility holding companies.

> [Even high-grade **industrial bonds** can be] affected as to volume of business and earnings in a major degree by a period of business stagnation.

> Recent years seem to have shown clearly that it is difficult if not impossible to guarantee successfully **real estate mortgages**...Present mortgage holdings may suffer by a lowering of interest rates.

Gross noted that while certain investment advisors believed that nonprofits should own "the **common stocks** (emphasis added here and below) of great American corporations…at best only a modest percentage of a corporation's funds should be used in the purchase of equities."

On the positive side, Gross's advice was the same as William Boult's had been in 1930: **railroad bonds** were the best choice for gift annuity fund managers. Gross predicted that they would remain attractive in the years ahead: "Senior railroad bonds of good roads are still in the prime investment class. They will continue to rate high in an investment way."

Alas, these longtime stalwarts would soon fall by the wayside:

> The casualties in the area of obligations secured by steel, brick, and mortar during the depression are notorious. Nowhere in the whole area of corporate obligations did defaults even begin to approximate those which occurred among **railroad bonds**, which have always been the outstanding example of secured obligations. Furthermore, defaults in the real estate mortgage loan field were also widespread and serious.[116]

No national data is available on the asset-allocation history of gift annuity reserve funds from 1927 to 1954. The first CGA survey on investment returns and asset allocation was presented at the ninth COA in 1955. Questions on investment returns and asset allocations are now included in a series of ACGA surveys that began in 1994. It is worth noting that among US life insurance companies, railroad bonds fell from 18 percent of total assets in 1927 to just 5 percent in 1950. Mortgages fell from 43 percent of total assets in 1927 to 15 percent in 1945.[117]

Also at the **fifth conference,** Huggins presented a substantial, eleven-page report entitled "The Mortality among Annuitant Lives." Conducted independently of the CGA, a gift-annuitant-mortality study among fourteen Protestant-affiliated organizations with 6,631 annuity contracts "had not been completed, and only partial information concerning them could be given" at the conference. Publication of the conference report was delayed, allowing Huggins time to address the findings: "The information gained from the completed studies makes the paper of far greater value."[118]

Huggins compared the gift annuitants' data with male and female life expectancies in seven mortality tables constructed from data on annuitant and insured lives provided by life insurance companies. He found that among the gift annuitants, overall deaths were "running lighter than expected," and the average residuum for two lives was lower than expected, primarily because of the "too liberal annuity rates."

This wide-ranging comparative survey of gift-annuitant-mortality experience as of 1934 allowed Huggins to articulate many actuarial principles that are fundamental to rate setting: payments contingent upon an expected average life, distribution of longevity risk among larger groups of annuitant lives, healthy lifestyles and economics of typical gift annuitants, self-selection favoring longer-lived annuitants, longer average female lives compared to those of males, and the important distinction between average life expectancy and the "distribution of death in a given group." The timing of deaths over a range of years has a direct financial impact on the charitable residuum.

For his rates calculations, Huggins selected the Combined Annuity Table of Mortality, which had a built-in setback of four years for female lives. Huggins adjusted downward "at the younger and the older ages" to provide additional safety in the payment rates, and he recommended lower rates for two-life gift annuity contracts. Conference participants adopted his recommendations.

On September 1, 1939, Adolph Hitler unleashed a blitzkrieg that ignited World War II. When the **sixth COA**[119] **met on October 4–5, 1939,** Americans knew that fundamental economic changes were likely, but no one was certain of the size or shape of the changes to come. Few could imagine the horrors of the next six years. Wilton A. Pierce of the Chase Bank Investment Service captured the general mood:

> All of you must be conscious of the very great change that has come about in recent weeks because of the belligerency abroad. You probably will agree that the frightfulness of it all will have a very definite effect upon not only our psychology, but very definitely upon our economy.

This sixth conference, convened nearly five years after the fifth, was the first to meet for two days, demonstrating an ambitious expansion of the COA's objectives.

On top of all the domestic changes affecting gift annuity programs, events in Europe began to create massive uncertainties for nonprofit leaders, millions of clients who depended on philanthropic services, and potential donors. World War II began one month before the conference with Hitler's invasion of Poland on September 1, 1939. Would the United States follow England and France into war? Would war bring inflation and a rise in interest rates, as had happened in previous wars?

Complicating the task of conference planners, average annuitant lives continued to grow longer. Investment returns had deteriorated during ten years of economic depression. The federal and many state governments had enacted legislation or issued rulings affecting gift annuities. Everyone in the business of issuing life annuities was under enormous pressure from constantly increasing American longevity and from the steady decline in interest rates, which had fallen to unprecedented depths.

The committee decided that the conference must focus on the CGA's core objectives. They invited Charles C. Dubuar, principal actuary for the New York State Insurance Department, to discuss the state's new gift annuity law. Gilbert Darlington, chairman of the COA, reviewed the legislative landscape. Several speakers addressed the economic situation and provided investment advice for gift annuity fund managers.

Presentations by three actuaries had helped participants at the third conference in 1930 understand the importance of George Huggins's system of best practices. The sixth conference featured an explanation of New York's newly enacted legal framework for investing gift annuity reserve funds, as well as two investment presentations.

New York State had imposed wide-ranging and important new restrictions on gift annuities issued by nonprofit organizations. The COA played a role in drafting the gift annuity provisions of the state's insurance law,[120] formally assisted nonprofits in compliance with the law, and modified the committee's general policies to conform with New York.

Confronted with adverse mortality and investment-return experience, New York State had enacted a complete rewrite of its insurance law. Until 1939, whether the investment of gift annuity reserves was subject to the same restrictions as life insurance reserves was an open question. Now, for nonprofits offering gift annuities in New York, it was the law.

Charles Dubuar elaborated on the four principal requirements for nonprofits issuing gift annuity contracts: "Adequacy of reserves; the rates shall be noncompetitive with those of life companies; the funds shall be segregated; and the investments shall be made in eligible securities."[121]

Dubuar described some of the specific investment restrictions mandated by the new law:

Annuity funds must be invested generally in the type of securities permitted domestic [i.e., New York–based] life companies...U.S. Government bonds, the bonds of any state or the municipality of any state, corporate bonds... preferred stocks...mortgage loans...and real estate used solely for home office purposes...The law does not allow a domestic life company to purchase common stocks.

He noted that nonprofit organizations had grace periods to bring their reserve funds into compliance with the law, recognizing that immediate divestment of common stocks would force the recognition of severe capital losses because of the stock market crash. Fund managers "will not be required to disturb their present investment portfolio during the next ten years." By the next conference in 1941, New York would come to regret this policy.

Somewhat counterintuitively, Wilton Pierce asserted that New York's investment restrictions for gift annuity reserve funds permitted "greater latitude" in asset allocation because nonprofits could now invest their annuity reserves in corporate bonds that were not secured by physical assets and in preferred stock.[122]

While gift annuity fund managers could choose among new classes of permitted assets, they searched in vain for adequate yields. Richard P. Cromwell, president of an investment firm in Boston, summed up the alarming fall in available interest rates: "It is a well-recognized fact that investment yields have been declining for several years. Bond yields reached a new all-time low this summer, and…yields are still so low, that a few years ago they would have been considered fantastic."

Cromwell noted that the federal government was encouraging banks to buy bonds for their own accounts and crediting government bonds held by banks as if they were gold, thus increasing excess reserves, and that the Federal Reserve was making loans that normally would have been made by banks, a policy that had "discouraged private enterprise." While events may occur to raise interest rates, he saw no reason for optimism: "It can only be said that most of the factors now operative are tending to maintain interest rates at low levels, and that these factors are likely to dominate the trend for some time."

Kenneth W. Moore from the Presbyterian Board of Missions discussed the question of the earnings assumption for rate calculations: "One might say 3 percent is safe today as a base in the annuity field. Others might say lower." He was not encouraging toward new gift annuity programs:

> I am frank to say, annuities do not look as attractive [to nonprofits] a business today as they did not so long ago. The low yield on and shrinkage of investment, the increased competition, the dissolution of large estates, lower incomes, increasing and uncertain taxation, this year in particular war conditions, and the uncertainty of the future, the fluctuating value and purchasing power of the dollar, and international confusion are not favorable at present.

Moore argued in favor of a payment rate cap of 6 percent or even 5 percent:

> A 5 percent or 6 percent rate, practically guaranteed, is a wise investment [for a donor] today, over against the low yields of 3 percent and less, with such terrible losses in principal. I would say, therefore, that the [annuity payment] rate is **our most serious problem which must be considered in this year of crisis.** (emphasis added)

Gilbert Darlington acknowledged that George Huggins had recommended lower annuity rates, but the 1939 conference deferred action "in view of the uncertainty of future interest rates due to war conditions." In this case, Huggins proved to be right.

In his report titled "Rates for Annuity Agreements," George Huggins discussed in detail the requirements of the New York Insurance Law for gift annuity programs, recent annuitant-mortality experience ("There has been continually increasing longevity among annuitant lives"), and the case for more cautious earnings assumptions:

During the few years which have elapsed since our last conference, there have been radical changes taking place in our economic life, and these have an important bearing on our consideration of annuity rates. The most far-reaching problem is due to the continually lowering rate of return on investments…we are confronted by the fact that interest rates at the present time are far lower than they were five (5) years ago.

While recognizing the need to make gift annuities attractive to donors ("There is undoubtedly a minimum point of annuity rate below which it would be difficult to obtain new gifts"), Huggins recommended a conservative new table of lower rates and a payment cap of 7 percent.

Conference participants were reluctant to adopt such low rates, so they deferred action until the impact of the war became clearer. Darlington summed up the conference findings:

While careful consideration was given to the annuity rates prepared by Mr. George A. Huggins, in view of the uncertainty of future interest rates due to war conditions…it was *Resolved*, That the Committee on Annuities be requested to publish in booklet form the papers read at the this Conferences by the several speakers; and also the proceedings of the Conference, including their decision to defer action on the matter of annuity rates.

By the time of the **seventh conference (April 29, 1941),**[123] war was raging in Europe and Asia, though US combat troops would not enter the fight until Japan bombed the naval base at Pearl Harbor on December 7. The agenda that April was shorter than that of the sixth conference and was contained within a single day.

For gift annuity fund managers, the investment outlook had become desperate. Gilbert Darlington noted that participants at the 1939 COA had deferred action on lowering rates: "There were

245

some present who felt that interest rates might rise substantially as the war progressed," but "experience has shown that modern governments have much stronger control over interest rates than was possible during and after the first World War."[124]

The two main goals of the conference were:

1. "To consider the question of adopting a lower standard of uniform annuity rates" because "interest rates on all classes of securities have declined very substantially."
2. To comply with New York's new requirements for a surplus of 25 percent to be added to the minimum allowable gift annuity reserves, recently enacted as an amendment to its insurance law.

Dr. Marcus Nadler from the Graduate School of Business Administration at New York University spoke on "Rates of Yield on Invested Funds Under Existing Conditions, and the Probabilities as to the Future." Like Darlington, he reminded conference participants of many people's mistaken expectations when war broke out in Europe in 1939. Many had thought the following:

The period of low-money rates had come to an end, and that money rates would go up…Later events, however, proved that they were wrong. It is, therefore, of importance to analyze what the chances are that money rates will go up. The cost of money and the present supply of and demand for money should be analyzed without any wishful thinking.

Nadler believed that the wartime experience of Great Britain in controlling national interest rates was instructive for Americans:

If Great Britain, with a public debt larger than the national income, can maintain low-money rates, then it is quite

246

obvious that the United States Government can do it too…In conclusion, I see no material change in the money market. To be sure, bonds will fluctuate, depending upon news from abroad and political developments here; but if you analyze the demand and supply factors, the power of the government over the money market, and the rate of interest on savings deposits, you must inevitably reach the conclusion that money rates will remain low.

Based on Nadler's presentation and Darlington's findings that current CGA rates were dangerously close to the maximums allowable under New York law, conference participants approved the reduced-rate table calculated by Huggins in 1939.

Charles C. Dubuar returned to the conference for a progress report on compliance with New York's law after its first two years. He was generally very pleased with the self-regulation evidenced by the conferences on annuities but took issue with nonprofit investment practices for gift annuity reserves. While he acknowledged the ten-year grace period granted to nonprofits under the 1939 Insurance Law, he expressed the Insurance Department's disapproval that the reserve funds of some organizations were much more heavily invested in common stocks than the law allowed:

A substantial portion of the reserves held for the protection of annuitants is being supported only by speculative securities. The Department desires to inject a word of caution against following such a practice. From the viewpoint of annuitants, the only fair and conscientious policy for a contracting annuity corporation is to place its funds so that there will be a minimum of risk to its annuitants.

Dubuar cautioned against nonprofits taking advantage of the ten-year grace period to add new stocks to their reserve fund portfolios:

Section 45 permits an annuity corporation domiciled in New York to hold ineligible investments, such as common stocks, until January 1, 1950 before being required to dispose of them. However, the law does not permit a domestic corporation to make new purchases of ineligible investments; and if this is being done, it should be discontinued by any domestic corporation.

He encouraged nonprofit gift annuity fund managers in other states to comply with investment laws governing commercial life insurance: "In the case of corporations located in other states, investments may be made in accordance with the laws of such other states regulating life insurance companies."

Huggins gave a brief two-part report, beginning with "Rate of Mortality among Gift-Annuitants Lives" and concluding with his rate recommendations. He described several recent gift-annuitant mortality studies. One was by a single unnamed nonprofit (possibly ABS) whose actual residuum following annuitant deaths in the fiscal year 1939–40 was just 80.5 percent of the expected value, and just 81.9 percent over the previous five years, attributed to low mortality rates.

The second mortality study was conducted by "three major boards of a denominational body," also unnamed. Huggins commented that their results were "somewhat more favorable," though the number of actual deaths was less than expected. Taken together, these nonprofit gift-annuitant studies were not adequate to stand on their own:

In our gift-annuity mortality studies, we do not have sufficient experience to develop our own tables of mortality. Therefore, we have to take as our yardsticks standard tables of mortality among annuitant lives, and to measure our actual experience from year to year, and cumulatively, against the yardstick, and then to modify the standard tables to conform as nearly as possible to our own experience as a basis for calculating rates and setting up and maintaining reserves.

Part B of Huggins's report was entitled "Rates for Gift-Annuity Agreements," in which he resubmitted the conservative rates recommendations he had presented in 1939, summarized in his presentation:

> The basis of these rates has already been outlined; i.e., the Combined Annuity Mortality Table with interest at 3½ percent, with ages set back two years on the female life basis, and calculated in accordance with a formula designed to produce an average residuum of 70 percent of the amount of the original gift, with the scaling down of the rates below age 55 until they reach 2½ percent at age 35, and letting that rate apply at any lower ages. At the higher-age bracket, the rate is held at 7 percent from 80 and upwards.

> The rates now submitted are on the basis of lower mortality and lower interest rates, both of which are in accordance with the trends which have developed so acutely since the present uniform rates were adopted [in 1934].

Participants at the 1941 conference adopted his recommended assumptions and annuity payment rates.

The Postwar Era: Golden Age of American Capitalism (1946–59)

As in the prewar conferences in 1939 and 1941, when uncertainty reigned, it was not at all clear in the months following the end of World War II how economic conditions would change in the United States, as more than seven million veterans returned from duty overseas. How effectively would America's industries make the transition to peacetime production? After twenty-five years of tight monetary controls, would the Federal Reserve allow open markets to set interest rates? And if so, would there be wage and price inflation, as had happened after previous wars?

The economic historian Robert J. Gordon recently analyzed the post–World War II "Great Leap Forward." The war created pent-up demand for consumer goods, encouraged savings, and broadened higher education through the GI Bill. On the supply side, there was "a vast expansion of the nation's capital stock," as the government paid for weapons factories that were converted after the war to civilian production and invested in infrastructure, such as interstate highways, dams, and bridges:

> To the surprise of many economists, after the stimulus of wartime spending was removed swiftly in 1945–47, the economy did not collapse. Some mysterious elixir had converted the production achievements of the Arsenal of Democracy into a postwar cornucopia of houses, automobiles, and appliances.[125]

Gordon finds that productivity growth rose much faster from 1941 to 1972 than in the years from 1890 to 1940: "By 1941, productivity was 11 percent above trend, then reached 32 percent above trend by 1957 and 44 percent above trend in 1972," a "productivity growth miracle."[126]

The narrative of the gift annuity conferences held in 1946, 1955, and 1959 changed from managing scarcity during a severe economic depression to managing the fruits of exceptional economic growth.

The green shoots of America's economic miracle had barely begun to sprout in the spring of 1946. Dr. Marcus Nadler's predictions at the 1941 conference about the direction of interest rates proved to be exactly right: when the **eighth conference**[127] **opened on April 10, 1946,** rates in the United States had never been lower. Gilbert Darlington observed that "interest rates have declined substantially since 1941, when the present uniform rates were adopted. This is true of interest on real estate mortgages, as well as on bonds, and preferred and common stocks."[128]

Darlington provided an overview of the Committee on Gift Annuities's return assumption for rate setting, which had been 3.5 percent since 1941. By 1946, most US life insurance companies had adopted a 2 percent return assumption. Beginning in 1942, the US Treasury required new gift annuities to be valued for tax purposes using a 2.5 percent return. New York State had even told several nonprofits to use a more conservative return to value their gift annuity reserves than the 3.5 percent required under its own law.

Rays of hope began to shine. Professor B. H. Beckhart of Columbia University provided an insightful analysis of the history of interest rates in the United States, predicting that the Federal Reserve would soon relax its long control of interest rates and allow fixed-income yields to be controlled by "competitive forces of the market." He foresaw that the rates on government and corporate bonds would begin to rise.[129]

Two weeks after the conference (on April 25, 1946), the Fed did begin pulling back. Dr. Beckhart added a brief update to the printed conference report with breaking news:

> The Federal Reserve System has taken the first step towards the ultimate goal of allowing the yields on Government obligations to be determined by the competitive forces of the market. Once these rates are determined by competitive forces of the market, all rates will similarly be determined. **The fact that the first step towards this ultimate goal has been taken would seem to indicate that the turning point in the bond market has occurred.** (emphasis added)

Whether or not donors were feeling renewed confidence in future earnings, a speaker on marketing testified that new gift annuities could be realized if a nonprofit were willing to invest in the effort:

> One institution which has been unusually successful in stimulating an interest in annuities has six salaried men on its payroll who spend every day making calls in geographical areas assigned to them. They are required to make a specified number of calls each day and to report every night in writing to the institutions headquarters how many calls they have made and what financial results have been achieved. Manifestly, such a salaried list of workers is not possible for many organizations, but that institution is on the right track.[130]

Positive signs for the economy and the prospect of higher interest rates in the future competed with the brutal facts of recent history. A case could be made for staying the course with then-current gift annuity rates, hoping that conditions would improve.

George Huggins had a more conservative view. He pointed out that nonprofits had been losing more money than expected from their annuity reserve funds, and that their return assumptions were out of step with the life insurance industry, which had adopted lower return assumptions in the face of greater annuitant longevity: "The life insurance companies which issue annuities have had to abandon mortality table after mortality table as their experience showed lowering mortality among their annuitant lives; i.e., further lengthening of annuitant lives as a group."[131]

As he did so well, Huggins cited the history of mortality data to bolster his case:

> In recent years there have been material increases in the longevity of our population. For example, the Metropolitan Life Insurance Company announces that among its industrial policyholders [i.e., group employee plans] life expectancy from birth in 1942 was 64.18 years with a slight recession

later. This compares with 63.56 in 1943; 51.64 in 1919–20; 46.63 in 1911–12; and 34.00 for the period 1879–89.

Not only had trends in annuitant mortality moved against nonprofits but investment earnings also had. Huggins reviewed the history of his return assumptions. In 1927, he had created the first national rate table based on a 4.5 percent return. That was reduced to 4 percent at the fifth COA in 1934, and had dropped steadily ever since:

> The assumed interest rate later had to be dropped to 3½%, then 3% and then 2½%, and today many commercial insurance company annuities are being offered on a 2% interest rate. Almost all of the non-profit agencies, however, are still using the 1941 rate based upon an assumed yield of 3½%.

Huggins encouraged nonprofits to accommodate to the reality of low returns:

> Taking all factors into consideration and in the interest of conservatism, we have used the rate of 2½% in our calculations of proposed annuity rates. This is only adopting the standard already accepted by life insurance companies for some years, but not adopting the lower current rate of 2% that is now largely in force.

High payment rates and greater longevity were clear and present dangers for nonprofits issuing annuities. The logical conclusion drawn from these negative conditions was for nonprofits and their future annuitants to accept drastic changes in rate-setting assumptions.

Huggins's most stunning recommendation was that nonprofits should lower their expectations for the charitable residuum target:

> A very important consideration confronting us is to what extent the organization should be the gainer by the gift. In

other words, how much of the total gift should be absorbed in the annuity payments and how much should go for the benefit and purposes of the organization…**In the rates proposed, it is our thought that the organizations should share some of the losses under these adverse conditions that have developed.** We are, therefore, proposing a set of rates with a **50% residuum as contrasted with the 70% residuum** which has been the basis of our rates to date. (emphasis added)

Huggins proposed very complex changes in America's rate-setting assumptions. These included lowering to a 2.5 percent return from its current 3.5 percent, the new 50 percent residuum target, and a brand-new factor: "an expense loading equivalent to 5 per cent of the total gift" for marketing and administration. All these changes and the proposed rate table were duly approved by the committee on resolutions that morning for consideration by the conference in the afternoon.

There is no record of the debate over these radical changes. Were the effects of the very conservative proposals too complicated for conference participants to sort out, given the relatively brief amount of time available to absorb and analyze them? Did people share Dr. Beckhart's optimistic vision of a turning point in investment returns?

The conference report makes clear only that there was resistance. An alternative motion was proposed: "In order to test the general sentiment of the Conference, it was moved and seconded: Resolved, that the Conference recommends that no change of rates be made at this time but that the whole matter of rates be referred back to the Committee on Annuities for further study."

Voting as individuals, not as representatives of their organizations, conference participants decided 23–19 *not* to make any changes in the rates that had been adopted in 1941 but to ask the CGA to look carefully at the proposed changes and make a decision at the next conference.

LEADERS OF THE GIFT ANNUITY MOVEMENT DECLARE INDEPENDENCE

Participants at the eighth COA in 1946 could not know that in 1950, the sponsor of the Committee on Annuities would no longer exist, that the committee would restructure itself as an independent, unincorporated association, and that a ninth Conference on Annuities would not convene until 1955.

When the National Council of Churches of Christ succeeded the Federal Council late in 1950, the committee "had no official status" with the National Council for nearly a year. On October 2, 1951, its Joint Department of Stewardship and Benevolence approved a resolution: "That the previously constituted Committee on Annuities of the Federal Council of Churches be continued as a separate committee under the Division of Christian Life and Work of the National Council of Churches, U.S.A."[132]

The NCCCA recognized that the work of the CGA was professional and nonsectarian in nature, "largely in the field of technical and expert counselling on actuarial problems, taxation, legislation, annuity rates, interest rates, terminology and the like."[133] However, friction soon arose in several areas. A professional, technical committee on gift annuities fit uneasily under the umbrella of the National Council's evangelical-education program. The council imposed a bureaucratic approval process for any CGA contact with federal and state officials. Most importantly, minutes of the CGA show considerable frustration that the council took in all income from the conferences and sales of publications but did not provide a budget to fund expenses.[134] As a result, no gift annuity conferences were held after 1946 until the committee declared its independence and provided its first freestanding conference in 1955.

During the years when the committee could not act freely, Gilbert Darlington and George Huggins were invited to speak on behalf of the CGA at a large **Conference on Wills, Annuities,**

and Special Gifts organized by the council on December 15–16, 1952. This conference was attended by 387 people. Huggins presented a detailed analysis of a national gift annuity mortality study, and Darlington gave a masterful overview of "Taxation, Legislation, and Regulation."[135]

Prior to the conference, Huggins invited fifteen nonprofit organizations issuing gift annuities to complete a survey on their mortality experience. He proudly reported using cutting-edge technology to compile the results: "From the lists submitted, an IBM punch card was prepared for each life included in the studies and therefore, the summarizing of the data was accomplished through IBM machine procedure."[136]

A total of 26,718.5 life years were reported.[137] Male annuitants were dying pretty much as expected, but females were living much longer than projected when the then-current CGA rate table was developed in 1934: "The ratio of the 905 actual deaths to those expected on this basis is 80.13% which indicates that there was approximately a 20% mortality deficiency in the mortality experience among the female gift annuitant lives."

Recall that Huggins had proposed new rate tables at the 1939 COA, which deferred action because of the war. The new rates were adopted in 1941. He proposed several conservative changes to the tables in 1946, but action was deferred to the next conference, which was not held until 1955.

Huggins found that organizations could adjust to increased longevity by using his recommended rates: "The 1946 recommendations would seem to have been confirmed by the experience of the five-year period under consideration." He did calculate new rate tables to illustrate what the rates would be based on current gift-annuitant mortality experiences, an expense load of 5 percent, and investment assumptions of 2.5 percent and 3 percent in place of the 3.5 percent that had been the policy of the CGA since 1941.

Data for the American Bible Society was reported separately from the national survey. The ABS residuum was running lower than expected: "Namely, a 74.8% ratio of the actual to expected reserves released by death," which "confirms dramatically…that the actual mortality experience is at a lower rate" than assumed in the outdated CGA rate tables.

Participants at this conference in 1952 had no power to act on CGA rates and were not asked to do so. Huggins's highest investment assumption for his sample illustrations remained a conservative 3 percent. There was no investment presentation at the 1952 conference, and Darlington did not suggest a higher-return assumption, but he noted that in recent years, "interest rates have risen substantially" and "the yield on highest grade bonds and preferred stocks has also risen," just as Dr. Beckhart had predicted at the 1946 COA.

Darlington summarized a cautious easing of the investment restrictions mandated by New York, "the largest state in population and wealth," which had begun to allow a very small portion of gift annuity reserves to be invested in common stocks:

Section 81 of the Insurance Law of New York State permits a very small investment in common stocks, except in the common stock of an insurance company or a national or state bank or trust company, provided cash dividends have been paid for a period of 10 years preceding the investment and the companies have earned 4% per annum on their common shares outstanding during such period and also provided the stocks are registered on some National Securities Exchange. However, the amount that can be so invested is limited to 3% of the total admitted assets or one-third of the surplus of the company that has made the investment, whichever is smaller. Some legal opinions indicate that if the surplus exceeds the 10% required by law, that this excess surplus over the legal requirements may also be invested in common stocks. This, however, is only a legal opinion.[138]

Relations between the CGA and the National Council of Churches continued to deteriorate. The last straw was a directive to restrict membership on the Committee to people representing Protestant religious organizations affiliated with the council. In November 1952, the CGA approved the following motion: "We do not believe that the former Committee on Annuities of the Federal Council is best located within the framework of the Joint Department of Stewardship and Benevolence."[139]

The Committee on Gift Annuities began to operate independently in 1953. Members of the committee composed a constitution and bylaws, which participants at the ninth COA approved in October 1955. The CGA became an independent, unincorporated nonprofit organization, making clear that it "shall in no way be a legal agent for any Sponsors of the Committee."[140] While remaining in close contact with the Council of Churches, the CGA was no longer restricted to Protestant church-affiliated organizations; its new constitution specifically empowered the board of the new CGA "to draw its members from other groups who are not members of the National Council." Its governing body expanded to a maximum of twenty-five members. All the founding board members were from church-related organizations, except for Dr. Theodore A. Distler, executive director of the Association of American Colleges.[141]

To help fund its activities, the CGA began asking for gifts in 1955. Organizations attending the conferences made ten-dollar contributions and were considered to be sponsors. The ninth COA approved a resolution that "the Committee on Gift Annuities be empowered to request regular contributions from the Sponsors of the Committee on Gift Annuities to cover the expenses of the on-going work of the Committee, the amount and term to be discretionary with the Committee."

Gift income was sorely needed, since the CGA ran on a shoestring. A treasurer's report dated February 7, 1956, showed income from "registrations and other fees" of $2,471 and expenses of $2,305.38, resulting in a cash balance of $165.62.

Freed from any religious denomination, the ninth COA expanded its secular representation to include nonprofits such as the ASPCA. Staff from colleges and universities such as Dartmouth, Pittsburgh, Pomona, and Vassar attended. Representatives from consulting organizations such as the American Association of Fund-Raising Counsel (AAFRC), the Howell Advertising Agency, and the John Price Jones Company participated, as well as the Teachers Insurance and Annuity Association (TIAA).

Attendance at the gift annuity conferences expanded from 62 people in 1946 to 126 in 1955 and 198 in 1959. At the twelfth conference in 1965, the committee chairman celebrated the fact that attendance had more than doubled to 418, representing 303 nonprofit organizations.[142]

The core functions of CGA continued virtually unchanged, but its economic and political contexts were very different indeed. The conference agendas in 1955 and 1959 each stretched over two days to give a larger number of nonprofit leaders the knowledge needed to take advantage of opportunities in gift planning during an era of rapid American economic growth.

FROM BUST TO BOOM

Happier days returned for the American economy, as reported at the **ninth conference**[143] **held on October 3–4, 1955**. Gilbert Darlington opened the conference by reciting welcome facts about the trends in yields:

> It is over nine years since the Eighth Conference met…Since then there has been an almost steady rise in the interest earned on invested funds by the life insurance companies

of the United States—from 2.88 percent in 1947 to 3.24 percent after taxes in 1954. The long decline in interest rates from the 1920's terminated in 1947. For the life insurance companies this meant a drop from 5.8 percent in 1923 to 2.88 percent in 1947.

These years saw "the greatest of all secular bear bond markets"[144] in which the yield index rose to record heights. Dr. Marcus Nadler reported on a very different economic environment in 1955 than during his conference appearance in 1946:

> Right now we are in the midst of the greatest boom that we have ever had in peace time in our history. To prove my point, employment is over 65½ million people. The total number of unemployed is less than 2½ million.[145] The demand for credit is very great. Building activity is at a high level. The demand for mortgages is very great. Business activity is in the midst of a boom.[146]

Nadler remarked on the high animal spirits among American investors and consumers:

> A wave of optimism has swept the country from one end to another. This wave of confidence (one may call it overconfidence) is based on the belief that nothing can happen to the country…This wave of confidence has had an impact on the saving, spending and investing habits of the people. People save less and spend more. People today are less interested in putting money in a savings bank than they are in buying equities.

In expressing concern that consumer borrowing for nonessential items must eventually swing back to more responsible levels, Nadler's remarks in 1955 resembled Alan Greenspan's warning about "irrational exuberance" during the dot-com bubble in the 1990s:

Private indebtedness has increased at a rate which, in my opinion, cannot be maintained...People apparently today are willing to mortgage their future in order to meet any desire or even yen...they are also willing to take a trip somewhere on the installment plan and borrow money from the bank to pay the hotel bill. Now, that cannot go on indefinitely.

Nonprofit fund managers jumped into equity markets. For example, 45 percent of Harvard University's endowment was invested in common stocks in 1951, compared with just 8 percent in 1900.[147]

The CGA conducted a national survey just prior to the ninth COA. Charles Baas, assistant treasurer for the ABS, asked people registering for the conference to respond to a series of questions regarding their organization's investment returns, asset allocation, and levels of gift annuity reserve funds. Forty-three responded. Among the findings:

- The average investment return was 4.3 percent on combined asset values of $40 million. Baas does not give the time period; possibly, this was for the twelve months prior to the conference.
- Gift annuity reserve fund balances averaged 90.4 percent of the amount originally transferred.

Baas observed that smaller institutions frequently restricted their investments to long-term government bonds. He encouraged them to hold more assets in "eligible securities of higher income-producing character, such as preferred stocks and mortgages" so that annuity payments were assured and that "the generous gift donated when the contribution was made will be available for use in the work of the institution."

Reserve fund asset allocations among the forty-three nonprofits were as follows:

Asset Values Combined

Asset	Percent (%)
Bonds	44.2
Preferred [stock]	15.3
Common [stock]	28.4
Mortgages	10.2
Others	1.9
	100

The changing economic landscape and investment conditions for gift annuity reserve funds can be illustrated by comparing the asset allocation recommended by William Boult in 1930, the actual allocations reported in the 1955 survey, and the model portfolio assumed in 2017 for the ACGA Rates Report[148]:

Asset Allocations for Gift Annuity Reserves

Asset Class	1930 Conference	1955 Survey	2017 ACGA
Fixed Income	**65.0%**	**44.2%**	**55.0%**
Government bonds	10.0%	0.0%	0.0%
Railroad bonds	25.0%	0.0%	0.0%
Public utility bonds	25.0%	0.0%	0.0%
Industrial bonds	5.0%	0.0%	0.0%
Bonds (unspecified)	0.0%	44.2%	0.0%
10-year treasury bonds	0.0%	0.0%	55.0%
Real Estate Mortgages	**30.0%**	**10.2%**	**0.0%**
Stocks	**5.0%**	**43.7%**	**40.0%**
Preferred stocks	5.0%	15.3%	0.0%
Common stocks	0.0%	28.4%	0.0%
Equities (unspecified)	0.0%	0.0%	40.0%
Other	**0.0%**	**1.9%**	**0.0%**
Cash and equivalents	**0.0%**	**0.0%**	**5.0%**

In 1955, a live question for gift annuity managers battered by the Depression and World War II was this: How long would the good times last? Mindful of how badly nonprofit organizations and their donors had suffered in previous decades, and recognizing that many participants had not attended the previous conference in 1946, George Huggins spoke on the "live and changeable subject" of "mortality among annuitant lives" in what was his longest, most wide-ranging in its references, and most philosophical, presentation. It included seven charts, plus two pages of recommended rates.

Huggins surveyed the major changes in rates recommendations since 1927, when the best available mortality table was that by Emory McClintock. Compelled by data showing "the steady lengthening of life among annuitants," actuaries prepared new annuitant-mortality tables. Huggins reported that he had changed the mortality table used as a "yardstick" for his rate calculations in 1931, 1934, and 1952.

To provide perspective on scientific discoveries in mortality experience, Huggins pointed out that the earliest estimates of the value of annuities were reported by Ulpian in ancient Rome. A more accurate mortality table was produced by the mathematician and astronomer Edmund Halley in 1693. Improvements were introduced by Richard Price's Northampton Table in 1785, which was used by many British life insurance companies.

Huggins showed conference participants a table comparing the value of one dollar for an annuity using the Northampton Table of 1785 with "our current mortality experience under gift annuities" using the Standard Annuity Table. The value of an annuity contract for an annuitant aged eighty in 1955 was 91.85 percent greater than it had been in 1785. Huggins observed that "this is one increase in cost that is not due to the increase in the cost of living [i.e., inflation] but to the increase in the periods of living."

Huggins then summarized the major national gift-annuitant-mortality studies conducted for the 1952 conference, which had been updated by the Bible Society through December 31, 1954. The results showed that the Standard Annuity Table, with calculations based on female lives and ages set back one year, was a reliable, conservative yardstick.

He then constructed an extremely complex schedule comparing current gift annuity rate recommendations at various ages with what the rates would be if calculated using investment assumptions of 2.5 percent, 3 percent, and 3.5 percent; with rates calculated under two additional mortality tables known as a-1949 and the Group Annuity 1951 Table; with maximum annuity rates allowable by the State of New York; and with "specimen annuity rates in use by a group of life insurance companies."

Taking all this data into account, Huggins presented his new gift annuity rate proposals for one and two lives. At the previous COA in 1946, he had recommended conservative changes in rate-setting assumptions, but the conference deferred making any changes because of the uncertain postwar economy. In 1955, he modified some of his assumptions: he kept the residuum target of 50 percent and a 5 percent expense load but assumed an investment return of 3 percent (vs. 2.5 percent in 1946), increased the payment rates slightly for annuitants age seventy-three and older, and raised the maximum-rate cap for single lives aged eighty and older from 7 percent to 7.4 percent.

The conference adopted Huggins's recommendations, with one change: participants voted to extend the rates for annuitants up to ninety years of age. This had no impact for single-life contracts, which were capped at a maximum rate of 7.4 percent, beginning at age eighty. Two-life rates between eighty and ninety years of age were a bit higher than Huggins had recommended, though the top rate for two ninety-year-olds was 7.2 percent.

The **tenth Conference on Gift Annuities**[149] **was held on December 1–2, 1959**. This was the second conference designed by an independent Committee on Gift Annuities. It was the first after a constitution and bylaws were approved in 1955, and it was the first in which nonprofit organizations became financial sponsors of the committee.

Many new leaders appeared as the governing body expanded to twenty-two members. In a rare personal address to the tenth conference, George Huggins graciously "expressed his great satisfaction in the strength of the Committee on Gift Annuities and in its dynamic leadership." He predicted that "he would probably not be present at the Conference four years hence," and, in fact, he died of a heart attack within a month. Gilbert Darlington had suffered a heart attack in December 1958 and had stepped down as chairman of the CGA, though he continued to serve as a volunteer for another two decades.

Darlington was succeeded by his colleague Charles Baas of the American Bible Society. Sydney Prerau, who later hired Conrad Teitell as his partner, made his first COA presentation. The conference featured an enthusiastic presentation on charitable-remainder trusts by Dr. Roland Mathies of Wittenberg University and the final actuarial report by Huggins.

At the previous conference in 1955, the combined face value of gift annuity accounts among conference participants was reported to be $40 million. In 1959, participants reported having "at least a total of 59,030 annuity agreements outstanding with an original principal value of $84,865,155."

Charles Baas opened the 1959 conference by welcoming recent increases in interest rates:

At the 1955 Conference the current net rate of interest earned on invested funds by U.S. Life Insurance companies, before Federal income taxes, was reported as 3.46 percent. This rate has risen to 3.85 percent in 1958 and no doubt will be even higher when 1959 figures are available. The rate of income earned on invested gift annuity funds is, of course, an important factor in determining gift annuity rates.

Baas reported that fear of inflation was leading some donors to favor receiving variable payments from life-income trusts (an early form of charitable remainder trusts) over fixed payments from gift annuities:

> Emphasis on the future possibility of inflation have [*sic*] placed doubts in the minds of many prospective donors as to the wisdom of making investments guaranteeing fixed annual return. These doubts plus favorable Internal Revenue treatment of capital gains resulting from the transfer of appreciated property in exchange for various agreements offering fluctuating life income,[150] has lead [*sic*] many of the organizations represented here today to embark on some sort of life income program.

Sixty nonprofits responded to a preconference questionnaire that, among other things, asked about issuing life-income trusts. Roland Mathies reported that at least thirty-four of the sixty organizations encouraged these trusts, and that nearly all of those thirty-four offered tax-free payments to beneficiaries by investing trusts in tax-exempt bonds. He felt that more donors and nonprofits could benefit from life-income trusts: "It is practically impossible to find a life income arrangement that cannot be worked, if you have an agreeable donor and if you have competent advice…it is the simplest method of obtaining a gift and returning the income."

As a result of the increasing popularity of life-income agreements, in 1961, the CGA voted to expand the reach of its mission, approving a motion "that the responsibility of the Committee on Gift Annuities be broadened so that it takes a similar interest in the field of life income agreements as it does on gift annuities."[151] Future COA agendas would often include presentations on charitable-remainder trusts and pooled-income funds. For example, the agenda for twelfth conference in 1965 included four presentations on life-income agreements and trusts. Participants received a life-income manual: "This is a first-class document that not only provides the tools for computing the Federal Tax implications for Life Income Agreements but has suggestions for administering Life Income Agreement Plans, including an approved form of Agreement."[152]

There was no need to develop a national process for rate setting or best practices for CRTs as there had been for CGAs, so gift annuities continue to be the major focus for ACGA research and conference presentations.[153]

While the improving economy encouraged gifts through charitable-remainder trusts, donors continued to make gifts through annuity contracts. In his conference presentation, George Huggins noted a strong continuing interest in gift annuities:

> As you are well aware, gifts subject to annuity agreements are playing an increasingly important role in philanthropic giving. They are more and more sought by individuals who are willing to make gifts for the benefit of the causes in which they are interested but who need some income during their future lifetime and in some cases during the lifetime of a designated beneficiary.

Dr. John W. Harriman surveyed the economy, stock market, and interest rates for the tenth conference. Harriman was an economist with Tri-Continental Corporation, professor of finance with the Graduate School of Business Administration at NYU, and a member of the Finance Committee for ABS. During this time of the Cold War with the Soviet Union, he injected the first note of anticommunism in the conference reports: "Sound direction of capital promotes the development of the economy and strengthens the private enterprise system within the Free World. This is my sermon for today!"[154]

Harriman celebrated the recent strength of the American economy:

The postwar period has been one of marked economic progress...This expansion has brought increased profits and higher dividends and has been a major reason for the sustained rise in common stock prices. This expansion has also caused the demand for funds to press hard on the supply with the result that interest rates have increased steadily.

He projected continuing expansion in the "decade of the sixties":

The underlying forces of growth will operate to push the economy to successively higher levels. Five such forces can be distinguished: (1) increasing population [the "baby boom"], (2) higher personal income, (3) rising consumer expenditures, (4) research and development on a massive scale, and (5) heavy spending by business for plant and equipment.

Harriman recommended investing gift annuity reserve funds in common stocks:

Common stocks are favored as long-term investments by economic growth, increased cyclical stability and capacity to offset inflation. These qualities have made stocks the outstanding investment medium in the postwar period, a situation which has been increasingly recognized by the serious investors. Since 1952 the number of shareholders in American corporations has risen from 6.5 million to 12.5 million, the common stock holdings of N.A.I.C. member investment companies from $4.3 billion to an estimated $13 billion, those of educational and charitable institutions by substantial but unknown amounts.

Trends in interest rates are of great importance for annuity fund managers. Harriman predicted it was likely that higher rates would continue:

It is necessary...for those who are concerned with long-term contracts such as bonds, mortgages and annuities to have reasonably definite opinions on the future of interest rates. These opinions must be based on certain assumptions regarding general business conditions and the policies of Government agencies...As far as interest rates are concerned the outlook is definitely for a continuation of the present high level for the foreseeable future. In other words, barring a true depression or a drastic change in our money policy, high interest rates appear likely to continue for the decade of the sixties. To me this indicates that an annuity rate [i.e., investment assumption] of 3 per cent is unrealistically low and that 3.5 per cent would be a reasonable and logical figure.

George Huggins gave his tenth and final conference presentation in 1959, a masterful "Report of Actuary on Mortality Experience Studies." This was based on a new survey by CGA that included 32,684 lives and 129,075 life years of exposure among seventy-nine gift annuity programs from January 1, 1954, through December 31, 1958.[155] Huggins compared this new gift-annuitant-mortality experience with the survey results in 1952.

The results were disturbing. Huggins showed that while the 1952 mortality study reported a favorable margin of safety, the current study revealed that gift annuitants were living much longer:

The current study clearly shows that the basis of the present gift annuity rates rather than having a comfortable mortality margin of 5.78% now shows a deficit of 2.74%...The trend to lower mortality with correspondingly longer periods of life expectancy means longer periods of annuity payments with a resultant increase in the cost of the annuity program.

Continued use of the Standard Annuity Table (1937) would be possible, though offsetting the ages by two or even three years for accuracy would produce "distortions." Huggins found that a newer American Annuity Table (1955) would "conform more closely to the current mortality experience...with a reasonable over-all margin against the further lengthening of lives."

In an appendix, which was probably added to the written report after discussion at the conference, Huggins comments on the relative importance of trends moving in opposite directions: "very favorable" investment performance and the "adverse experience" of longer life expectancies. How much weight should be given to future investment assumptions?

Huggins produced a chart comparing the current rate recommendations based on recent mortality studies and a 3 percent return assumption with rates using a return of 3.25 percent and 3.5 percent, and with the maximum annuity rates allowable under the New York State Insurance Law. Taking all the factors into account, rates based on a return assumption greater than 3 percent might produce rates higher than the law permitted.

The conference approved Huggins's recommendation to make no changes in the rates adopted in 1955, despite the improved economic situation.

After serving for thirty-two years as consulting actuary for the Committee on Gift Annuities, George Augustus Huggins died on December 30, 1959.

COMPARISONS BETWEEN THE CONFERENCES IN 1927 AND 1959

A brief comparison of some aspects of the first Conference on Annuities held in 1927 with the tenth conference in 1959 shows how far the national system of gift annuities developed during George Huggins's lifetime.

1927 Conference (#1)	1959 Conference (#10)
Sponsored by Federal Council of Churches of Christ in America.	Independent Committee on Gift Annuities funded through conference fees and sponsor gifts.
Proposed a national system for rate setting and other best practices; 70% residuum target.	Incremental refinements included a 5% expense load, modified rates at older and younger ages, and a 50% residuum target.
Speakers included two ABS staff and Huggins. No presentation on economic conditions or investment projections for use in rate setting and reserve fund management.	NYU finance professor presented an independent economic report. Top actuary from New York State spoke on twenty years of gift annuity regulation. Independent consultant Sydney Prerau analyzed CGA taxation.
No national gift-annuitant data. McClintock Annuitant Mortality Table (1899) was the best available, though outdated.	Huggins conducted and compared surveys of gift annuity programs in 1952, 1955, and 1959 to adjust recent annuitant-mortality table.
Focus on gift annuities.	In-depth exploration of life-income trusts (CRTs).

The chart highlights changes. There were many continuities over these first ten conferences. Huggins presented an actuarial report at each. From the start, active debate over his rate-setting assumptions was expected and encouraged. Rev. Gilbert Darlington also presented at every one of the first ten conferences on gift annuity legislation, regulation, and taxation. Despite temporary resistance by the National Council of Churches, the national Committee on Gift Annuities was always free to work directly with federal and state officials.[156]

HOW GIFT ANNUITIES SHAPED AMERICAN PHILANTHROPY

Reforming the practices of American nonprofit organizations was neither easy nor simple, but the Committee on Gift Annuities was extremely successful. In a statement before the US commissioner of internal revenue in 1955, Huggins listed what the committee had accomplished:

> During this period, through a series of conferences and by the adoption of uniform rates we have practically eliminated competition in annuity rates between organizations issuing gift annuity agreements. We have taken the lead in establishing good practices in advertising literature; in the wording of the annuity agreements; in discretion as to what is acceptable as the consideration for gift annuities when other than cash; in the investment of the funds; in the segregation of reserves; and in the keeping of records and accounts. We have endeavored to keep abreast of supervisory and tax laws and regulations and to keep our constituency informed accordingly.[157]

It is quite a list, yet it is too modest. Huggins and fellow CGA members enabled nonprofit gift annuity programs to recast their fundraising practices based on sophisticated uses of longevity data and long-term investment models, in order to manage the risks of life-income gift fundraising programs. Businesslike practices enabled nonprofits to avoid the worst consequences of the Depression in the 1930s and the recent Great Recession. There are many other benefits from the actuarial revolution.

Increasing sophistication compelled nonprofits to rely on the services of professional specialists, such as actuaries, investment and tax advisors, attorneys, and software developers. For-profit service providers have become essential partners for nonprofit gift-planning programs. Commercial-service providers are now major funders of national professional conferences and other training activities for nonprofit staff.

To this day, national and local gift-planning conferences provide opportunities for philanthropic planners from diverse nonprofit and for-profit organizations to meet face to face and share their best ideas in a spirit of friendly collaboration. This was the vision of Dr. Alfred Williams Anthony in the 1920s.

Written reports from the early conferences addressed virtually every aspect of a gift annuity program long before other reference materials appeared. National standards of best practices addressed ethical marketing, accurate accounting, responsible rate-setting, and keeping the charitable gift element primary. These standards for nonprofits are voluntary. Gift annuity programs developed through experience, not as a result of public or private mandates.

Gift annuity programs spawned a national alert system for legislative, judicial, and regulatory issues affecting philanthropy. In 1848, Luther Bradish ably outlined the legislative and judicial landscape underlying life-income gifts. From 1927 through 1959, Gilbert Darlington provided a process for understanding and shaping state and federal policies through research, information-sharing, and lobbying.

National research has been a bedrock for nonprofit decision making ever since Arthur Ryan presented a survey report at the first conference in 1927. Gift annuity research conducted by nonprofit organizations is particularly important, since the federal government does not collect data on gift annuities, as it does for charitable remainder trusts and other split-interest gifts.[158] The valuation of life interests in gift annuities using mortality data and actuarial analysis, introduced in 1927, is now standard practice for charitable gifts structured as remainder trusts, pooled-income funds, retained-life estates, and lead trusts. This standardization makes it possible to collect and report meaningful data on such gifts.

George Huggins inaugurated the tradition of tracking and comparing national and individual organization mortality studies and the use of transparent investment assumptions based on current and projected economic conditions. Other groundbreaking national gift annuity surveys were published by Paul Cassat in 1930, Arthur Wellck in 1933, and William Venman in 1962.

Frank Minton began a modern series of national gift annuity survey reports published by the ACGA in 1994, 1999, and 2004. The author supervised the ACGA survey reports in 2009 and 2013. The scope of these research reports has expanded over time. The 1994 survey asked twenty-five questions, and the report was twenty-six pages; the 2013 survey asked forty-five questions and was fifty-five pages. Reviewing statistical highlights from the 2013 report at the thirty-second conference, held in April of 2016, Barlow Mann described the ACGA data-gathering project as "gargantuan."[159]

The conferences on gift annuities are the world's longest-running series for nonprofit fundraisers, business officers, and associated professional advisors. Among many high-level presentations on gift planning, the thirty-second conference featured a general session for six hundred participants on the gift annuity rate-setting process, with charts on the history of fixed-income-investment yields and long-term trends in stock prices. A panel presentation explored in depth the elements and history of rate setting, including the validity of a gift-annuitant-mortality study commissioned by ACGA in 2010.[160] George Huggins would have felt quite at home.

Thanks to the events in this book, charitable gift planning is more effective in funding services that save lives and make life more tolerable. America is a better place as a result. Gift planners have good reasons to be proud of our history.

Notes

1. Alfred Williams Anthony, preface to the conference report (Various 1927a). See full report in Appendix V. The thirty-two conference reports for the years 1927–2016 are available online at no charge at the ACGA website: www.acga-web.org/resources-top/surveys-reports-conference-pa-pers-and-brochures.

2. Baas 1991, 71.

3. From the website of Huggins Actuarial Services, Inc.: "Huggins & Company was originally formed in 1911 and, in the 1970s, became part of the Hay Group, a leading international employee benefits consulting firm...In 1987, Ernst & Young LLP purchased Huggins's insurance actu-arial consulting practice. Ernst & Young continued to use the Huggins name for the actuarial services group within their insurance industry practice. [In 2003, Ronald T. Kuehn] acquired the Huggins actuarial practice from Ernst & Young, along with several key employees, and re-established Huggins as an independent actuarial consulting firm" (see www.hugginsactuarial.com/about-us/history-of-huggins). Three Huggins actuaries have been members of the CGA and the ACGA board from its founding in 1927 to the present day: George A. Huggins (1927–1959); Charles L. Burrall Jr. (1961–1984); and Michael Mudry (1978–present; now an emeritus member).

4. The other was Rev. Gilbert Darlington of the American Bible Society.

5. In his preface to the third conference report, Anthony noted that after the first two conferences, "booklets containing the papers presented have been published and circulated quite widely, which have had an important effect upon standardizing and stabilizing policies and methods in harmony with sound principles of law and of ethics." He pointed out that the third report "penetrates somewhat more fully into the principles and details of methods and plans than its predecessors have done." Various 1930, 4.

6. Various, 1931, preface, by Alfred Williams Anthony. The foreword to the fifth conference report encouraged people to buy the whole series:

"Previous conferences had considered various phases of the annuity business, the reports of which were printed and copies of which are still available. They constitute a valuable compendium of information on the annuity plan as used by religious, charitable and educational organizations and institutions for securing gifts" (Various 1934).

7   Darlington described the first nine conference reports as "still authoritative" but noted that "unfortunately, some of these Reports are out of print." From "Taxation, Legislation, and Regulation," in Various 1952, 110.

8   See conference proceedings and reports at http://www.acga-web.org/resources-top/surveys-reports-conference-and-brochures.

9   Charitable gift planning is one of many aspects of modern life regulated by statistical thinking: "Statistics has become known in the twentieth century as the mathematical tool for analyzing experimental and observational data [such as observing the average length of American annuitant lives]. Enshrined by public policy as the only reliable basis for judgments as to the efficacy of medical procedures or the safety of chemicals, and adopted by business for such uses as industrial quality control, it is evidently among the products of science whose influence on public and private life has been most pervasive" (Porter 1986, 3). The evolution of statistical thought is illuminated by Chatterjee (2003, reprinted with corrections 2005). For a superb historical narrative and extensive bibliography, see Bouk (2015).

10   For the mathematical formulas on charitable gift annuities, see IRS 2009a. For remainder trusts, IRS 2009b.

11   Charles L. White, "Reinsurance of Annuities," in Various 1930, 25.

12   Ernest F. Hall, "The Place and Use of Annuities," in Various 1931a, 35–38.

13   Kenneth W. Moore, "Securing Annuity Gifts," in Various 1939, 34.

14   Huggins, "Danger Points and Protective Essentials in the Annuity Business," in Various 1931c, 11–23.

15   Huggins, "Uniform Rates: Agreements and Terminology: Reserves and Accounting," in Various 1930, 12.

16   Huggins, *Danger Points and Protective Essentials*, 14.

17   After a "false start" from 1926 to 1929, bond yields continued a long, unbroken descent. In 1920, the annualized average yield for corporate

and municipal long-term bonds was 5.27%; in 1932, the average yield was 4.61%. Bond prices rose, and yields fell steadily in the United States' "greatest bull bond market": by 1946 the annualized average yield was 2.45% (Homer 2005, 346–56).

18   Founding members of the Committee on Financial and Fiduciary Matters (CFFM), which convened the conferences in March and April of 1927, included Everett M. Ensign, executive secretary of the National Association of Life Underwriters; Leroy A. Mershon, secretary of the Trust Division of the American Bankers Association; Frank H. Mann, president of Union Guarantee and Mortgage Company and treasurer of the Federal Council of the Churches of Christ in America; and seven other representatives of national charitable organizations. Roster published in Various 1923.

19   Various 1927, 97–99.

20   "Report of the Committee on Findings" in Various 1927a, 150. The "Findings" were of such importance that they were published separately before the full conference report (CFFM 1927b).

21   Anthony, in Various 1925.

22   Anthony 1928.

23   Anthony 1927, 12–13.

24   Various 1931a.

25   Huggins, "Proper Handling of Annuities and Creation of Committee on Annuities," *Cooperation in Fiduciary Service*, 152.

26   Alfred Williams Anthony, preface to Various 1927.

27   "Report of the Committee on Findings," in Various 1927a, 152.

28   "The report of the Committee on Findings was the basis of discussion of the afternoon session and was finally adopted unanimously by the conference" (Various 1927a, 46).

29   The *Wise Public Giving* series included publications on bequests, life insurance, community trusts and foundations, life-income trusts, and gift annuities, among other philanthropic topics.

30   "In the judgment of those present it would be wise to have another meeting concerning annuities giving special attention to promotion methods" (Various 1927a, 48).

31   No roster of conference participants was published for the second through the seventh conference reports. In his preface, Alfred Williams Anthony noted there were fifty-nine people enrolled (compared with forty-eight at the 1927 conference), and that "twenty of the fifty-nine represented colleges and universities."

32   The National Committee on Planned Giving (NCPG, which became the Partnership for Philanthropic Planning on January 1, 2009, and the National Association of Charitable Gift Planners in October 2016) was created after ten years of discussion and planning. NCPG held its first organizational conference in 1986 and was incorporated in 1988. See Brown 2017.

33   Charles White testified to the broad appeal of gift annuity programs in his conference presentation of March 1927: "The writer of this paper has shared in the experience that probably many others have had, of being requested to send information and whatever literature he had bearing on the subject, to representatives of organizations widely scattered, including Roman Catholic and Jewish groups." The author has not found records of the early history of gift annuities issued by those groups.

34   Preface to Thompson 1952.

35   In a dissertation entitled *Gift Annuity Agreements of Colleges* submitted to the University of Michigan in 1962, the author expresses regret that his survey of 438 colleges and universities fell short in reporting on Catholic and Jewish organizations: "It was originally intended to include Catholic colleges in the survey, but the variation in their financial reports was deciding. Only two Jewish institutions were listed [in *American Colleges and Universities, Eighth Edition* (1960)], one a graduate school and the other a teachers college" (Venman 1962, 64). A summary of highlights that was published as a booklet noted that Venman's survey "was sent to 438 private, non-Catholic, non-Jewish accredited liberal arts colleges and universities in the continental United States. While no Catholic colleges or junior colleges were covered by the survey, there is no reason why they could not make use of such agreements" (Venman n.d., 20). Naturally, there is no reason why Jewish colleges like Yeshiva College and Brandeis University could not issue gift annuities.

36   "At its founding, the ABS opened itself to partnership with Catholics in distributing the Bible. But as Catholic immigration to the United States surged after 1830, the ABS spurned any Catholic associations and committed its work to spreading the Protestant Bible as a weapon against Catholicism. ABS publications warned against the growing 'Catholic menace,' and ABS agents derided the Catholic Church for promoting superstitions and heretical rituals among its members" (Young 2016). John Fea has written that relations between ABS and the Catholic Church were "at times downright hostile" from the nineteenth century until the Second Vatican Council (1962-1965). See Fea (2016, 243–52). Old prejudices are not easily overcome. The author had a discussion at the ACGA Conference in April of 2016 with a staff member for a national Catholic organization who said that "until recently there was a sense that our organization did not get involved with the ACGA."

37   "Constitution and By-laws of the Committee on Gift Annuities," in Various 1959, 101.

38   Dr. Ashton A. Almand, "History of the Committee on Gift Annuities," in Various 1971, 82.

39   Bruyn was appointed head of fund raising for Mount Holyoke College in 1923 and was awarded the Alumnae Medal of Honor for eminent service by Mount Holyoke in 1947. See https://www.mtholyoke.edu/archives/history/alumnae_medalists_year. She served as national chair of the American Alumni Council (predecessor to the Council for Advancement and Support of Education, CASE) in 1939–1940.

40   Conference Data: Attendance, in Baas 1991, 106.

41   Baas 1991, 98.

42   "The earliest defined-benefit pension plans were established on a pay-as-you-go basis without advance funding or the assistance of actuaries. Benefits were paid when they became due, and there were no actuarial calculations of currently accruing costs or of projected benefits and costs. George Huggins began pension actuarial calculations in America in 1904" (Grubbs 1999, 34). Huggins was "the ranking authority of his era on clergy pensions," according to the Society of Actuaries. See "Historical Background" at https://www.soa.org/About/History/about-historical-background.aspx.

Analysis of employee-pension costs was not a priority for companies in the nineteenth century because "pensions were generally gratuitous in nature and employers could, at their option, choose who was to receive a pension and the scope of the pension that would be made available...A second reason for the slow evolution of pension cost analysis was that early pensions generally were provided on a pay-as-you-go or assessmentism basis. Under this scheme the incidence of cost is negligible during the early years of the pension plan when there are only relatively few retired employees. It takes a number of years before the ultimate cost of the plan becomes apparent...Since no one was concerned that the cost of a pension plan could impose a serious financial problem, an analytical solution for this problem was not sought...Although the need for a detailed analysis of the implications of the accrued liability was firmly established by 1915, a considerable period of time elapsed before actuaries began to quantify systematically the approaches for dealing with this problem" (Shapiro 1985, 82, 86).

43 Huggins testified before the Senate Finance Committee in 1935 concerning the new Social Security Act on behalf of twenty-two "denominational pension systems, including 110,000 ministers, serving 135,000 churches, and representing 25,000,000 church members." See https://www.ssa.gov/history/pdf/s35huggins.pdf.

44 See Grubbs's (1999) discussion of the actuary's role as pension consultant and in funding insurance-company contracts in "The Public Responsibility of Actuaries in American Pensions" (35).

45 Huggins, "Actuarial Basis of Rates," in Various 1927, 9.

46 Members of the committee often used the phrase "rate of interest" where today we would use "investment return."

47 For example, George Sutherland on "Investments": "It is an absolutely unsafe business proposition to accept money on the annuity plan and... depend upon the benevolence and generosity of the contributing constituency to supply a sufficient income to meet these obligations...any individual would be very unwise to give his funds to an organization which does not carefully invest such funds in good generally sound investments, retaining them in such investments during the entire lifetime of the donor" (Various 1929b, 37).

280

48   The first American annuitant mortality table was published by Emory McClintock in 1899, "based on the annuity experience of fifteen American companies prior to 1892. There was a large amount of foreign business included, about three-fourths of the lives being European" (Nelson and Warren Consulting Actuaries, n.d., 1956?, 61. Also see Hustead 1988, 14.

49   Wellck, 1933.

50   Various 1952, 105.

51   ACGA, 2014, 20.

52   Huggins, "Proper Handling of Annuities and Creation of Committee on Annuities," in Various 1927a, 97–99.

53   There was little or no tax advantage to accepting a lower gift annuity payment in the 1920s.

54   Resistance to the idea of actuarially determined lower payment rates for young annuitants continued through at least 1934. A major goal of the fifth conference was that the uniform national rate table (or "schedule") "should be lower than the schedules being used by most organizations." Conference participants insisted on higher payments for annuitants aged thirty-five and younger: "The committee had proposed a rate of 2.5% for younger ages up to 30 years of age. The conference voted that the rate should be changed to 3% for ages up to and including 35 years of age." Ernest F. Hall, foreword to Various 1934.

55   ACGA rates calculations in 2017 assume an annualized investment return of 4.25% minus 1% annually for expenses.

56   For how insured lives became rated by risks, see Bouk 2015.

57   In 2012, ACGA introduced a new factor: whether the calculated payment rate produces at least a 20 percent present value for the charitable residuum.

58   The formal title of the current ACGA rates paper is "Explanation of the ACGA Gift Annuity Rates Effective January 1, 2012" (Smyrna, GA: ACGA, updated May 2017). This and previous Rates Committee reports are available on the ACGA website at http://www.acga-web.org/surveys-reports-conference-papers-and-brochures/76-suggested-maximum-rate-schedules.

59   Huggins, "Summary of Annuity Rates of Conferences on Annuities," in Various 1946, 21.

60 ACGA 2014, 13.

61 See http://www.acga-web.org/about-gift-annuities-top/gift-annuty-best-practices.

62 Zollman 1924, 564, 566.

63 Huggins, "Proper Handling of Annuities and Creation of Committee on Annuities," in CFFM 1927a, 98.

64 Huggins, Actuarial Basis 1927, 9.

65 Huggins, "Report on the Mortality Experience Studies," Various 1959, 16.

66 Ernest Hall, chair of the SOA, observed that offering high rates "induces investment bargaining, which is contrary to the basic principles of annuities of charitable organizations" ("The Trend Toward Uniformity," in Various 1931b, 7).

67 Huggins, "Annuity Rates and Reserves," in Various 1929b, 30.

68 Huggins, "Danger Points and Protective Essentials," in Various 1931c, 12–13.

69 Charles L. White, "Annuities," in CFFM 1927a, 87–88. White became a founding member of the Committee on Annuities.

70 "Actuarial Basis of Rates," in Various 1927b, 9.

71 The most recent ACGA report found that "96 percent of the charities responding to the 2013 survey reported that they always or usually follow the ACGA rates, consistent with responses in previous surveys" (ACGA 2014, 13).

72 "Actuarial Basis of Rates," in Various 1927b, 8.

73 Huggins, "Danger Points and Protective Essentials," in Various 1931c, 12.

74 Huggins, "Report on the Mortality Experience Studies," in Various 1959, 16.

75 Huggins, "Gift Annuity Rates and Mortality Experience," in Various 1955, 31.

76 "Actuarial Basis of Rates," in Various 1927b, 8.

77 "From 1900 to 1960, the elderly [i.e., age sixty-five-plus] increased tenfold, while the population under age sixty-five was only 2.2 times larger" (National Institute on Aging 1997, 6). "In 1900 average life expectancy at birth for the world as a whole was only around 30 years, and in rich countries under 50. The figures are now 67 and 78 respectively, and still rising," though not nearly as rapidly (*Economist* 2009).

78   "The populations of developed societies have grown old at an amazing pace. Within the last hundred years…the populations of Europe, North America, Australasia, and Japan have become far and away the oldest human populations of which we have knowledge…this represents a unique occurrence in human history" (Laslett 1995, 3, 27). Angus Deaton has shown that in recent years, the life expectancy of white, middle-aged US men and women has begun to decline because of suicides and drug poisonings. See, for example, Case (2015). On the other hand, life expectancy among African-Americans has lengthened: "The death rate for African-Americans (blacks) declined 25 percent from 1999 to 2015… But disparities still persist between blacks and whites. Although blacks as a group are living longer, their life expectancy is still 4 years less than that of whites" (Centers for Disease Control and Prevention 2017). Overall, American life expectancy at birth reached a high of 78.9 years in 2014 and declined to 78.8 years in 2015. See Xu 2016.

79   For a description of the mathematical processes involved in creating a new mortality table in the 1920s, see R. D. Murphy 1922.

80   ACGA and many states adopted a dynamic, generational 2012 Individual Annuity Reserving Table for commercial and charitable annuities issued after January 1, 2015. This is the first annuitant-mortality table intended to incorporate annual improvements in mortality experience, thus alleviating the need to create new mortality tables. See the American Academy of Actuaries/Society of Actuaries Payout Annuity Table Team (2011) and an analysis by PG Calc at http://info. pgcalc.com/2012-iar-a-new-kind-of-mortality-table, also downloaded April 26, 2017. The ACGA Rates Committee continues Huggins's practice of fitting standard annuitant mortality tables to the actual experience of charitable-annuitant lives as determined by national surveys of nonprofit gift annuity programs.

81   Nelson and Warren Consulting Actuaries [1956?], 25, 27.

82   Huggins, "Rate of Mortality Among the Gift-Annuitant Lives," in Various 1941.

83   Actuary Edward W. Marshall told participants at the fourth COA in 1931 that annuity reserves "shall be invested in certain prescribed investments

to yield a rate of interest at least equal to the rate on which the reserve is based " ("Reserve Valuations of Annuity Funds," in Various 1931, 22).

84   The Society of Actuaries (2002) has published an interesting conference discussion entitled "Asset Allocation for Life Insurers" that compares asset allocation strategies and constraints for individual investors, defined-benefit pension plans, and life insurance reserves. See https://www.soa.org/ library/proceedings/record-of-the-society-of-actuaries/2000-09/2002/ january/rsa02v28n179ts.pdf.

85   Federal policymakers determined in 1962 that the investment in an annuity contract would be valued as if it were an annuity sold by a life insurance company, and the surplus or projected residuum would be deductible as a charitable gift: "In Revenue Ruling 62-136 the Service ended seven years' uncertainty on the question of when they would tax capital gain in the charitable annuity...In a companion ruling, the Internal Revenue Service published a table for determining the cost of a single life annuity. Revenue Ruling 62-137 held that charitable annuities were sufficiently comparable to commercial annuities to be valued according to similar standards" (Desmond 1967, 49–50).

86   Various 1927b.

87   "A period of monetary deflation such as the world is facing now may redound to the benefit of annuitants, and may lead to a revival of annuity business on a large scale" (Kopf 1927, 229).

88   Various 1929b.

89   George F. Sutherland, "Investments," in Various 1929b.

90   Battered by years of subsequent experience, Huggins's return assumptions for rate-setting would decrease as investment opportunities withered: down to 4 percent in 1934, 3.5 percent in 1939, 2.5 percent in 1946.

91   Robinson, "Economic Changes as Affecting the Investment of Charitable Funds," in Various 1929a, 99–124.

92   According to the US Bureau of Labor Statistics, in December 2016 there were about 7.5 million unemployed workers, and the unemployment rate was 4.7 percent. See http://www.dlt.ri.gov/lmi/laus/us/usadj.htm.

93   See http://tradingninvestment.com/100-years-dow-jones-industrial-average-djia-events-history-chart/2/. Investment risk is familiar to every

gift annuity fund manager whose reserve accounts suffered during the Great Recession. The Dow reached a prerecession high of 14,164.43 on October 9, 2007, and fell to 6,594.44 on March 5, 2009. See https://www.thebalance.com/dow-jones-closing-history-top-highs-and-lows-since-1929-3306174.

94   Darlington, "Change in Interest Rates," in Various 1955, 3.

95   For more details on rates and return assumptions, see Appendix VI: CGA Rates Chart, 1927–59 (Single Life).

96   "The greatest of all secular bear bond markets, which began in April of 1946, and probably ended in September 1981, carried prime long American corporate bond yields from their lowest recorded yields to their highest. The yield index rose from 2.46 to 15.49% for seasoned prime issues and up to 16.5% (industrials) and 18.0% (utilities) for high-quality new issues" (Homer 2005, 366).

97   ACGA, 2015, 5.

98   Various 1930.

99   "The entire bond market advance of 1929–1931 has been called a false start" (Homer 2005, 352).

100   Cited by Rainard B. Robbins (1933, 210).

101   Originally published in Various 1930, 81–100; quotes are from 81–82. Reissued as *Administration and Investment of Annuity Funds*, WPGS no. 35.

102   Introduction to Various 1931c, 9.

103   Francis M. Knight, "The Investment of Reserve and Other Trust Funds," in Various 1931c, 59.

104   Various 1931b.

105   Alfred Williams Anthony, preface to Various 1931.

106   Edward W. Marshall, "Reserve Valuations of Annuity Funds," in Various 1931b, 22.

107   Huggins, "Uniform Maximum Rates," in Various 1931b, 10–11.

108   Piper, "Comments on Rates," in Various 1931b, 18.

109   Marshall, "Reserve Valuations of Annuity Funds," Various 1931b, 24.

110   Wellck, 1933.

111   According to the US Inflation Calculator at http://www.usinflationcalculator.com/.

112   Various 1934.

113   Ernest F. Hall, Foreword, in Various 1934, 3.

114   Lewis T. Reed, "Uniform Annuity Rates," in Various 1934, 20.

115   Gross, "Investment of Funds for the Safeguarding of Annuities," in Various 1934, 22.

116   Bell H. a. 1952, 45–85. Available at http://scholarship.law.duke.edu/cgi/viewcontent.cgi?article=2513&context=lcp, downloaded 12/31/2016.

117   Bell and Fraine 1952, 55, table 4.

118   Ernest F. Hall, foreword to Various 1934. The author was not able to find the mortality-study report analyzed by Huggins in 1934.

119   Various 1939.

120   Minutes of the CGA on December 28, 1937, show that Huggins had met with Charles Dubuar to discuss revisions in its insurance law concerning gift annuities. Members of the CGA discussed an early draft of the proposed revision and suggested several changes, which Huggins brought back to Dubuar.

121   Charles Dubuar, "The Regulation and Supervision of the Issuance of Annuity Agreements by a Charitable Society," in Various 1939, 8.

122   See discussion by Bell and Fraine 1952, 49ff.

123   Various 1941.

124   Darlington, "Why the Conference was Called," in Various 1941, 7.

125   Gordon 2016, 536.

126   Gordon 2016, 539.

127   Various 1946.

128   Darlington, foreword to Various 1946.

129   Beckhart, "Interest Rates and Possible Future Trends," in Various 1946, 6–11.

130   William P. Schell, "How to Stimulate Gifts on the Annuity Basis," *Annuity Agreements of Charitable Organizations*, 13.

131   Huggins, "Proposed Rates for Gift Annuity Agreements," *Annuity Agreements of Charitable Organizations*, 19.

132   Charles W. Bass, "Opening Remarks," in Various 1959, 7.

133   Minutes of a Special Meeting on Wills and Annuities called by the Joint Department of Stewardship and Benevolence, National Council of Churches, October 2, 1951.

134   "The committee felt that as its income from the registration of those who come to the conferences on annuities has been taken over by the National Council of Churches of Christ in the U.S.A. and that as the publication and sale of the studies and information prepared by the committee were also taken over by the National Council, that the National Council should each year provide in its budget, or from the sale of its publications, to reimburse the committee for actual amounts expended in preparing information about taxation, mortality experience, legislation, et cetera" (CGA minutes dated September 14, 1954).

135   Various 1952.

136   Huggins, "Rates, Mortality Experience, and Reserves," in Various 1952, 103. A letter from T. K. Thompson of the NCCCA dated December 22, 1952, shows that the National Council refused to reimburse the CGA for $979.22 spent on Huggins's survey, proposing instead to recover the costs by "solicitating [*sic*] the agencies which will profit from your study made on annuities." By September of 1954, Huggins had received only $622.40 from NCCCA.

137   "A life year of exposure may be defined as a period of one year in which a life of a given age was receiving an annuity." If one annuitant received five years of payments, that would be considered five life years of exposure.

138   New York State continues to be concerned about aggressive investment of gift annuity reserves: "Asset Liability Mismatch (ALM) Risk—Many organizations have a high degree of ALM risk and are holding a high concentration of assets with substantial volatility and/or credit risk. However, reserves are not being held for potential declines in asset values" (Emami 2016). See http://www.dfs.ny.gov/insurance/life/char_rsve_impt_2016.pdf.

139   Minutes of the Joint Department of Stewardship and Benevolence Committee on Annuities, November 28, 1952.

140   The committee incorporated as a nonprofit charitable organization in 1993 under the name it is known by in 2017: the American Council on Gift Annuities.

141   See the roster of CGA Board members in Various (1959, 103). Dr. Distler "relinquished membership" in December of 1959.

142   Charles W. Baas, "Opening Remarks," in Various 1965, 3.

143   Various 1955.

144   Homer 2005, 366.

145   Eleven million Americans were unemployed in 1933, more than 25 percent of the workforce, as cited earlier.

146   Nadler, "Interest Rates," in Various 1955, 11. The ninth conference report was the first to be published by the Committee on Gift Annuities and not by the Federal Council of Churches of Christ. The committee continued using the naming convention for its conference report, which became *Wise Public Giving* series No. 48. The tenth report in 1959 was WPGS No. 49.

147   Bell H. a., 1952, 77–78.

148   See ACGA 2017, 6.

149   Various 1959.

150   For a few years, the IRS enabled donors to give appreciated property through life-income trusts that were reinvested in tax-free securities, enabling trust beneficiaries to avoid paying capital gains tax on their trust income.

151   Minutes of the CGA dated April 12, 1961.

152   Various 1965, 9.

153   A survey of 102 organizations participating in the twelfth COA in 1965 reported that they were managing 47,517 gift annuity agreements with a value of $99,889,673. These organizations reported 2,453 life-income agreements with a value of $27,796,297 (Charles W. Baas, "Opening Remarks," in Various 1965, 4).

154   In subsequent years, fear of communism would lead to the McCarthy hearings and to congressional investigations into the abuse of private trusts and foundations for subversive political purposes. Concerns about public accountability and self-dealing among donors of charitable trusts resulted in the Tax Reform Act of 1969.

155   ABS reported on 9,236 living annuitants and 1,493 annuitants who died during the survey period. The next largest annuity programs were the Moody Bible Institute (4,805/926) and four programs of the United Presbyterian Church (2,981/461).

156   "Our Committee is entirely free to deal with any agency of the Government, either Federal or State, and has done so from the very beginning" (Darlington, "Address of Welcome," in Various 1955, 8).

157   Statement of George A. Huggins, Vice Chairman of the CGA, to the Commissioner of Internal Revenue, dated November 1, 1955. Copy located in the archives of the ACGA.

158   See SOI Tax Stats (Split-Interest Trust Statistics) at https://www.irs.gov/uac/soi-tax-stats-split-interest-trust-statistics.

159   Mann, "The 2013 Survey on Gift Annuities: Interpreting the Results," in Various 2016, 95.

160   David Libengood, James McPhillips, and Ronald A. Brown, "Still Vital After All These Years: ACGA Rates Suggestions," in Various 2016.

Appendix I

Important Events in the History of Gift Annuities

- c. 220 **Measuring the length of annuitant lives** is a cornerstone of actuarial science. In his report to the ninth Conference on Gift Annuities in 1955, George Huggins cited an **innovative Roman life table reported by Domitius Ulpianus (170–223)** for valuing testamentary annuities under a new tax law. Ulpian's mortality table was used for more than 1,400 years.

- c. 540 Saint Benedict (480–543) encouraged wealthy parents not to spoil their children with money but to **give to his religious community and receive income back for their lives**. His gift model was adapted from a classic Roman arrangement known as a *usufruct*. The Rule of Benedict was followed by thousands of medieval monasteries and remains in use today.

- c. 800–1000 The **laws for annuity contracts were different from laws for charitable trusts,** but there were times when their histories intersected (see *Bradish Report* of 1848, below). The earliest known documents for an Islamic charitable endowment known as a *waqf* date from

876; many waqfs operated like charitable trusts. Similar fiduciary arrangements developed in medieval Germany (Treuhand) and France (*cestui que use* or *trust*).

- c. 1000–1550 **Gifts known as *corrodies*** were popular among English donors who gave cash, real estate, or other property in exchange for the contractual right to receive a specified lifetime supply of food, shelter, drink, and/or cash payments from a monastery, hospital, or church. These gift arrangements ended when Henry VIII confiscated Catholic funds during the Reformation.

- 1225 The modern British legal historian Frederic W. Maitland **credited Franciscan monks with popularizing charitable trusts** under English law in the thirteenth century. A vow of poverty prevented the Franciscans from owning property, so cities such as Cambridge held buildings and farms in trust for their use.

- 1601 The **Statute of Charitable Uses** was enacted by the English Parliament to identify charitable trusts ("uses") that promoted the general welfare, contrasted with self-dealing for personal benefits. Its preamble contained a list of activities that became defined as charitable purposes in the laws of Great Britain and the United States.

- 1693 English mathematician and astronomer Edmond Halley published *An Estimate of the Degrees of Mortality of Mankind...with an Attempt to Ascertain the Price of Annuities upon Lives*, a mortality table based on experience and constructed using actuarial principles.

- 1759 The **Corporation for the Relief of Poor and Distressed Presbyterian Ministers and Distressed Widows and Children of Ministers** was chartered by Pennsylvania to provide survivorship annuities. Often cited as the earliest American life insurance company, contracts were available only to Presbyterian ministers and their families. Actuary Robert Patterson computed premiums for the Ministers Fund in 1792.

- 1762 The **Equitable Life Assurance Society** was founded in London. The Equitable pioneered the use of Edmond Halley's mortality data (1693) to calculate age-based premiums.

- 1774 Welsh actuary Richard Price published *Observations on the Proper Method of Keeping the Accounts, and Determining from Year to Year the State of the Society for Equitable Assurances on Lives and Survivorships*, a founding document of actuarial science applied to the operation of a life insurance company.

- 1783 Richard Price published **The Northampton Table**, the earliest mortality table constructed for use by life insurance companies, developed for the Equitable Life Assurance Society based in London. Huggins compared this with more recent mortality tables in a report to the ninth Conference on Gift Annuities in 1955 to demonstrate changes in American longevity.

- 1811 The merchant and philanthropist **Stephen Girard of Philadelphia** purchased the stock and buildings of the First Bank of the United States and founded Girard's Bank. He became one of the wealthiest and most generous Americans of all time (see his charitable-trust case, 1844).

- 1812 The **Pennsylvania Company for Insurance on Lives and Granting Annuities** was chartered as the first US company to sell life insurance and annuities to the public.

- 1815 English actuary Joshua Milne published *A Treatise on the Valuation of Annuities and Assurances on Lives and Survivorships; On the Construction of Tables of Mortality; and On the Probabilities and Expectations of Life*, including the groundbreaking **Carlisle Table of Mortality** based on the experience of two parishes from

1779 to 1787. Cited by Huggins at the first Conference on Annuities in 1927.

- 1815   In approving a charter to the Phoenix Bank, the Connecticut House of Representatives agreed to make a grant of $10,000 for the Bishop's Fund of the Episcopal Church. The senate did not approve the grant, initiating the **Bishop's Bonus controversy**. Benjamin Silliman received a grant for the Yale medical college, and in 1831 would collaborate with the Episcopalians to secure a grant for the Trumbull Gallery.

- 1816   The **American Bible Society was founded**. ABS issued its first gift annuity in 1843 (see below). In the 1920s, ABS became the world's leading issuer of charitable gift annuities and home to the Committee on Gift Annuities. John Jay, the first chief justice of the United States, served as president of the society from 1821 to 1828.

- c. 1825 **Peter Augustus Jay**, attorney, banker, and son of John Jay, was appointed treasurer of the New York Corporation for the Relief of Widows and Children of Clergymen of the Protestant Episcopal Church in the State of New York, which provided a survivorship-annuity program.

- 1829   Peter Jay was appointed **chair of the Legacy Committee of the American Bible Society,** responsible for reviewing and accepting complex proposed gifts and bequests, including life annuities.

- 1830   Actuary William Bard founded the **New York Life Insurance and Trust Company** and encouraged competitors to share mortality data. Peter Jay was selected as a trustee of the company.

- 1830   John Trumbull and Benjamin Silliman met in Trumbull's Manhattan apartment, just a few blocks from the future home of the American Bible Society in Astor

Place. **Trumbull offered to give his best paintings of the American Revolution to Yale College in exchange for "a competent annuity for my life."**

- 1831 **Benjamin Silliman** lobbied the Connecticut legislature in partnership with Charles Sigourney of Phoenix Bank and the Episcopal Church. Connecticut awarded grants of $3,000 for the church's Washington College and $7,000 for Yale, which spent $5,000 on constructing the Trumbull Gallery.

- Dec. 1831 John Trumbull and Yale President Jeremiah Day signed the **annuity bond and indenture contracts** drafted by Peter Augustus Jay. Yale agreed to pay Trumbull $1,000 per year for his life.

- 1832 **Trumbull Gallery** completed. Trumbull sailed with his paintings to New Haven to oversee their installation. Benjamin Silliman served as the unpaid director of the gallery.

- 1836 Yale's purchase of the sculpture *Jephthah and his Daughters* by Hezekiah Augur for $4,000 **angered Trumbull**, but he decided not to renegotiate the terms of his annuity contract.

- 1836 The **Girard Life Insurance and Trust Company** succeeded Stephen Girard's bank. See the challenge to Girard's testamentary charitable trust below (1844).

- 1841 Publication of **Trumbull's *Autobiography***, including the full texts of his annuity bond and indenture contracts with Yale. These legal documents were imitated by many nonprofit organizations, notably the American Bible Society.

- 1843 American Bible Society **issued its first annuity bond** to Boston merchant Joseph Keith.

- 1844 **Stephen Girard will contest**: The largest charitable trust to that point in US history ($5 million) was affirmed by the Supreme Court. The landmark decision in *Vidal v. Girard's Executors* found that charitable trusts predate the 1601 Statute of Charitable Uses, so are valid under US common law, even when a state has not adopted the English statute.

- 1847   **Death of Colonel John Trumbull**. Yale expected Trumbull to live for six years after signing his life-annuity contract and expected to pay him $6,000. He lived for nearly twelve and received $11,250.

- 1848   After issuing its first gift annuity in 1843, the American Bible Society had second thoughts. *On the Matter of Accepting Trusts*, written by a committee chaired by Luther Bradish, provided general rules for managing a robust gift annuity program.

- 1850   **US Census** began to gather and report **mortality data**.

- 1857   Benjamin Silliman wrote his *Reminiscences* describing the events involved with arranging Yale's gift annuity contracts and constructing the Trumbull Gallery, a rare personal narrative on the planning process for a life-income gift.

- 1858–66   **Actuary Elizur Wright**, the "Father of Life Insurance Regulation," served as commissioner of insurance for the State of Massachusetts. Year after year, Wright calculated the required reserve values for every insurance contract issued in Massachusetts.

- 1869   Elizur Wright received a US patent for his **Arithmeter**, a high-resolution slide rule he used and sold to life insurance companies to calculate the values and reserve requirements of life insurance policies and annuities.

- 1889   **Actuarial Society of America** founded. Its headquarters were in Astor House on Broadway and Vesey Street in Manhattan.

- 1899   Publication of **Emory McClintock's Table of American Annuitant Lives,** the first American annuitant mortality table. Previous mortality tables were developed for life insurance contracts. Average insured lives were shorter than average annuitant lives because of self-selection. Huggins used the McClintock table for his gift annuity rate calculations in 1927.
- 1905   **Armstrong Committee** formed by the New York state legislature investigated and reported stock manipulation and other abuses in the American life insurance industry.
- 1906   Hundreds of life insurance firms voluntarily adopted the **American Life Convention**, reforming their business practices. Sales of life insurance and commercial annuities rose dramatically.
- 1914–1920s   **Henry Albert Collins, "The Annuity Man,"** published a series of books and pamphlets touting gift annuities. Many American nonprofit organizations began issuing annuity bonds as a fundraising activity. Unsafe business practices arose in the absence of public regulation and voluntary norms for protecting annuitants as well as the issuing nonprofits.
- 1917   A **federal income-tax deduction for charitable gifts** was introduced in the War Revenue Act (Public Law No. 65-50).
- 1919   **First Lieutenant Frank Mann** was hired as secretary of the Ways and Means Committee of the American Bible Society. With help from Ivy Lee, the "father of public relations," ABS launched an international gift annuity campaign.
- 1920–30   The American Bible Society received **16,309 inquiries about gift annuities and issued 4,615 gift annuity contracts** during these years.

- 1923   With support from the superintendent of insurance, the New York state legislature enacted an **insurance law that regulated gift annuities as life insurance products**.

- 1925   **George Augustus Huggins**, a Philadelphia actuary, was hired to perform a general audit of the gift annuity program of the American Bible Society.

- 1925   After successful lobbying by Gilbert Darlington of the American Bible Society and George Huggins, the New York State Insurance Law **affirmed the right of nonprofit organizations to issue gift annuities.** The law exempted nonprofits from registering as commercial life insurance firms but required actuarial standards for valuing gift annuity reserve funds.

- 1925   Dr. Alfred Williams Anthony of the Federal Council of Churches of Christ in America organized a **Conference on Financial and Fiduciary Matters,** bringing together leading financial firms and leaders of US nonprofit organizations. Frank Mann of the Bible Society spoke on gift annuities.

- 1926   **The Methodist Episcopal Church appointed a Committee on Annuities** to study gift annuity practices among its member organizations. The committee identified many practices in need of reform among eighty-eight Methodist organizations issuing gift annuities.

- March 22–24, 1927 Speaking at the Conference on Financial and Fiduciary Matters, George Huggins persuaded the Federal Council of Churches to **form a national committee** "to study and recommend the proper range of rates, the form of contracts, the amount and type of reserve funds and the nomenclature to be used, to ascertain and advise as to the legislation in the United States and the various states regarding annuities, their taxability, etc. This committee is requested to make an immediate study of the matter of rates and to call a conference of interested parties on this matter at the earliest possible date."

- April 29, 1927 **First Conference on Gift Annuities** convened in Manhattan. George Huggins presented "**Actuarial Basis of Rates**," the foundational document for calculating the financial implications of life-income gifts to charity. He recommended a maximum single-life payment rate of 10.5 percent for annuitants aged eighty and older, but the Committee on Gift Annuities capped the maximum rate at 9 percent. Huggins made actuarial presentations at ten gift-annuities conferences before his death in 1959.

- 1927–89 The **American Bible Society** provided the Committee on Gift Annuities with extensive, free administrative support, such as financial accounting and reporting, mailings, and database management. The Annuity Board of the Southern Baptist Convention became the second host of the Committee in 1989. Now an independent 501(c)(3) organization, the American Council on Gift Annuities has never had its own professional staff.

- Apr. 30, 1928 The Methodist Church adopted a uniform gift annuity payment rate schedule with a **maximum rate cap of 8 percent** for annuitants aged eighty and older, lower than the 9 percent committee rate.

- Nov. 9, 1928 **Second Conference on Gift Annuities**. Presentations on marketing, accounting, and investing, as well as on legislation and rates.

- 1927–35 **Sales of commercial annuities** grew during the Great Depression as buyers sought financially stable institutions to protect their principals and provide secure incomes. For example: Forty-one life insurance companies doing business in New York issued 118,999 annuity contracts in 1928 and 203,897 contracts in 1931.

Life insurance company income from annuities rose from $52 million in 1927 to $491 million in 1935.

- Nov. 17, 1930 **Third Conference on Gift Annuities**. Paul Cassat of Vassar College reported results of a gift annuity survey among ninety nonprofit organizations with more than $25 million in gift annuity reserve funds.

- Jan. 6–7, 1931 A national Methodist Church conference on gift annuities **criticized the American Bible Society** for its high payment rates and its use of "annuity bond" terminology.

- Mar. 17, 1931 **Fourth Conference on Gift Annuities** featured presentations by three actuaries. Huggins recommended a more conservative rate schedule with a cap of 8 percent; conference agreed. The American Bible Society adopted the gift annuity rate table recommended by the conference and agreed to stop promoting "annuity bonds."

- 1932 Publication of *The Liberal Arts College*, based on a survey of thirty-five colleges related to the Methodist Episcopal Church. Thirty-two colleges had gift annuity programs, and 640 annuity contracts had been issued since 1920. The face value of 851 existing annuity contracts was $6.2 million. The value of annuity reserve funds was $5.6 million, and endowments totaled $31.5 million.

- 1933 Arthur Albert Wellck published an ambitious survey of the 296 largest US colleges and universities and reported that 153 were offering gift annuities. *The Annuity Agreements of Colleges and Universities* presented important research on gift annuity administration, investment, and risk management. A total of 1,738 gift annuity contracts was reported. Wellck estimated that colleges were managing more than $35 million in gift annuity reserves.

- Nov. 20, 1934 **Fifth Conference on Gift Annuities**. Huggins reported results of a gift-annuitant-mortality study among fourteen national Protestant organizations managing 6,631 annuity contracts with a face value of $11.8 million.

- 1937 **Stanford University launched its R-Plan,** encouraging professional advisors to help wealthy donors plan their charitable giving.
- 1937 George Huggins consulted with the principal actuary of the Department of Insurance for New York State concerning **revisions to the New York State Insurance Law** concerning gift annuities.
- 1939 In cooperation with the Committee on Gift Annuities, New York State enacted an insurance law **requiring nonprofit organizations to obtain a certificate** allowing them to issue gift annuities. The law prohibited the investment of gift annuity reserves in common stocks.
- Oct. 4–5, 1939 **Sixth Conference on Gift Annuities**. Major presentations on the New York State Insurance Law. The committee encouraged every nonprofit issuing gift annuities to maintain a segregated reserve fund based on New York's actuarial methods. No action taken on rates because of economic uncertainty at the start of World War II.
- Apr. 29, 1941 **Seventh Conference on Gift Annuities.** Maximum gift annuity rate was capped at 7 percent for ages seventy and older, the lowest maximum rate ever.
- 1944 **Pomona College Plan** developed by advertising expert Allen Hawley. Restricted by college trustees from promoting life-income gifts among its alumni, Pomona advertised successfully in national newspapers.
- Apr. 10, 1946 **Eighth Conference on Gift Annuities**. Columbia University professor of banking analyzed trends in interest rates and the economy. Uncertain about postwar economy, participants voted to make no changes in payment rates.

- 1948 *How Tax Laws Make Giving to Charity Easy*, by J. K. Lasser, was one of the first charitable gift planning manuals.
- 1949 **Alger Hiss** was forced to resign as head of the Carnegie Foundation for International Peace. Accused of being a communist spy, Hiss was convicted of perjury. Concern arose over public accountability of private charitable foundations and trusts. Richard Nixon and Joseph McCarthy came to national prominence because of this case.
- 1950–51 The Federal Council of the Churches of Christ in America was succeeded by the **National Council of Churches**, which was concerned that some organizations represented on the Committee on Gift Annuities were not affiliated with the council. The committee formally joined the National Council in October of 1951. There was a gap of nine years between the eighth Conference on Gift Annuities in 1946 and the ninth conference in 1955.
- 1952 A House Select Committee investigated **whether charitable trusts and foundations "are using their resources for un-American and subversive activities."**
- Dec. 15–16, 1952 The **Conference on Wills, Annuities, and Special Gifts**, sponsored by the National Council of Churches and held just before a large Conference on Financial and Fiduciary Matters, drew 387 attendees. George Huggins and Gilbert Darlington made gift annuity presentations. Sydney Prerau (later a principal partner of Prerau and Teitell), representing J. K. Lasser, made a presentation entitled "**Tax Aspects of Giving**."
- 1954 **Internal Revenue Code** enacted. This monumental tax-reform act made many changes in the tax treatment of charitable gifts, including larger deduction limits and clarification of gift annuity taxation.

- Oct. 3–4, 1955   The **Committee on Gift Annuities** became an independent, unincorporated nonprofit organization at the **ninth conference**. Attendance doubled to 126 (and reached 418 at the twelfth conference in 1965). Huggins reported results of the **first national gift-annuitant-mortality study conducted by the committee.**

- 1956   Publication of ***Voluntary Support of America's Colleges and Universities 1954–55*** by the Council for Financial Aid to Education. Colleges and universities reported receiving $4.7 million in gift annuities and $6.6 million through charitable trusts, roughly $100 million in outright gifts, and $35.7 million in bequests.

- Dec. 1–2, 1959   **Tenth Conference on Gift Annuities.** Huggins presented a masterful report on his new national gift-annuitant-mortality study.

- Dec. 30, 1959 **Death of George Augustus Huggins** (1881–1959).

- 1961   After prompting the US Treasury Department for a tax ruling, the Committee on Gift Annuities began publishing ***Tax Implications of an Annuity Gift*** (the "***Green Book***") with tables for hand calculating the tax and financial implications of a gift annuity contract.

- 1962   **US congressman Wright Patman (D-Texas)** launched a series of populist hearings on self-dealing financial abuses by creators of charitable trusts and foundations. Patman was the first person invited to testify at the Ways and Means Committee tax-reform hearings in 1969, condemning the use of charitable trusts and foundations for "deliberate evasion of fiscal and moral responsibility to the Nation."

- 1962   Publication of ***Gift Annuity Agreements for Colleges***, by William C. Venman, based on a survey of

438 US colleges and universities, in which 160 colleges reported having gift annuity programs, and 112 reported 4,625 gift annuity contracts with a face value estimated at $50 million.

- 1964 **Conrad Teitell** began presenting planned-giving seminars with charitable-tax expert Sydney Prerau. Teitell spoke at every Conference on Gift Annuities from 1968 to 2016.
- 1966 *The Case for Deferred Giving*, important essays published by the American Alumni Council, forerunner of the Council for Advancement and Support of Education (CASE).
- 1969 After ten months of hearings on charitable-trust and foundation abuses, Congress passed the *Tax Reform Act of 1969*. TRA '69 clarified the rules for charitable-remainder and lead trusts, imposed prohibitions against self-dealing, and stimulated growth in the number and value of life-income gifts to charity.
- 1971–77 Charitable gift planners formed **local, regional, and national planned-giving councils** for technical training, networking, research, and sharing of best practices. Early councils included the Planned Giving Group of Greater New York (1971), CANARAS Planned Giving Council (1974), Minnesota Planned Giving Council (1976), and the Planned Giving Group of New England (1977).
- 1974 The Northwest Area Foundation initiated a **Deferred Giving Project** to encourage and support programs at eighteen colleges in Iowa, Minnesota, Oregon, and Washington. Eleven colleges participated in a second round, beginning in 1977.
- 1976 **Charles Johnson** joined the Lilly Endowment staff and led a series of strategic-grant initiatives supporting planned giving.

- 1982 The Northwest Area Foundation sponsored a national **Deferred Gift Development Roundtable** in Minneapolis. A second roundtable was held in 1984.
- 1983–85 **Gift calculation software firms founded**, such as Philanthro Tec (1983), Crescendo (1984), and PG Calc (1985). In 1994, the ACGA published a list of eleven planned-gift software vendors.
- 1985–87 **Michael Boland, Charles Johnson, and Richard Wilson** led a series of meetings and conferences aimed at raising the professional competence and business practices of charitable gift planners. Their efforts resulted in a national professional organization for gift planners.
- 1986 **Tax Reform Act** increased tax rates for capital-gain income, closed popular methods of reducing taxes ("loopholes"), and opened the door to questionable practices. Some financial planners began promoting the use of charitable-remainder trusts as tax shelters and asked nonprofit organizations to pay finders' fees in exchange for a remainder interest.
- 1987 The **National Committee on Planned Giving (NCPG)**, a federation of planned-giving councils, appointed its first officers. NCPG was supported by a grant from the Lilly Endowment and received administrative services from the Center on Philanthropy at Indiana University/Purdue University at Indianapolis (IUPUI).
- 1988 **First public NCPG Conference** held in Indianapolis.
- 1989–90 Creation and publication of the **CANARAS Convention** and the **CANARAS Code** on ethical gift-planning behavior.
- 1989 **Second NCPG Conference** was marked by anger over the lack of opportunity for council participation and

a proposed national training and certification process for charitable gift planners.

- 1991 **Model Standards of Practice for the Charitable Gift Planner** adopted by the National Committee on Planned Giving and the Committee on Gift Annuities.
- 1993 The Committee on Gift Annuities became incorporated under Texas law as the **American Council on Gift Annuities**.
- 1994–97 A **national class-action lawsuit** in Texas alleged price-fixing by nonprofits using payment rates recommended by the Committee on Gift Annuities. The plaintiffs sought triple damages for annuitants. Congress enacted the **Philanthropy Protection Act of 1995,** affirming the validity of a national gift annuity rate schedule and mandating disclosures for annuitants. The **Charitable Donation Antitrust Immunity Act of 1997** resolved the lawsuit by protecting pooled investment funds by banks serving nonprofit annuity programs.
- 1994–2013 ACGA conducted a series of **five national gift annuity surveys** and published extensive survey data and brief analyses.
- 2001 Because of lobbying by nonprofit organizations, New York State adopted a **prudent-investor standard**, broadening the admitted assets for gift annuity reserve funds after sixty-two years of restricting investments in common stocks (see 1939). New Jersey followed in 2004.
- Jan 1, 2009 The National Committee on Planned Giving changed its name to the Partnership for Philanthropic Planning.
- 2001–02 ACGA commissioned a **gift-annuitant-mortality study** involving 24,445 gift annuity contracts.
- 2010 ACGA commissioned another **gift-annuitant-mortality study** involving 47,075 gift annuity contracts.

Gift-annuitant mortality exceeded expectations: there were 50 percent more deaths than predicted by ACGA's current methodology.

- Apr. 6–8, 2016   The **thirty-second Conference on Gift Annuities** was held in Saint Louis, Missouri.
- 2016 The Partnership for Philanthropic Planning (PPP) changed its name to the **National Association of Charitable Gift Planners**.

Appendix II

Yale's Annuity Bond with John Trumbull[1]

Know all men by these presents, that we, the President and Fellows of Yale College in New Haven, are held and firmly bound unto John Trumbull, of the city and state of New York, Esquire, in the sum of twenty thousand dollars lawful money of the United States of America, to be paid to the said John Trumbull, his certain attorney, executors, administrators or assigns, for which payment we bind ourselves and our successors firmly by these presents, sealed with our corporate seal, and dated the nineteenth day of December, in the year of our Lord one thousand eight hundred and thirty one.

The condition of the above obligation is such, that if the above bounden obligors shall and do yearly and every year for and during the natural life of the said John Trumbull, well and truly pay or cause to be paid to him or to his certain attorney or assigns, an annuity or clear yearly sum of one thousand dollars lawful money of the United States of America, in even quarterly payments to be made on the four following days in the year, that is to say, on the first day of October, the first day of January, the first day of April, and the first day of July in every year, by even and equal portions, the first payment thereof to begin and be made on the first day of October, in the year of our Lord one thousand eight hundred and thirty two—then the above obligations to be void, else to remain in full force and virtue.

—Jeremiah Day, President of Yale College

Signed by the President of the College, in my presence. Witness the seal of the College. Certified,

—Elizur Goodrich, Secretary of Yale College

Notes

1   From Trumbull 1953, 288–89.

Appendix III

Yale's Indenture with John Trumbull[1]

This indenture, made the nineteenth day of December, in the year of our Lord one thousand eight hundred and thirty one, between John Trumbull, of the city and state of New York, Esquire, of the first part, and the President and Fellows of Yale College in New Haven, of the second part, witnesseth, that the said John Trumbull, in consideration that the parties of the second part have executed a bond or obligation, whereby they have bound themselves to pay to him during his natural life an annuity of one thousand dollars a year, in the manner and at the times specified in the conditions of the said bond; and also in consideration of his good will toward Yale College, and his desire to promote its prosperity, hath granted, bargained, sold and conveyed, and hereby doth grant, bargain, sell and convey, to the parties of the second part and their successors, all the pictures or paintings mentioned in the schedule to this indenture, annexed, to have and to hold the same upon the conditions and for the purposes herein mentioned, provided always and nevertheless, and these presents are upon condition, that if the said annuity, or any part thereof, shall be behind or unpaid by the space of fifteen days next after any of the days of payment whereon the same ought to be paid, pursuant to the condition of the said bond, or if default shall be made in any of the covenants or agreements herein contained, on the part and behalf of the parties of the second part, or their successors, to be kept and performed then and from henceforth, it shall and may be lawful for the said John Trumbull, his executors, administrators or assigns, to retake and repossess the said paintings, and the same to have again, repossess and enjoy, as in his first and former estate, any thing herein contained to the contrary notwithstanding. And it is covenanted and agreed by and between the parties to these presents, in manner following, that is to say, that the parties of the second part shall erect upon land belonging to them in New Haven, a fire-proof building for the reception of the said paintings, which building shall be finished on or before the first day of October, in the year of our Lord one thousand eight hundred and thirty two, and shall be of such form and dimensions as shall be approved of by the said John Trumbull, and the said paintings shall be placed and arranged in the said building, under the directions and superintendence of the said John Trumbull, and the said paintings after they shall be so placed and arranged, shall be exhibited, and the profits of such exhibition shall be received by the parties of the second part, and applied in the first place toward the payment of the said annuity during the life of the said John Trumbull, and the whole of such profits after his death (except in the case hereinafter mentioned,) shall be perpetually appropriated toward defraying the expense of educating poor scholars in Yale College, under such regulations as the said President and Fellows, and their successors, shall from time to time see fit to make. And if the profits of such exhibition shall not, during the life of the said John Trumbull, be sufficient to discharge the said annuity, then the said parties of the second part may borrow as much money as may be necessary for that purpose, and the profits of the said exhibition, after the decease of the said John Trumbull, shall be applied to discharge the principal and interest of the debt which shall thus have been incurred, and after the said debt shall be extinguished, then the whole profits of the said exhibition shall be applied toward defraying the expense of the education of poor scholars, in manner aforesaid. And it is further expressly agreed, that the said paintings shall never be sold, alienated, divided or dispersed, but shall always be kept together, and exhibited as aforesaid, by the said parties of the second part, and their successors, and that the profits of such exhibition shall be sacredly applied to the purposes before mentioned, and to no other.

In witness whereof, the parties to these presents have interchangeably executed the same, that is to say, the said John Trumbull hath to one part of these presents set his hand and seal, and the said President and Fellows of Yale College, in New Haven, have to another part of these presents caused their corporate seal to be affixed, on the day and year first above written.

—Jeremiah Day, President of Yale College

Signed by the President of the College, in my presence. Witness the seal of the College.

—Elizur Goodrich, Secretary of Yale College

Schedule referred to in the annexed instrument, being a list of the paintings thereby conveyed to the President and Fellows of Yale College, in New Haven.

Eight original paintings of subjects from the American Revolution, viz.

1. The Battle of Bunker's Hill
2. *The Death of Gen. Montgomery at Quebec*
3. *The Declaration of Independence*
4. *The Battle of Trenton*
5. *The Battle of Princeton*
6. *The Surrender of Gen. Burgoyne*

7. *The Surrender of Lord Cornwallis*
8. *Washington Resigning his Commission*[2]

Our Savior with little children

The woman accused of adultery

Peter the Great at Narva

Madonna and Children, copied from Raphael

Saint Jerome, Madonna, &c., copied from Correggio

Infant Savior, Saint John and Lamb

Holy Family

Saint John and Lamb

Maternal Tenderness

Portrait of President Washington

Do. of Alexander Hamilton

Do. of Rufus King

Do. of Christopher Gore

Six frames, each containing five miniature portraits of persons distinguished during the Revolution[3]

—Jeremiah Day, President of Yale College

Notes

1   From Trumbull 1953, 285–88.

2   Note by Theodore Sizer in his edition of Trumbull's *Autobiography* (1953, 287): "These are the eight originals of the celebrated 'national history' series, begun in 1785 and finished in 1822."

3   Six frames (thirty miniature portraits) were thus committed to Yale;

another six had been allocated to Hartford. Trumbull also decided to give these frames, containing twenty-eight miniature portraits, to Yale. He installed all fifty-eight portraits in the new gallery in 1832.

Appendix IV

Luther Bradish, *On the Matter of Accepting Trusts* (1848)[1]

which were approved.

Mr. Bradish from the Select Comee. appointed at the stated meeting in February made the following Report which was unanimously adopted and directed to be placed upon the Minutes.

The Select Comee. to whom were referred the Proposition of Mr. Amos Wright to give to this Society Two thousand Dollars upon condition of receiving from the Society the payment annually during his life of a sum equal to its Interest; and also a Preamble & Resolution upon the same general subject, presented for the consideration of the Board by Mr. Woolsey, respectfully submit the following,

Report: In whatever aspect the subject referred to the Committee may be viewed, whether regard be had to the question of Interest it presents, the Principles it involves, or the Consequences to flow from its decision, its importance will be Conceded by all. Duly impressed with this importance the Committee have felt it their duty to give to the subject their most careful attention. In an ordinary case, the Committee would have felt their deliberations upon this subject somewhat embarrassed by the former action of the Board in regard to it. But they deem its right decision of such paramount importance as to supersede every other consideration; and to render it the duty of the Committee to enter upon its examination as if it were now presented for the first time. While, therefore, the Committee entertain all proper deference and respect for the past action of the Board and its Committees upon this subject, they will proceed to its consideration uninfluenced by anything but what may appear to them its own intrinsic merits and the true Principles it involves.

As the decision of the Board in the particular case now before it may establish a general rule for its future government in all cases presenting the same or analogous facts the Committee will consider the subject with reference to such general rule, as well as to the particular case in hand.

The Subject under consideration presents two general Questions, viz.

1st. Would the receiving by the American Bible Society of Donations under the circumstances, and upon the conditions proposed in the particular case in question be legal? and if so

2nd. Would it be expedient?

To an affirmative decision upon the general subject it is necessary that both these preliminary Questions should also be decided in the affirmative; because however desireable in point of Interest the receiving of such donations may be, yet if that would be illegal or even of doubtful right that should of course decide the general Question: So too if the question of legality be conceded yet if the receiving of such Donations upon the terms proposed would be, inexpedient that also should govern the decision of the question and settle the general rule.

First then would the receiving of such donations by this Society upon the terms proposed be legal?

The transaction would be either –

1st Simply a matter of Contract; or

2nd A Trust.

If simply a matter of Contract then no doubt could for a moment be entertained that it would be entirely lawful.

If a Trust, then is it such a Trust as this Society may rightfully and effectually take and execute?

Perhaps upon no branch of the Law have opinions been more variant, or the Law itself undergone greater changes than that which regards the capacity of Corporations to take and execute Trusts. The ancient and extreme Doctrine undoubtedly was that a Corporation could not be a Trustee; and this whatever might be the character of the Corporation or the object of the trust. A Doctrine so extreme and severe as this could not long be sustained by the increasing intelligence and common sense of the world. We therefore see it early relaxing in the case of Religious corporations and in favor of charitable uses. So strong was this early tendency of the public mind in England, that in order to remove all doubt, express statutes were passed in the 39th and 43rd of Elizabeth, recognizing such trust powers and charitable uses as legal and giving the Courts of Equity jurisdiction over them. The latter of these statutes more particularly has been denominated and generally known as "The Statute of Charitable Uses."

In the adjudications under this Statute the opinion has been held and repeatedly expressed by most of the learned Judges of England and has now there become the settled doctrine that this Statute was not the enactment of new law, but merely declaratory of that which had long existed. That Grants or Devises to Corporations for charitable uses, long previous to the passage of that statute and of course independent of it had been recognized as legal, and congnizance had been taken of them by the Courts of Equity. Of this opinion were Lords Ridesdale, Loughborough, Northington, Eldon, Chief Justice Wilmot, Chancellor Sugden, Sir Joseph Jeckyll, Sir John Leach and others. This opinion has been expressed by these Judges in several cases which came before them for adjudication, and which are reported in the Books. Mr. Shelford too in his admirable Treatise on Mortmain Ch. IV Sec. 1. 2. says "That the King as Parens Patriae has a superintending power over all charities abstracted from and antendent to the statue of 43 Eliz", which paternal care and protection is delegated to the Court of Chancery" and further that "this statute (43 Eliz) did not create new Law with respect to charitable uses but only a new and ancillary jurisdiction by commission" subject to "the controlling jurisdiction of the Court of Chancery as it existed before the Passage of that Statute." For this he refers to several authorities of acknowledged weight.

    In this country it is exceedingly important to sustain this opinion, for the statute of the 43d of Elizabeth not having been re-enacted in many of the States of the Union, and being in some others where it had been re-enacted, wholly repealed, if it were the enactment of new law and not according to that opinion merely declaratory of the existing law, our Courts of Equity would be divested of an important branch of their supposed jurisdiction, and our Common Law of some of its valuable provisions. It is certain that the doctrine in regard to charitable uses is of very ancient date. It has been supposed to have been derived from the civil law and early incorporated into the Common Law of England. Of this opinion were Lords Thurlow and Eldon, and to this opinion Judge Story also seems to incline. But the civil law was introduced into England about the year 1138. While it seems to be a well established fact that the Law of Charitable uses existed and was in operation there long prior to that Period indeed that it is co-eval with the introduction of Christianity itself, from which it evidently sprung. It has been truly said that wherever Christianity went, charity and the Law of charitable uses went with it. It has been supposed that Christianity was introduced into England about the time it was into Rome by St. Paul and St. Peter. At latest it certainly came there with St. Augustine in 597, when the Arch Bishop of Canterbury was appointed to the office which has continued ever since.

    Thus the law of charitable uses in England seems to have been as ancient in its origin, as it has been uniform in its observance. But this Law authorizing Corporations to take, by Grant or Devise, estates *in trust for charitable uses*, has been gradually relaxing; and in the application of its Principles, becoming more and more general, until Jeremy in his Treatise on Equity Jurisdiction Book 1, Ch. 1 S1.2 advances the Doctrine which in its latitude, would and have been deemed startling "*That a Corporate body may be a Trustee, not merely for charitable purposes within the 43d of Eliz. but in all cases in which an Individual may be a Trustee*." This Doctrine is sustained by the Decisions in the cases reported in 1 Ves.536, 2 vern 412,454. Hob 136, 2 Swanst 590, 1 ves 468, 2 Bro P. C. 235 and 2 Ves Jun46. Such indeed seems now to be the settled Law of England.

    In this country with some exceptions in the settlement of the Law upon this subject, the tendency has been to the extreme modern doctrine in England. The law of charitable uses was very ably discussed, deliberately considered and well settled by the Court of Chancery of Vermont, in the important case of "the Executor of Joseph Burr VS Richard Smith and others" reported in 7 Vermont Rep 241. In the Decision in that Case, This Society, while yet merely an association, was interested as one of the beneficiaries under the Trust, which was there drawn into question, but which was sustained by the final judgment of the Court. That case is one of great interest, not only as a leading one in that state upon its general subject, and the great care with which it was considered, but especially for the argument of unrivalled ability pronounced in it by Mr. Wood of our own Bar. Of this argument it has been well said by one, who, from his long and intimate knowledge of this interesting branch of the Law and of all that has been produced upon it by the best judicial minds of Europe, is as competent to judge as he is fastidious in his opinion of merit and chary of his compliments "that at the time it was published it was the best thing upon the subject in the Language." This argument and the Decision of the Court in this case fully recognize the doctrine of charitable uses and the power of corporations to take by Grant or Devise estates in trust for such uses.

In the very interest case of "Vidal and others vs Girards Executors" in the Supreme Court of the United States, reported in 2 Howards R 127 and so ably argued by John Sergeant, Horace Binney and Daniel Webster, Judge Story in delivering the opinion of the Court, goes beyond the Decision in the Vermont case and seems to adopt the extreme Doctrine of Jeremy. He says, "although in early times it was held that a Corporation could not take & hold Real & Personal Estates in trust upon the ground that there was a defect of one of the requisites to create a good Trustee, viz, a want of confidence in the person; yet that doctrine has been long since exploded as unsound and too artificial, and it is now held that where the Corporation has a legal capacity to take and hold Real and Personal Estate, there it may take and hold it upon trust, in the same manner and to the same extent as a Private Person may do" – "That there is no positive objection in point of Law to a Corporation taking Property upon a trust not strictly within the scope of the direct purposes of its institution, but collateral to them; nay for the benefit of a stranger or of another Corporation." In regard to this latter principle he puts himself upon the authority of the cases of McIntire Free School vs The Zanesville Canal Co. 8 Ohio Rep 217 and especially that of The Trustees of Phillips Academy vs King Executor &c 12 Mssts Rep 546. This latter case perhaps more than any other in this country has carried the principal in regard to the capacity of Corporations to take & execute trusts, to the extent of the extreme doctrine laid down by Jeremy. This was the case of a Legacy of Thirty thousand Dollars bequeathed by Mary Norris to the Trustees of Phillips Academy in Andover, for the purpose and to the use and benefit of the Theological Institution, otherwise called "The Divinity College of Andover", upon Special Trust, that the Trustees of the Academy should invest and manage the capital sum as the Theological Institution should direct, and that the latter should receive the whole Income of the said Trust Fund.

Here it will be perceived that the Academy was in no respect a beneficiary under this trust, but that in taking and executing the trust, she was a mere naked Trustee without interest. And yet the court sustained this bequest, and fully affirmed the power of the first corporation to take and administer the trust for the use and benefit of the Second Corporation as the exclusive certui que trust.

Judge Thatcher, in delivering the opinion of the Court in this case, expressed his surprise that the Power of Corporations to take and execute such trusts should ever have been called in question; and accounts for it upon the supposition that the Principles deduced from the ancient prescriptive Corporations had without due consideration, been applied by the writers upon this subject, to modern Corporations, which being creatures of the Law, may take and exercise any Powers with which the creative Power in its wisdom and sovereignty may invest them and not inconsistant with the constitution of the Government.

The Courts and writers of our own State have occupied upon this subject a more middle ground, a ground equally removed from the ancient strictness and the unlimited doctrine of Jeremy. While they recognize the power in Corporations to take and execute trusts, yet this is submoda and only admitted in well defined cases and upon specific conditions. It must be either among their specified powers or those necessarily incident thereto. The objects of the Trust should be within the general scope of the declared objects of the Corporation, and not foreign to its institution. The Corporation should have either a direct or collateral interest in the Trust. This is the Doctrine of 2 Kents com 279.5 "ed the case of 8 John Rep 422, 2 John Ch R 384. and 1 Page ch R 214 and it is sustained by the decision in the cases in 3 Pick Msstts. Rep. 257, 1 Penn Rep 49 and 6 Conn Rep 304. Indeed it is believed to be as yet the more general doctrine of this country, and in the language of the admirable treatise on Corporations by Angell and Ames "This appears to us more expedient than the ancient strictness of the Law in this particular, and more conformable to principle than the unlimited Doctrine asserted by Jeremy". The tendency however here as well as in England undoubtedly is to the latter Doctrine. Even our own great Commentator Chancellor Kent says that "at this day the only reasonable limitation is that a corporation cannot be seized of Land in trust for purposes foreign to its institution" see 2 Kents Conn 279.

The case above cited from 1 Paige ch Rep 214, is so analogous in its facts and the general principles it involves, with that presented in the proposition of Mr. Wright, and referred to the Committee and the Decision of it so clear and conclusive that it requires a more particular notice. It was the case of Howe Executor of Anderson deceased and was as follows.

Nicholas Anderson, the Testator gave to St. Georges Church in New York a Legacy of Four thousand Dollars in trust that the same should be put out at interest or vested in Public Stocks, and that the income thereof should be paid to his Housekeeper for life; and after her death the Income thereof to be applied to the purchase of a Church Library, the support of a Sabbath School in the church and other church purposes, to which the Church contributions may be applied agreeably to the Canons of the Episcopal church.

Chancellor Walworth, in delivering the opinion of the Court of Chancery in this case says "It is a general rule that Corporations cannot exercise any powers not given to them by their charters or acts of incorporation; and for that reason they cannot act as Trustees in relation to any matter in which the Corporation has no interest. But wherever the Property is devised or granted to a Corporation partly for its own use and partly for the use of others, the right of the Corporation to take and hold the property for its own use, carries with it as a necessary incident, the Power to execute that part of the Trust which relates to others. In this case the substantial part of the Legacy is for the benefit of the Corporation, and the income thereof after the death of the Housekeeper, is to be applied to some of the purposes to which the Rector, Church Wardens, and Vestrymen were authorized to apply the general funds or temporalities of the Church under their Management. The Testator had a right to limit his bounty to a part of the objects to which they might appropriate the general funds of the Corporation. He also had a right to direct when the Income should be applied for that purpose. If the Corporation receive the Legacy it must be re-

1912.   Managers   -   March 2, 1840.

ceived charged with the payment of the Interest or Income to the Housekeeper for Life. The Corporation must execute the trust in her favor
to enable them to obtain the fund which is afterwards to be appropriated
to Corporate purposes. The Legacy must therefore be paid over to the
Rector, Church Wardens and Vestrymen as the Representatives of the Cor-
porators who are bound to carry into effect the Testators will in respect
to the same."

It will thus be perceived that this case is almost precisely par-
allel in its facts, and entirely so in its principles, with that now in
hand; and that if the chancellors opinion in that case be sound Law, and
it has never been questioned, it is conclusive upon the legal questions presented as well in the particular case now before us as in the proposed
general Rule.

The affirmative of the Question of Legality then being conceded, the
Committee proceed to submit their views,

2dly. on the Q uestion of Expediency.
It will be readily admitted that it is as well the duty, as it is
unquestionably the right of the American Bible Society to increase her
corporate funds in every legal and proper manner, in order thereby to en-
large her means of accomplishing the great & beneficient purposes of her
institution. But in the report of a former Committee of this Board upon
this subject the apprehension is expressed, "That from the confidence felt
in this Society, this disposition of funds might if encouraged become a
favorite one with its friends, that ultimately a large debt might thus be
incurred, the interest upon which might become burdensome, and our future
patrons be disposed to contribute less liberally to an Institution thus
heavily taxed for monies long since expended."

If the view here presented be correct and the apprehension it expresses well founded, it should be conclusive upon the whole subject. But
with great deference the reasoning of this paragraph seems to your present
Committee to proceed upon an assumption of the very Question in discussion;
and the evils it apprehends are rather incidental to a supposed mismanagement of the funds to be received in the manner proposed, than consequences
necessarily flowing from the receiving of such funds in that way.

That the confidence reposed in this Society will render such a disposition of funds as that contemplated a favorite one with its friends,
if encouraged your Committee do not doubt. But if this be within the Corporate powers, and the legitimate functions of this Society as has been
already shown and it would increase its means of usefulness by aiding in
the accomplishment of its great and beneficial purposes, it should be a
subject rather of congratulation than of regret.

If however as is supposed in the former report upon this subject
the donations in question were to be received and immediately expended
leaving the Society for the future without any additional means, charged with
the performance of the conditions upon which those donations had been accepted then indeed the result apprehended in that Report might be realised.
This would be an additional burden without any corresponding additional
strength to bear it. But this as before remarked has regard not to the

receiving of the funds but to their subsequent management and the result apprehended is in the judgment of your Committee in no respect necessary.   Such result may be obviated in either of the two following modes, viz.

1st. By depositing with a Trust Institution such a part of the donation received as may be sufficient to purchase or sustain an Annuity equal to the sum, the payment of which is the condition of the Donation.   Or

2nd. By setting apart and investing either in Bond & Mortgage or the Public Stocks of the United States or of the State of New York and placed under the management of the Society itself through its proper offices a similar part of the donation.

As the former mode if carried out would render this Society, except under a special contract releasing her, a Guarantor of the Annuity and of course of the continued solvency of the Institution issuing it, there might be some objection to its adoption.

In the second mode suggested the Society itself would be the exclusive manager of the portion of the donations set apart for the performance of their conditions and would therefore incur no risk except from her own want of wisdom and prudence.

In either mode ample provision might be made for the performance of the conditions of the donations and a considerable surplus of those donations still remain to be applied in the sound discretion of the Society to the furtherance of her great objects. That the deep interest felt by many in those objects, as well as the peculiar situation of such individuals would induce frequent and important donations to this Society upon the terms in question, your Committee fully believe. Independent of the experience of the past they can readily imagine that the future may present many cases of aged persons in the possession of wealth from which they are soon to be separated but the use of which during their lives is essential to their comfort, might with a view of relieving themselves from the trouble, the responsibility, and the risk of its management by themselves or others their Agents, desire to give that wealth upon the terms proposed to a Society in whose objects they feel a deep interest and a strong desire to contribute to their promotion. This feeling is not a little strengthened by the new difficulties which modern legislation presents in regard to testamentary dispositions of Estates generally and especially to the creation by will of valid and effectual trusts. These have given rise to the strong desire in all, as far as may be practicable to execute their own wills in their own life time.   It is natural that this should be so.   In giving effect therefore to these feelings in the way proposed, the Donor and the Recipient would be benefitted.   Charitable Corporations like the American Bible Society in the language of the great and good Chancellor Kent are from their peculiar structure and perpetual succession "proper and safe depositaries of Trusts"; especially of trusts not foreign to their institution, but directly in aid of their declared objects.   Shall this Society then in view of the great good she might accomplish both for charitably disposed individuals and in furtherance of her own objects, still shrink from the responsibility of assuming such trusts in the way proposed? That responsibility would not be the tithe of that now incurred in many of her ordinary and daily operations.

1914.   managers   -   March 2, 1848.

If by adopting the course proposed and thus giving exercise and
effect to individual benevolence, the means of this Society would be so
increased as to enable her to place in the hands of a single additional be-
nighted Pagan or destitute Infidel the living oracles of Light and Life, and
thus under the blessing of God become the means of reclaiming from error and
bringing to a knowledge of the Truth one additional human soul, how immeasur-
ably would this outweigh all the considerations that even the most shrinking
timidity or the most extreme fastidiousness could possibly suggest against
the plan proposed? Deeply impressed however as the Committee are with this
view of this subject, they yet fully concur in the practical, plain and
homely truth "that there is a right way of doing even right things." They
are, too, fully aware that the character of the American Bible Society con-
stitutes, under Heaven, her strength. They would therefore be among the
last to jeopard that character by recommending either the assumption and
exercise of a questionable power or the adoption of a doubtful expediency.
But firmly believing as they do that the course proposed is clearly within the Corporate powers, and entirely in harmony with the appropriate functions
and legitimate objects of this Society; and that its adoption would be as expedient, as its principle is sound, the Committee are unanimously of opinion
that the Society not only has the right, but that it is her duty to adopt
the Plan proposed as a general rule for her future action.

The Committee have not prepared and therefore do not submit for the
consideration of the Board, a resolution embodying in form such general
rule, and defining its specific provisions. This could not well be done.
They would therefore, respectfully recommend that under the assertion of
the general principle of the Legality and Expediency of the plan proposed,
each individual case should be left to be determined according to its own
peculiar circumstances, by the sound discretion of the Society at the time
such case is presented.

In regard to the particular case of Mr. Wright referred to the Committee it being embraced in the general subject, and fully within the reasoning of this Report, the Committee recommend that his proposition be accepted,
and that it be referred to the Standing Committee on Publication and Finance
to be carried into effect upon proper and safe conditions.

    All which is respectfully submitted,

                                    (signed) L. Bradish   )
                                              E. J. Woolsey) Comee.
New York, March 2d, 1848.   Benj. L. Swan)

Notes

1   Minutes of the Ways and Means Committee of the American Bible
        Society (1848).

Appendix V

George Huggins, "Actuarial Basis of Rates" (1927)

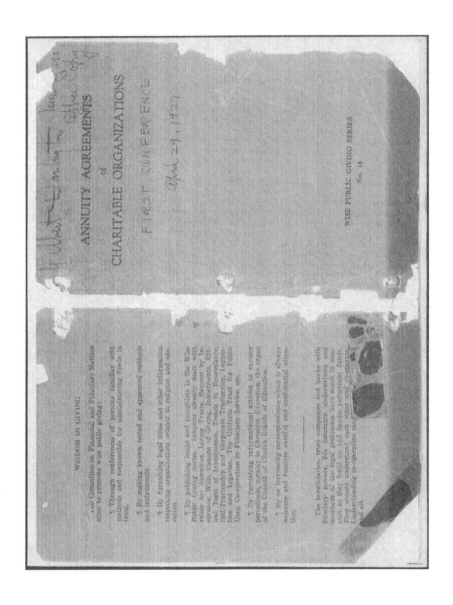

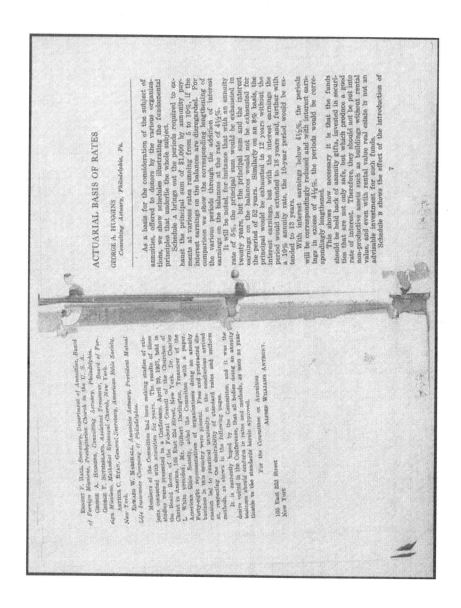

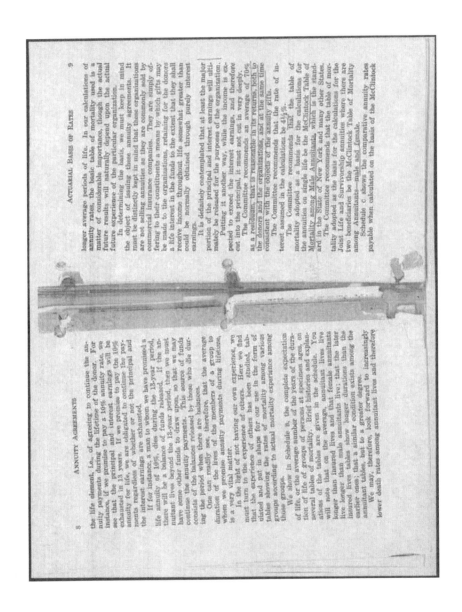

ANNUITY AGREEMENTS

the life element, i.e., of agreeing to continue the annuity payments during the lifetime of the donor. For instance, if we promise to pay a 10% annuity rate, we see that the principal and interest earnings will be exhausted in 13 years. If we promise to pay the 10% annuity for life, we are obligated to continue the payments regardless of whether or not the principal and the interest earnings are exhausted.

If for instance, a man to whom we have promised a life annuity of 10%, dies during the 13-year period, there will be a balance of funds released. If the annuitant lives beyond the 13-year period, then we may have some other funds to draw upon, so that we may continue the annuity payments. This source of funds consists of the balances released by those who die during the period when there are no business. One can readily see, therefore, that the average of the lives of the members of a group, during which we promise annuity payments during lifetime, is a very vital matter.

In the light of not having our own experience, we must turn to the experience of others. Here we find that the experience of others has been studied, tabulated and put in shape for our use in the form of tables showing the rates of mortality among various groups according to actual mortality experience among these groups.

We show in Schedule B, the complete expectation of life, or the average number of the years of the duration of life of groups of persons at specimen ages, on several tables of mortality. Brief histories and explanations of the tables are given in the schedule. You will note that on the average, annuitant lives live longer than insured lives and that female annuitants live longer than male annuitant durations than the insured lives table show longer durations among the earlier ones; that a similar condition exists among annuitant tables, but to a greater degree.

We may, therefore, look forward to increasingly lower death rates among annuitant lives and therefore

ACTUARIAL BASIS OF RATES

longer average periods of life. In our calculations of annuity rates, the basic table of mortality used is a matter of considerable importance, though the actual future results will naturally depend upon the actual future experience of the particular organization.

In determining the basis, we must keep in mind the object of issuing these annuity agreements. It must be distinctly kept in mind that these organizations are not selling annuities as they are commonly sold by commercial insurance companies. They are simply offering to their constituents a means by which gifts may be made to the organizations, retaining (or the donors a life interest in the funds to the extent that they shall receive income throughout life somewhat greater than could be normally obtained through purely interest earnings.

It is definitely contemplated that at least the major portion of the principal and interest earnings will ultimately be released for the purposes of the organization.

Putting it another way, while the income is expected to exceed the interest earnings, and therefore cut into the principal, it must not eat in very deeply.

The Committee recommends an average of 70%, as a residuum, that is reasonable in its returns, both to the donors and the organization, and at the same time consistent with the object of the annuity gift.

The Committee recommends that the rate of interest assumed in the calculations be 4½%.

The Committee recommends that the table of mortality adopted as a basis for the calculations for the annuities on single life be the McClintock Table of Mortality among Male Annuitants, which is the standard in the State of New York and many other States.

The Committee recommends that the table of mortality adopted as the basis for the calculations for the Joint Life and Survivorship annuities where there are two beneficiaries be the McClintock Table of Mortality among Annuitants—male and female.

Schedule C shows the comparative annuity rates payable when calculated on the basis of the McClintock

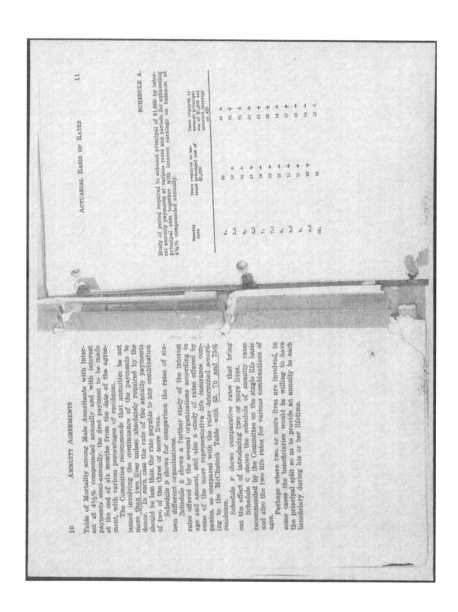

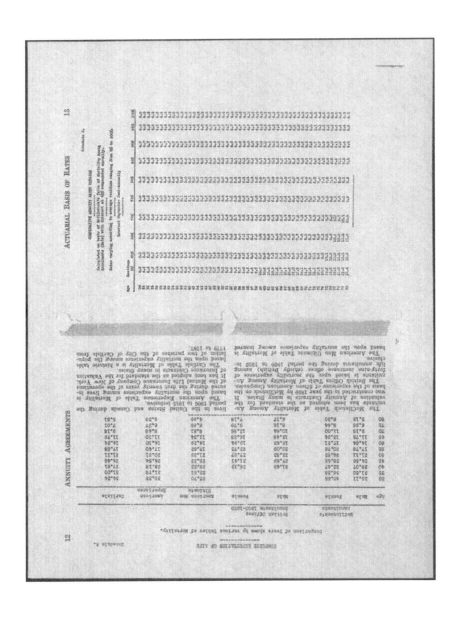

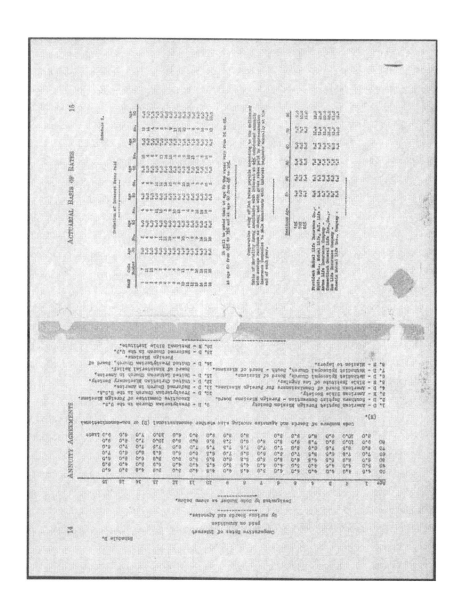

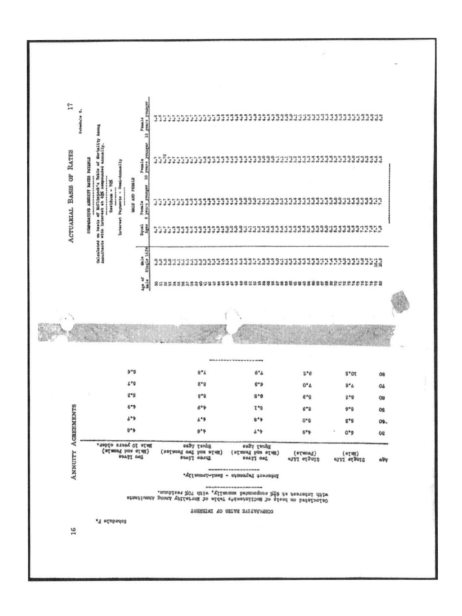

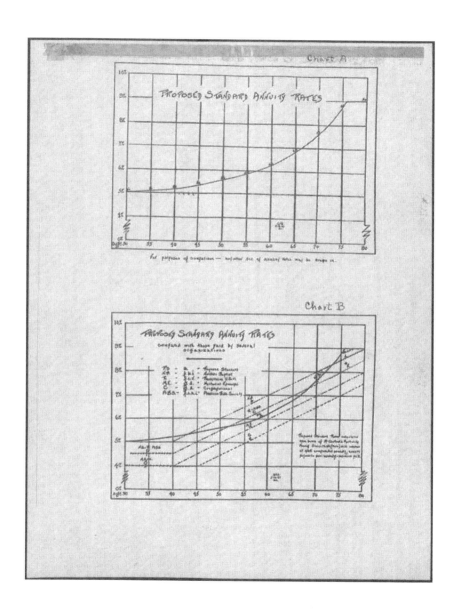

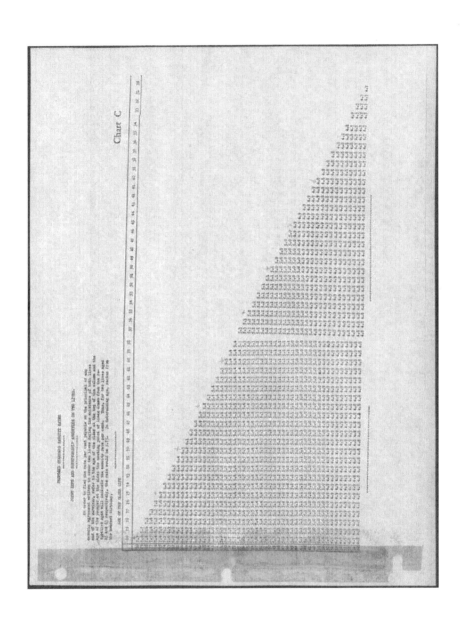

Chart C

Appendix VI

CGA Rates Chart, 1927–59 (Single Life)

Gift Annuity conferences	Rate age 70	Rate age 80	Assumed return	Mortality table	Age setback	Residuum target	Historical notes
1: April 29, 1927	7.6%	9.0% for age 76+ [10.5% for age 80+]	4.5%	McClintock Table of Mortality Among Male Annuitants (1899)	0	70%	George Huggins recommended a top rate of 10.5% for annuitants age 80+ [brackets] but conference participants voted to cap the rate at 9% for annuitants aged 76+. Huggins produced a revised rate table for the conference report. For 1927–31, the rates for a single-life annuity were based on a male life, thereafter on a female life.

CGA Rates Chart, 1927–59 (Single Life)

2: November 9, 1928	7.6%	9% for age 76+	4.5%	McClintock	0	70%	No substantial report on rates. Discussion of whether investing in common stocks is right for gift annuity reserve accounts if not okay for commercial annuities that are restricted by law.
3: November 17, 1930	7.6%	9% for age 76+	4.5%	McClintock	0	70%	Stock market crashed in October 1929, marking start of the Great Depression, but bond yields remained high (temporarily). No substantial report on rates.

337

| 4: March 17, 1931 | 6.7% | 8.0% | 4.5% | American Annuitants Table (1927) | 0 | 70% | Three actuarial presentations on gift annuity rates and reserves. Huggins noted lower death rates among commercial annuitants. He presented rate calculations for male and female lives; Conference voted to keep a unisex table but changed base to a female life and to cap rates at 8%. No change to 4.5% return assumption. One presenter discussed a 5% annual-expense load; that was not adopted for rates calculations until 1955. |

5: November 30, 1934	6.2%	8.0%	4.0%	Combined Annuity Mortality Table, Female Lives (1934)	0	70%	Low interest rates led to an "urgent request" for a lower payment schedule. First report on a gift-annuitant-mortality study showed unfavorable mortality experience and a low residuum for two-life CGAs due to "too liberal annuity rates." Adjusted rate table accordingly. Huggins noted that a 4-year setback for female lives was built into the Combined Annuity Table.

| 6: October 4–5, 1939 | 6.2% [5.5%] | 8.0% [7.1%] | 4.0% [3.5%] | Combined Annuity Mortality Table, Female Lives (1934) | 0 [2] | 70% | A year of crisis. War began in Europe a month before the conference. Bond yields at an "all-time low." Huggins notes lower returns and increasing annuitant longevity, recommending a 2-year setback. Illustrates rates with investment assumptions of 4%, 3.5% and 3%. Selects 3.5% return for safety and to attract new gifts. Huggins proposed lowering rates [brackets]. Committee deferred action pending economic effects of the war. |

7: April 29, 1941	5.5%	7% for age 80+	3.5%	Combined Annuity Mortality Table, Female Lives (1934)	2	70%	Committee adopted Huggins's conservative recommendations from 1939 because of lower interest rates, the results of gift-annuitant actuarial surveys, and NY State Insurance Code mandates for gift annuities. United States entered WWII in December 1941 following attack on Pearl Harbor.

| 8: April 10, 1946 | 5.5% [5.1%] | 7.0% [6.9%] | 3.5% [2.5%] | Combined Annuity Mortality Table, Female Lives (1934) [Standard Annuity Table, 1937] | 2 [1] | 70% [50%] | WWII ended in June 1945, followed by start of Cold War. Huggins recommended major changes: one-time 5% expense load, drop in investment assumption, new mortality table, and a 50% residuum. The committee voted to make no changes because of uncertain postwar economy. |

9: October 3–4, 1955	5.5%	7.4%	3.0%	Standard Annuity Table (1937)	1	50%	Next conference held nine years after the end of WWII. Huggins's longest, most detailed, and most philosophical report to date analyzed results of two recent gift-annuitant-mortality studies. Reserve funds began allocating significant amounts to common stocks. Committee on Gift Annuities became an independent body, adopted a 50% residuum target and 5% expense load.

| 10: December 1–2, 1959 | 5.3% | 7.2% | 3.0% | American Annuity Table (1955) | 0 | 50% | Strong economic trends. First conference report since 1928 to encourage buying common stocks ("the outstanding investment medium in the post-war period") for inflation protection of reserve accounts. The last report by Huggins compared new gift-annuitant-mortality experience with survey results in 1952, found favorable experience and good fit with new American Annuity Table. Investment experience had been more positive, but New York mandated a 3% return assumption, so Huggins used that in his rate calculations. |

Appendix VII

Summary of Conference Presentations on Reserve Fund Investment Policies and Allocation (1927–2017)

Gift annuity conferences	Investment presentation(s)	Major financial topics	Recommended asset allocation	Assumed return for rate setting	Assumed return for reserves
1: April 29, 1927	No separate presentation on investments. Gilbert Darlington described NY Insurance Law of 1925.	Are gift annuity reserve fund investments subject to the laws restricting commercial life insurance annuity investments?	Arthur Ryan: Gift annuity reserves "should be invested in securities suitable for insurance companies operating in the state in which the institution is incorporated."	4.5% (No expense load for investment and admin fees until 1955.)	NY 4%, CA 3.5%
2: November 9, 1928	"Investments," George F. Sutherland	Investing reserve funds "not an especially difficult under-taking." Gift annuities are not legally required to follow life insurance investment laws.	Recommends investing in guaranteed mortgage-backed bonds, public-utility, and railroad bonds.	4.5%	NY 4%, CA 3.5%

| 3: November 17, 1930 | "Administration and Investment of Annuity Funds," William T. Boult | Gift annuity fund managers are "morally bound" to observe investment restrictions imposed on life insurance firms. Diversified bond portfolio (maturity, locality, and type). | "Depreciation in market values of stocks of fifty per cent. and more, has occurred within the last fourteen months." Recommends guaranteed mortgages on improved real estate (30%); railroads (25%); public utilities (25%); governments (10%); industrials (10%); preferred stocks (5%); industrials (5%). Avoid real estate; common stocks "should be shunned." | 4.5% | NY 4%, CA 3.5% |

"Reinsurance of Annuities," T. A. Stafford and Charles L. White	Avoid financial risks by purchasing commercial annuities	Stafford advocated investing the net amount after purchasing a commercial annuity and not using it until the contract terminates. White recommended spending the proceeds: "A great sum would be available at once to pay debts, to avert the abandonment of key enterprises whose continued life hangs in the balance, and to maintain strongly the present work during a period of world depression."
"Annuity Agreements, Cautions and Restraints," Alfred Williams Anthony	Chair of the sponsoring organization for the Committee on Gift Annuities cautioned against "reinsuring" gift annuities	Will charities become partners or agents of insurance companies? Will donors like the idea of sharing their gifts with a for-profit enterprise? Will prospective donors buy a commercial annuity rather than making a gift?

N/A: January 6–7, 1931	"The Investment of Reserve and Other Trust Funds," Francis M. Knight; national conference on gift annuities held by Methodist Church	Invest reserves for safety, yield, and marketability. Advocates "intelligent diversification."	Bond portfolio: utilities (30–40%); railroads (20–30%); industrials, real estate, and foreign governments (10–20% each)	4.5%	N/A
4: March 17, 1931	No separate presentation	Actuary Edward Marshall: gift annuities "have not as yet been required to comply with the laws governing life insurance companies."	Actuary K. B. Piper: "I know of no satisfactory method of forecasting interest rates."	4.5%	NY 4%, 3.5%

				4.0%	N/A
5: November 30, 1934	"Investment of Funds for the Safeguarding of Annuities," John H. Gross	Chairman Ernest Hall: residuum of 70% "impossible to obtain…because of the low income on safely invested securities." Gross: "It seems impossible to be certain that bonds which are high-grade today will continue to maintain that status."	Senior railroad bonds "are still in the prime investment class"; underlying mortgage bonds of "good" operating utility companies "appear to be secure"; industrial bonds are subject to economic "stagnation"; real estate mortgages have proven "difficult if not impossible to guarantee"; avoid common stocks		
6: October 4–5, 1939	"Outlook for Interest Rates," Richard P. Cromwell	Bond yields "reached a new all-time low this summer" and "are still so low, that a few years ago they would have been considered fantastic."	No specific recommendations. General conclusion: "Most of the factors now operative are tending to maintain interest rates at low levels…these factors are likely to dominate the trend for some time."	Huggins recommended 3.5%. Fearful of war, the conference made no changes, kept 4%.	NY 3.5%

"Investment Planning under Revised Insurance Law of the State of New York," Wilton A. Pierce	Financial controls imposed by the Federal Reserve and other government agencies have resulted in "planned fiscal policies, planned economics and pegging of the prime security markets" that "have become a seemingly chronic situation."	1939 NY Insurance Law prohibited non-profits from investing gift annuity reserves in common stocks. Few specific recommendations. Mentions Norfolk & Western railroad and public-utilities bonds.

| 7: April 29, 1941 | "Rates of Yield on Invested Funds Under Existing Conditions, and the Probabilities as to the Future," Dr. Marcus Nadler | Darlington: "Since November 20, 1934, interest rates on all classes of securities have declined very substantially." Nadler: "The chances are that money rates in the U.S. are going to remain low...Money is one commodity which the government can control and does control under present conditions." | Metropolitan Life reduced its annuity rates 23% from 1935 to 1940. "Where insurance companies or pension funds can buy government bonds to yield 2¾ percent, it would be unwise for them to buy corporate bonds that yield less than 3 percent, because there is nothing better than government obligations." | Surprised by the Fed's ability to keep interest rates low, the conference reduced assumed earnings to 3.5%. | N/A |

8: April 10, 1946	"Interest Rates and Possible Future Trends," Dr. B. H. Beckhart	Darlington: "Interest rates have declined substantially since 1941... This is true of interest on real estate mortgages, as well as on bonds, and preferred and common stocks." Beckhart: "The decline in the average yield on long-term bonds and the greater decline in short as compared to long-rates since 1931 are the result of commercial bank purchases of the [US national] debt."	Since 1941, most US life insurance companies assumed a return of 2.5% or 2%. Predicts that as governmental financial controls are eased and normal markets are restored, interest rates will rise, and so will prices for commodities, real estate, and common stocks.	Huggins recommended an earning assumption of 2.5%. Uncertain about the postwar economy, conference made no changes, kept assumption at 3.5%.	NY: 3.5%. "No one can predict when New York State and other states may adopt more conservative valuation tables for annuity reserves based upon present interest rates."

N/A: December 15–16, 1952	Reorganization of Federal Council of Churches left no sponsor for Committee on Gift Annuities. Huggins & Darlington presented at a Conference on Wills, Annuities, and Special Gifts.	Charles P. Taft on Cold War political economy: "It was the separation of economic power, business, that is, from identity with government, that gave the economic base for the Puritan Revolution from which most of our American democratic ideas are derived."	Darlington: the gift annuity rates adopted in 1941 are still in effect, while "interest rates have risen substantially…The yield on highest grade bonds and preferred stocks has also risen." While NY permits only a "very small investment in common stocks," other gift annuity reserves "can be invested in a diversified portfolio including common stocks and investment company stocks."	3.5%	N/A
9: October 3–4, 1955	"Interest Rates," Dr. Marcus Nadler	US business is "in the midst of the greatest boom that we have ever had in peace time in our history."	"People today are less interested in putting money in a savings bank than they are in buying equities…What the equity market will do, I don't know." No specific recommendations.	3% (One-time 5% expense load subtracted from original amount transferred.)	US Treasury regs assume a 2% return, reducing value of donor's tax deduction. NY 3%, CA 2.5%

10: December 1–2, 1959	"Interest Rates and Investment Outlook," Dr. John W. Harriman	Political economy: "Sound direction of capital promotes the development of the economy and strengthens the private enterprise system within the Free World."	"Common stocks are favored as long-term investments by economic growth, increased cyclical stability and capacity to offset inflation [emphasis added]. These qualities have made common stocks the outstanding investment medium in the post-war period... High interest rates appear likely to continue for the decade of the sixties."	3% (One-time 5% expense load subtracted from original amount transferred.)	NY 3%, CA 2.5%. Life insurance companies earned 3.85% in 1958.
32: April 5, 2016	"Explanation of the ACGA Gift Annuity Rates Effective January 1, 2012," updated June 2015, affirmed by ACGA board in April 2016 and April 2017	"History has shown that, in well-diversified portfolios, asset allocation (not investment manager selection or individual security selection) is the primary driver of investment return."	Model portfolio for rate setting: 40% equities, 55% 10-year US Treasury bonds, 5% cash and equivalents.	4.25% (Minus 1% annual load for investment and admin fees = net return of 3.25%.)	N/A

Abbreviations Used

ABS　　American Bible Society

ACGA　American Council on Gift Annuities

CFFM　Committee on Financial and Fiduciary Matters

CGA　　Committee on Gift Annuities

COA　　Conferences on Annuities

FCCCA　Federal Council of the Churches of Christ in America

NYL&T　New York Life Insurance and Trust Company (not same as today's NY Life)

SOA　　Subcommittee on Annuities, forerunner of the Committee on Gift Annuities and the American Council on Gift Annuities

WMC　　Ways and Means Committee of the American Bible Society

WPGS　*Wise Public Giving* series

Glossary of Terms

actuarial science: The professional discipline that applies mathematical and statistical methods to assess and manage risk in insurance, finance, fundraising, and other industries and professions.

annuitant: A person receiving annuity payments.

annuity, or commercial annuity: A contractual obligation to pay a stated amount to an annuitant, generally for life. "A person purchases an annuity from a Company, when he pays a gross sum, on the condition that the Company will pay him an annual allowance as long as he lives…the money paid and received is fixed by calculation, founded on tables of observation, by which is determined the number of years an individual of any age has a chance of living."[1]

annuity bond: In 1831, attorney Peter Augustus Jay characterized the contract between John Trumbull and Yale College as a blend between a debt investment (bond) and a life annuity (normally issued by a life insurance company). While the principal of a bond is returned to the bond owner when a bond matures, the *charitable residuum* of a gift annuity is used for philanthropic purposes.

charitable-remainder trust (also see "trust"): A form of charitable gift in which a donor transfers money to a trustee under the terms of a trust agreement. The trustee makes payments annually or more frequently to one or more beneficiaries for their lives or a term of years. The trust remainder (*residuum*) is transferred to one or more nonprofit organizations when the trust terminates.

gift annuity, or charitable gift annuity: A contract between a donor and a nonprofit organization in which the donor transfers money to a nonprofit, which agrees to make fixed payments annually or more frequently for the lives of one or two annuitants, in the expectation that an amount of money (the *residuum*) will remain to support a philanthropic purpose when the contract terminates.

life-income agreement: An early form of charitable remainder trust that paid beneficiaries the actual income earned by the trust portfolio. The Tax Reform Act of 1969 mandated the use of annuity trusts and unitrusts.

mortality table: "A table that shows the rate of deaths occurring in a defined population during a selected time interval, or survival from birth to any given age. Statistics included in the mortality table show the probability of a person's death before their next birthday, based on their age. Death-rate data help determine prices paid by people who have recently purchased life insurance [and gift annuities]. A mortality table is also known as a 'life table,' an 'actuarial table,' or a 'morbidity table.'" (Investopedia.com)

residuum, or charitable residuum: The amount remaining for use by a nonprofit organization after the death of an annuitant or termination of a charitable-remainder trust.

risks and gift annuities: For nonprofits issuing annuity contracts, the main risks are from annuitants living longer and thus receiving more payments than expected and from investment returns that are lower than expected. For an annuitant, the main risk is that the nonprofit will default on its payment obligations

trust: A relationship between parties with respect to property in which one party has the responsibility of managing the property as a fiduciary for the benefit of the other.

Notes

1   Rates and Proposals of the New-York Life Insurance and Trust Company, no. 38 Wall Street, for Insurance on Lives, Granting Annuities, Receiving Money in Trust, and the Management of Trust Estates (New York: Clayton & Van Norden, Printers, 1830), 11.

Bibliography

ABS. 1927. *Bible Society Record* 72, no. 7 (July): 111–12.

ACGA. 2005. *Report and Comments on the 2004 American Council on Gift Annuities Survey of Charitable Gift Annuities*. Indianapolis: ACG.

———. 2006. *ACGA in Touch* 6, no. 2.

———. 2014. *Report and Comments on the ACGA 2013 Survey of Charitable Gift Annuities*. 2nd ed., corrected on June 25, 2014. Smyrna, GA: ACGA.

———. 2015. *Explanation of the ACGA Gift Annuity Rates Effective January 1, 2012*. Updated June 2015. Smyrna, GA: ACGA.

———. 2017. *Explanation of the ACGA Gift Annuity Rates April 2017*. Smyrna, GA: ACGA.

Act for Liberty to Erect a Collegiate School. 1701. Connecticut, S. o. 1701.

American Academy of Actuaries/Society of Actuaries Payout Annuity Table Team. 2011. *2012 Individual Annuity Reserving Table*. September. Retrieved from http://www.actuary.org/files/publications/Payout_Annuity_Report_09-28-11.pdf.

American Council of Life Insurers. 2016. *Life Insurers Fact Book, 2016*. Retrieved from https://www.acli.com/-/media/ACLI/Files/Fact-Books-Public/2016LIFactBook.ashx?la=en.

American Law Institute. 2003. *Restatement of the Law Third, Trusts*. Vol. 1. Philadelphia: American Law Institute.

Anthony, A. W. 1918. *The Home Missions Task*. New York: Home Missions Council.

―――. 1923. Roster of the CFFM. *Wise Public Benefactions and their Creation under The Uniform Trust for Public Uses*. WPGS no. 4. New York: FCCCA.

―――. 1925. *Funds for the Future, With Special Reference to Christian Education*. CFFM Conference. WPGS no. 7. New York: CFFM.

―――. 1927. *Linking Christian Education with Financial Agencies: What Has Been Done and What It Means, a Report for 1926*. New York: FCCCA, 1927.

―――. 1927b. *Cooperation in Fiduciary Service: Papers Presented at a Conference on Financial and Fiduciary Matters*. CFFM Conference. WPGS no. 14. New York: Abbott Press & Mortimer-Walling.

―――. 1928. "Fiduciary Service for Charitable Organizations." *Christian Education*, 239–43.

―――. 1929a. *Changing Conditions in Public Giving*. CFFM Conference. WPGS no. 32. New York: Abbott Press & Mortimer-Walling.

―――. 1931a. *Philanthropy for the Future: A Long-Range Look at Economic Policies in the Field of Charity*. CFFM Conference. WPGS no. 36. New York: CFFM.

"Assured Income Bonds." 1921. *Record of Christian Work Advertising* (December): 1090.

Augur, H. 1837. *Connecticut Herald*. November 21.

Baas, C. 1991. *Committee on Gift Annuities: A History*. Dallas: ACGA.

Bean, J. 1968. *The Decline of English Feudalism, 1215–1540*. Manchester, UK: Manchester University Press.

Beardsley, E. E. 1868. *The History of the Episcopal Church in Connecticut from the Death of Bishop Seabury to the Present Time*. Vol. 2. New York: Hurd and Houghton.

Bell, A. A. "2007; revised 2009. Valuing Medieval Annuities: Were Corrodies Underpriced?" *ICMA Centre Discussion Papers in Finance DP2007-15*. ICMA.

Bell, H. A. 1952. "Legal Framework, Trends, and Developments in Investment Practices of Life Insurance Companies." *Law and Contemporary Problems* 17, no. 1: 45–85.

Bell, J. M. [1991?]. *The ABS Annuity Story: "Pioneers in Gift Annuities."* New York: American Bible Society.

"A Better Way." 1905. *The Baptist Home Mission Monthly* 27, no. 10 (October): 400.

Black's Law Dictionary. 2009. 9th ed. St. Paul, MN: Thomson Reuters, 2009.

Bouk, D. 2015. *How Our Days Became Numbered: Risk and the Rise of the Statistical Individual.* Chicago: University of Chicago Press.

Bremner, R. H. (1960) 1988. *American Philanthropy.* Rev. ed. Chicago: University of Chicago Press.

Brown, R. A. 2017. *The First Ethical Standards for Gift Planners: A Fledgling National Association Earns Its Wings.* April 11. Retrieved from www.gift-planninghistory.org.

Buel, J. D. 1984. *The Way of Duty: A Woman and Her Family in Revolutionary America.* New York: W. W. Norton.

Buley, R. C. 1953. *The American Life Convention, 1906–1952: A Study in the History of Life Insurance.* Vol. 1. New York: Appletin-Century-Crofts.

Burlingame, Dwight F., ed. 2004. *Philanthropy in America: A Comprehensive Historical Encyclopedia.* Santa Barbara, CA: ABC Clio.

Burns, E. 2015. *1920: The Year That Made the Decade Roar.* New York: Pegasus Books.

Burpee, C. W. 1914. *First Century of the Phoenix National Bank of Hartford.* Hartford: Phoenix National Bank.

Carter, H. 2016. "The Best and Worst Presidential Portraits." *New York Times.* December 29. Retrieved from http://www.nytimes.com/2016/12/29/arts/design/the-best-and-worst-presidential-portraits.html?rref=collection%2Fbyline%2Fholland-cotter&action=click&contentCollection=undefined&region=stream&module=stream_unit&version=latest&contentPlacement=2&pgtype=colle.

Case, A. 2015. "Rising Morbidity and Mortality in Midlife among White Non-Hispanic Americans in the 21st Century." *PNAS* 112, no. 49.

Cassat, P. 1931. "Annuity Agreement Business: Extent and Characteristics." *Methods and Plans in Using Annuity Agreements.* WPGS no. 34. New York: CFFM.

Centers for Disease Control and Prevention. 2017. "African-American Death Rate Drops 25 Percent." May 2. Retrieved from https://www.cdc.gov/media/releases/2017/p0502-aa-health.html.

CFFM. 1927a. *Cooperation in Fiduciary Service: Papers Presented at a Conference on Financial and Fiduciary Matters, Hotel Chalfonte, Atlantic City, NJ, March 22–24, 1927.* WPGS no. 14. New York: CFFM.

————.1927b. *Financial and Fiduciary Matters: Report of Committee on Findings.* WPGS no. 13. New York: CFFM.

Charter and Fundamental Laws of the Corporation for the Relief of Widows and Children of Clergymen of the Protestant Episcopal Church for the State of New York. 1807. New York: T&J Swords.

Chatterjee, S. K. (2003) 2005. *Statistical Thought: A Perspective and History.* Reprint, with corrections. Oxford: Oxford University Press.

Collins, H. A. 1914. *After Many Days: A Story.* Jackson, MS: Correlated Presbyterian Schools of Mississippi.

————. 1916a. *Life Annuity Bonds.* New York: Board of Foreign Missions of the Methodist Episcopal Church.

————. 1916b. "Pleased Annuitants." *Northwestern Christian Advocate* 64, no. 29 (July 12): 688.

————. 1918. *Ice-Cream Alley: A Novel.* Peoria, IL: J. W. Franks & Sons.

————. 1920. *His Master's Word.* Westerville, OH: Otterbein College.

Cooper, H. A. 1983. *John Trumbull: The Hand and Spirit of a Painter.* New Haven, CT: Yale University Press.

Cutlip, S. M. (1965) 1990. *Fund Raising in the United States: Its Role in America's Philanthropy.* Reprint, New Brunswick, NJ, and London: Transaction.

Darlington, G. 1952. "Taxation, Legislation, and Regulation." In *Conference on Wills, Annuities and Special Gifts.* New York: National Council of Churches of Christ in America.

Desmond, R. L. 1967. *Higher Education and Tax-Motivated Giving: The Federal Tax History of Life Income and Annuity Gifts.* Washington, DC: American College Public Relations Association.

Dubuar, C. 1939. "The Regulation and Supervision of the Issuance of Annuity Agreements by a Charitable Society." In *Annuity Agreements of Charitable Organizations.* New York: FCCCA.

Dwight, H. O. 1916. *The Centennial History of the American Bible Society.* Vol. 1. New York: Macmillan.

The Economist. 2009. "A Slow-burning Fuse." Special Report: Ageing Populations. June 25. Retrieved from http://www.economist.com/node/13888045.

Emami, S. 2016. "Important Notice Regarding Reserves for Gift Annuities." New York State Department of Financial Services.

Bibliography

Fea, J. 2016. *The Bible Cause: A History of the American Bible Society.* New York: Oxford University Press.

First Presbyterian Church. 1922. "Annuity Bonds of This Board." *Herald and Presbyter: A Presbyterian Family Paper.* July 5.

Fishman, J. 1985. "The Development of Nonprofit Corporation Law and an Agenda for Reform." *Emory Law Journal. Vol. 34*

Fishman, J. J. 2007. *The Faithless Fiduciary and the Quest for Charitable Accountability, 1200–2005.* Durham: Carolina Academic Press.

Fitzgerald, F. S. 1925. *The Great Gatsby.* New York: Charles Scribner's Sons.

Foster, M. S. 1962. *"Out of Smale Beginings…": An Economic History of Harvard College in the Puritan Period.* Cambridge, MA: Belknap Press.

Franklin, J. 2001. *Statististics and Probability before Pascal.* Baltimore: Johns Hopkins University Press.

Frier, B. 1982. "Roman Life Expectancy: Ulpian's Evidence." *Harvard Studies in Classical Philology* 86: 213–51.

Ganguin, B. A. 2005. *Fundamentals of Corporate Credit Analysis.* New York: McGraw-Hill.

Gordon, R. J. 2016. *The Rise and Fall of American Growth: The US Standard of Living since the Civil War.* Princeton: Princeton University Press.

Grant, J. 2014. *The Forgotten Depression.* New York: Simon and Schuster.

Grubbs, J. D. 1999. "The Public Responsibility of Actuaries in American Pensions." *North American Actuarial Journal* 3, no. 4: 34.

Hall, E. 1931. "The Place and Use of Annuities." In *Philanthropy for the Future: A Long-Range Look at Economic Policies in the Field of Charity.* New York: Committee on Financial and Fiduciary Matters.

Hammack, D. C. 2000. *Making the Nonprofit Sector in the United States: A Reader.* Bloomington: Indiana University Press.

Harper, R. J. 1983. "A Note on Corrodies in the Fourteenth Century." *Albion* 15: 95–101.

Harvey, B. 1993. *Living and Dying in England 1100–1540.* Oxford: Oxford University Press.

Helmholz, R. A. 1998. *Itinerae Fiduciae: Trust and Truehand in Historical Perspective.* Berlin: Dunker and Humblot.

Hess, A. M. 1980–2017. *Bogert Trusts and Trustees.* Rev. 2nd and 3nd ed. Thomson West.

Hilt, E. 2009. "Rogue Finance: The Life and Fire Insurance Company and the Panic of 1826." *Business History Review* 83 (Spring): 87–112.

Hirsch, F. E. 1941. "The Bard Family." *Columbia University Quarterly*, 222–41.

Historic Records Working Party. 1969. *The History of Individual Annuity Contracts.* Report H.R. 12. London: Insurance Institute of London.

History.com. 2014. *The Roaring Twenties*. October 18. Retrieved from http://www.history.com/topics/roaring-twenties/print.

Holden, R. 1967. *Yale: A Pictorial History.* New Haven, CT: Yale University Press.

Homer, S. A. 2005. *A History of Interest Rates.* 4th ed. Hoboken, NJ: John Wiley & Sons.

Horner, T. L. 1997. "Securities Regulation of Fundraising Activities of Religious and Othere Nonprofit Organizations." *Stetson Law Review* 27, no. 2: 473–530.

Huggins, G. A. (1928?). "Annuity Rates and Reserves." In *Conditional Gifts Annuity Agreements*. WPGS no. 31. New York: Abbott Press and Mortimer-Walling.

Huggins, G. A. 1931. "Uniform Rates: Agreements and Terminology: Reserves and Accounting." In *Methods and Plans in Using Annuity Agreements*. WPGS no. 34. New York: CFFM.

———. 1955. "Gift Annuity Rates and Mortality Experience." In *Gift Annuity Agreements of Charitable Organizations (9th conference)*, 31–34. WPGS no. 48. New York: Committee on Gift Annuities.

Hunter, A. 1937. "Mortality of Annuitants in the United States and Canada." *Journal of the Institute of Actuaries (1886–1994)* 68, no. 4: 508.

Hustead, E. C. 1988. "The History of Actuarial Mortality Tables in the United States." *Journal of Insurance Medicine* 20, no. 4: 14.

In the Matter of Howe, etc., Executor, and Anderson, Deceased. 1828. (New York Court of Chancery).

IRS. 2009a. *Actuarial Valuations, Version 3A: Remainder, Income, and Annuity Examples for One Life, Two Lives, and Terms Certain. For Use with Respect to Income, Estate, and Gift Tax Purposes, Including Valuation of Pooled Income Fund.* IRS Publication 1457, rev. 5-20. Washington: IRS.

———. 2009b. *Actuarial Valuations, Version 3B: Unitrust Remainder and Life Estate Examples for One Life, Two Lives, and Terms Certain for Use in*

Income, Estate, and Gift Tax Purposes. IRS Publication 1458, rev. 5-2009. Washington: IRS.

Jaffe, I. B. 1975. *John Trumbull, Patriot-Artist of the American Revolution.* Boston: New York Graphic Society.

Jaffe, I. B. 1976. *Trumbull: The Declaration of Independence.* London: Penguin Books.

Jay, J. 1905. *Memorials of Peter A. Jay Compiled for His Descendants By His Great Grand-son John Jay.* Holland: G. J. Thieme.

Johnson, A. E. (1929) 1957. *Dictionary of American Biography.* New York: Charles Scribner's Sons.

Jones, G. 1969. *History of the Law of Charity, 1532–1827.* Cambridge, UK: Cambridge University Press.

Jordan, W. 1959. *Philanthropy in England, 1480–1660.* London: George Allen & Unwin.

Journal of Education. 1927. "Education in Action." *Journal of Education* 105, no. 2 (1927): 48.

Kardong, T. G. 1996. *Benedict's Rule: A Translation and Commentary.* Collegeville, MN: Liturgical Press.

Katz, S. N. 1985. "Legal Change and Legal Autonomy: Charitable Trusts in New York, 1777–1893." *Law and History Review* 51. Retrieved from HeinOnline.

Kelly, B. M. 1974. *Yale: A History.* New Haven, CT: Yale University Press.

Kingsley, J. L. 1823. *Remarks on the Present Situation at Yale College, for the Consideration of its Friends and Patrons.* New Haven, CT: Yale College.

Knowles, C. E. 1929. *History of the Bank for Savings in the City of New York 1819–1929.* New York: Bank for Savings.

Kopf, E. W. 1927. "The Early History of the Annuity." *Proceedings of the Casualty Actuarial Society* 13.

Laslett, P. 1995. *Aging in the Past.* Berkeley: University of California Press.

Lewin, C. 2003. *Pensions and Insurance before 1800: A Social History.* East Lothian, Scotland: Tuckwell Press.

"Life Annuity Bonds." 1919. In *Methodist Year Book for 1918*, 156.

"Life Insurance—Company Income by Type: 1854–1998." (n.d.). Table Cj727-732. Retrieved from Historical Statistics of the United States Millennial Edition Online.

Living Trusts: What They Are, What They Serve, Their Advantages. 1927. WPGS 15. New York: Committee on Financial and Fiduciary Matters.

Lowenstein, R. 2015. *America's Bank: The Epic Struggle to Create the Federal Reserve.* New York: Penguin Press.

Maitland, F. W. (1909) 1936, 2011. *Equity: A Course of Lectures.* Reissued. Cambridge, UK: Cambridge University Press.

Mann, F. H. 1925, "Annuities." In *Safeguarding Funds: Financial and Fiduciary Matters*, 21–27. New York: J. E. Stohlmann.

"Millions in Liberty Bonds Stolen." 1921. *Record of Christian Work Advertising* (December): 1080.

Minton, F. 2017. *Charitable Gift Annuities: The Complete Resource Manual.* Cambridge, MA: PG Calc.

Monitor Institute. 2016. *Investing for Social & Environmental Impact: A Design for Catalyzing an Emerging Industry.* January 9. Retrieved from http:// monitorinstitute.com/downloads/what-we-think/impact-investing/ Impact_Investing.pdf.

Moorhead, E. 1989. *Our Yesterdays: The History of the Actuarial Profession in North America 1809–1979.* Schaumburg, IL: Society of Actuaries.

Moss, D. A. "The Armstrong Investigation." Harvard Business School Case 9-708-034. Rev. January 14, 2009. Cambridge, MA: Harvard Business School.

Murphy, R. D. 1922. *Construction of Mortality Tables from the Records of Insured Lives.* New York: Actuarial Society of America.

Murphy, S. A. 2010. *Investing in Life: Insurance in Antebellum America.* Baltimore: Johns Hopkins Press.

NAIC. 2014. Year-End 2014 Insurance Industry Investment Portfolio Asset Allocations, table 4. Retrieved from Capital Markets Special Report: http:// www.naic.org/capital_markets_archive/150622.htm.

National Institute on Aging. 1997. *Aging in the United States—Past, Present, and Future.* Retrieved from https://www.census.gov/population/international/ files/97agewc.pdf.

Nelson and Warren Consulting Actuaries. n.d. (1956?). *Principal Mortality Tables, Old and New.* St. Louis: Nelson and Warren.

"A New Officer at the Bible House." 1919. *Bible Society Record* 64, no. 2 (February): 22–23.

North, D. C. 1954. "Life Insurance and Investment Banking at the Time of the Armstrong Investigation of 1905–1906." *Journal of Economic History*, 14(3), 209–228.

North, E. M. 1964. "Annuity and Trust Agreements." Sec. G of ABS Historical Essay 20, part 2, *Financial Administration 1861–1900*. New York: American Bible Society.

———. 1966. "Annuities and Special Agreements." Sec. H of ABS Historical Essay 20, part 3, *Financial Administration 1861–1900*. New York: American Bible Society.

———. 1966. ABS Historical Essay 17, part 3, *Financial Administration 1861–1900*. New York: American Bible Society.

NY Life Insurance and Trust Company. 1830. *Rates and Proposals of the New-York Life Insurance and Trust Company, no. 38 Wall Street, for Insurance on Lives, Granting Annuities, Receiving Money in Trust, and the Management of Trust Estates*. New York: Clayton & Van Norden, Printers.

NYS Office of General Counsel. 2008. *OGC Op. No. 08-08-01*. (August). Retrieved from NYS Department of Financial Services: http://www.dfs. ny.gov/insurance/ogco2008/rg080801.htm.

Parker, J. A. 1928. *Insurance Law of New York*. Albany: NY State Printing and Publishing.

Poitras, G. 2000. *The Early History of Financial Economics, 1478–1776: From Commercial Arithmetic to Life Annuities and Joint Stocks*. Cheltenham, UK: Edward Elgar.

Porter, T. M. 1986. *The Rise of Statistical Thinking, 1820–1900*. Princeton, NJ: Princeton University Press.

Ransom, R. L. 1987. "Tontine Insurance and the Armstrong Investigation: A Case of Stifled Innovation." *Journal of Economic History* 47, no. 2: 379–90.

"Recent Decisions: Taxation. Annuity Bonds. Premiums." 1921. *Columbia Law Review* 21, no. 3: 294.

Reeves, F. W. 1932. *The Liberal Arts College: Based upon Surveys of Thirty-Five Colleges Related to the Methodist Episcopal Church*. Chicago: University of Chicago Press.

Robbins, R. B. 1933. *Proceedings of the Casualty Actuarial and Statistical Society of America*. Vol. 20.

Roe, M. J. 1993. "Foundations of Corporate Finance: The 1906 Pacification of the Insurance Industry." *Columbia Law Review* 93, no. 3: 639–84.

Rubin, M. 1987. *Charity and Community in Medieval Cambridge*. Cambridge: Cambridge University Press.

Ryan, A. C. 1927. "Administrative Policy." In *Annuity Agreements of Charitable Organizations*. WPGS no. 18.

"A Safe Investment." 1919. *Bible Society Record* 64, no. 1 (January): 31.

"A Safe and Productive Investment." 1919. *Bible Society Record* 64, no. 10 (October–December): 186.

Schoenhals, R. 1992. "The First Gift Annuity…and Many More: An Interview with J. Milton Bell." *Planned Giving Today* 3, no. 2 (February).

Scott, A. W. 1987. *The Law of Trusts*. 4th ed. Boston: Little, Brown.

Shapiro, A. F. 1985. "Contributions to the Evolution of Pension Cost Analysis." *Journal of Risk and Insurance* 52, no. 1: 82, 86.

Sharpe, R. F. 2008. *Is There "Security" in Planned Giving?* Chicago: ACGA.

Silliman, B. 1820. *Remarks Made on a Short Tour, between Hartford and Quebec, in the Autumn of 1819*. New Haven, CT: S. Converse.

———. 1842. *An Address Delivered before the Association of the Alumni of Yale College in New Haven, August 17, 1842 by Professor Silliman*. New Haven: B. L. Hamlen.

Silliman Family Papers. Yale University Library, New Haven, CT.

Sizer, T. 1967. *The Works of Colonel John Trumbull: Artist of the American Revolution*. New Haven, CT: Yale University Press.

Society of Actuaries. 2002. "Asset Allocation for Life Insurers." *Record*, 28, no. 1 (May 30–31). Retrieved from https://www.soa.org/library/proceedings/record-of-the-society-of-actuaries/2000-09/2002/january/rsa02v28n179ts.pdf.

Staiti, P. 2016. *Of Arms and Artists: The American Revolution through Painters' Eyes*. New York: Bloomsbury Press.

Stalson, J. O. 1942. *Marketing Life Insurance: Its History in America*. Cambridge, MA: Harvard University Press.

The Statute of Charitable Uses and the English Origins of American Philanthropy. 2016. July 4. Retrieved from http://www.hks.harvard.edu/fs/phall/01.%20 Charitable%20uses.pdf.

Stoddard, F. R. 1923. Letter from NYS superintendent of insurance to James A. Parsons, counsel to the governor, April 2. Albany, New York.

Such, R. 2009. "Stock Market Indicators: 1919–1939." Table Cb52-54. Retrieved from Historical Statistics of the United States Millenial Edition Online.

Tappan, L. 1870. *The Life of Arthur Tappan.* New York: Hurd and Houghton.

Thompson, T. 1952. Preface to *Conference on Wills, Annuities, and Special Gifts.* New York: NCCCA.

Tillotson, J. H. 1988. *Monastery and Society in the Late Middle Ages: Selected Account Rolls from Selby Abbey, Yorkshire, 1398–1537.* Suffolk: Boydell Press.

Trumbull, J. 1833. Letter to Wyllys Warner. October 7. New York, NY.

———. 1841. *Autobiography, Reminiscences and Letters of John Trumbull from 1756 to 1841.* New Haven, CT: B. L. Hamlen.

———. 1904. *Monumental News*, 16, no. 1. (January).

———. 1953. *The Autobiography of Colonel John Trumbull, Patriot-Artist, 1756–1843.* Edited by T. Sizer. New Haven, CT: Yale University Press.

Various. 1816a. *Bishop's Bonus, Seabury College, divine right of Presbyterianism, and divine right of Episcopacy, in a series of essays originally published in the Connecticut Herald, from November 21st, 1815, to January 9th, 1816, inclusive; together with.* New Haven, CT: Oliver Steele.

———. 1816b. *The Bishop's Fund and Phoenix Bonus: A Collection of the Pieces on this Subject, from the Connecticut Herald: with an Explanatory Preface, Notes, &c., and an Additional Piece by Hamilton.* Hartford: Printed at the Journal Office.

———. 1927c. *Annuity Agreements of Charitable Organizations: Papers, Findings and Conclusions of a Conference on Annuities.* First conference. WPGS no. 18. New York: Abbott Press and Mortimer-Walling.

———. 1929b. *Conditional Gifts Annuity Agreements.* Second conference. WPGS no. 31. New York: FCCCA.

———. 1930. *Methods and Plans in Using Annuity Agreements.* Third conference. WPGS no. 34. New York: FCCCA.

———. 1931. *Annuity Agreements, Their Promotion and Management.* Chicago: Committee on Annuities of the World Service Commission of the Methodist Episcopal Church.

———. 1931b. *Rules, Regulations and Reserves in Using Annuity Agreements.* Fourth conference. WPGS no. 38. New York: FCCCA.

————. 1931c. Methodist Annuity Conference. *Annuity Agreements: Their Promotion and Management*. Chicago: Committee on Annuities of the World Service Commission of the Methodist Episcopal Church.

————. 1934. *Annuity Rates and Federal Taxation of Annuities*. Fifth conference. WPGS no. 43. New York: FCCCA.

————. 1939. *Annuity Agreements of Charitable Organizations*. Sixth conference. WPGS no. 44. New York: FCCCA.

————. 1941. *Annuity Agreements of Charitable Organizations*. Seventh conference. WPGS no. 45. New York: FCCCA.

————. 1946. *Annuity Agreements of Charitable Organizations*. Eighth conference. WPGS no. 47. New York: FCCCA.

————. 1952. *Conference on Wills, Annuities, and Special Gifts*. NCCCA conference. New York: National Council of Churches of Christ in America.

————. 1955. *Gift Annuity Agreements of Charitable Organizations*. Ninth conference. New York: Committee on Gift Annuities.

————. 1959. *Gift Annuity Agreements of Charitable Organizations*. Tenth conference. WPGS no. 49. New York: Committee on Gift Annuities.

————. 1965. *Gift Annuity Agreements of Charitable Organizations*. Twelfth conference. WPGS no. 51. New York: Committee on Gift Annuities.

————. 1971. *Gift Annuity Agreements of Charitable Organizations*. Fourteenth conference. WPGS no. 53. New York: Committee on Gift Annuities.

————. 2016. *Changing Lives, Transforming Communities*. Thirty-second conference. Smyrna, GA: ACGA.

————. n.d. *Memorials of Connecticut Judges and Attorneys as Printed in the Connecticut Reports*. Vol. 15. Hartford.

Venman, W. C. 1962. "Gift Annuity Agreements of Colleges." PhD diss., University of Michigan. Microfilm.

————. n.d. *Gift Annuity Agreements for Colleges* (booklet). Ann Arbor: Center for the Study of Higher Education, University of Michigan.

Vidal v. Girard's Executors, 43 US. (2 How.) 127, 11 L. Ed. (1844).

Weaver, G. 1967. *The History of Trinity College*. Hartford: Trinity College Press.

Wellck, A. A. 1933. *The Annuity Agreements of Colleges and Universities*. New York: A. A. Wellck.

White, C. L.1927a. "Annuities." *Cooperation in Fiduciary Service*. WPGS no. 14.

New York: Abbott Press and Mortimer-Walling.

White, C. L. 1927b. *"Annuities," Financial and Fiduciary Matters: Report of the Committee on Findings.* WPGS no. 13. New York: CFFM of the FCCCA.

Whitehead, J. S. 1973. *The Separation of College and State: Columbia, Dartmouth, Harvard, and Yale, 1776–1876.* New Haven, CT: Yale University Press.

Winters, W. H. 1892. *History of the Library of the New York Law Institute.* New York: Doglas Taylor.

Xu, J. M. 2016. *Mortality in the United States, 2015.* Washington, DC: National Center for Health Statistics.

Yale University Art Gallery 2008. "Life, Liberty and the Pursuit of Happiness: American Art from the Yale University Art Gallery." New Haven, CT: Yale University Press.

Young, N. 2016. *Interpreting "The Bible Cause": Neil Young Reviews Fea's History of the American Bible Society.* June 1. Retrieved from https://histphil. org/2016/06/01/interpreting-the-bible-cause-neil-young-reviews-feas-history-of-the-american-bible-society/.

Zimmerman, J. H. 1967. *Public Relations, Financial Promotion and Support, 1901– 1930.* ABS Historical Essay 17, part 5. New York: American Bible Society.

Zollman, B. 1924. *American Law of Charities.* Milwaukee: Bruce.

Zunz, O. 2012. *Philanthropy in America: A History.* Princeton, and Oxford: Princeton University Press.

Index

Note: Page numbers in italics indicate figures; page numbers ending in "t" indicate tables. Notes are indicated with "n".